THE GENESIS FACTOR

THE GENESIS FACTOR

by ROBERT A. WALLACE

William Morrow and Company, Inc. in association with
Publisher's Inc.

Published jointly by

William Morrow and Company, Inc.   *and*   Publisher's Inc.
105 Madison Avenue   243 12th Street
New York, NY 10016   Del Mar, CA 92014

Dedication, p. v.
From "Little Gidding" in *Four Quartets* by T.S. Eliot, copyright 1943
by T.S. Eliot; renewed 1971 by Esme Valerie Eliot. Reprinted by
permission of Harcourt Brace Jovanovich, Inc. and Faber & Faber Ltd.

Library of Congress Catalog Card No.: 79–65876
ISBN: 0-688-03536-1

Printed in the United States of America

First edition

1 2 3 4 5 6 7 8 9 10

Book and Jacket Design: John Odam

We shall not cease from exploration
And the end of our exploring
Will be to arrive where we started
And know the place for the first time

—T. S. Eliot

CONTENTS

PREFACE

Images. Haunting remembrances of Nazi "doctors" measuring the cranial structure of schoolchildren while describing the characteristics of the pure Aryan to wide-eyed onlookers. Frightful images that have not been dimmed by time, but instead have resonated, gaining strength as our very fibers recoil sympathetically to the knowledge of what we are capable of. We now know more about the limits of human behavior and the postures that people can assume to defend what they are doing. We know that people can appear confident, even from a contorted stance. In other words, we are aware of our chilling ability to arbitrarily choose what we will believe and then to act strongly on the basis of that choice as if we somehow possessed a Great Truth. The knowledge that people have the ability to strongly embrace selected facts or even sheer irrationality has caused many concerned people to be acutely, even painfully, sensitive to our potential ability to harm each other. Their concern is not misplaced because we have shown that we can be dangerous to each other simply by adopting a certain set of ideas and ignoring information that is inconsistent with our opinions. We know that we act with little regard for truth or rationality. We know, now, that because of chilling flaws in our nature, a certain weakness in our mind or spirit, certain ideas must never be allowed a toehold in our culture. Among those ideas, as far as some people are concerned, is the notion that human behavior is genetically determined, that we are largely limited or gifted by our heritage, and that those inherent limitations or predispositions cannot be overcome by the proper cultural influences.

Of course, the great cultural programs of the 1960s were based on the opposite premise: that human behavior is infinitely modifiable by cultural molding. In the United States untold millions of dollars were spent in the expectation that disadvantaged elements in our society could be brought to behave like solid, predictable, and productive citizens, on time for work and unaddicted (except to work) if simply given the chance. The "chance" was presented in the form of relaxed standards, easier educational opportunities, loans, and professional training. It is true that in some cases the programs worked, but not frequently enough to mollify the public, who were paying the bills. With new programs the expenses have climbed higher, but at the same time money has become tighter and so have belts. Thus, new questions are being asked, but they have the disturbing ring of certain old questions. People wonder: Are we really changing our society with our present attempts at cultural modeling? Or *can* people be changed much? Precisely how much? Is our effort worth it? If we aren't totally modifiable, then what are our limits?

Here's where the problem arises. There is apparently a growing tendency to reject the "environmentalist" position, which assumes that if the information available to the human mind is carefully regulated by social programs, individual human behavior will be as society would have it. Put quite simply, that position is being given the fish-eye because so many of our social programs haven't worked—they haven't changed anything very much at all. But, at the same time, there has been a reticence to accept the logical alternative—that social behavior may not be very malleable after all, that our limits are rather fixed, that genetics may play a more important role than we thought. As Sherlock Holmes so often said, "When you have ruled out the impossible, whatever is left must be the truth, no matter how improbable." If the evidence forces us to the conclusion that our social programs are ineffective, then we are left with an alternative that few people care to admit in a humanitarian society. Alternatives, as we know, can be brutal. We're quick to admit that some of us are just naturally smart, but why the hesitance to look at the other side of the coin: some of us must be, by definition, just naturally dumb. And if dumbness is genetic, are there more dummies in some genetic groups than in others? Which groups? Which races? We have now gone one step further than simply rejecting the environmentalist position. See the problem?

And then there's the question of those well-known differences in the behavior of males and females. How do such differences come about? Are they molded through careful teaching, or are they in any way under the control of genes? Is it "natural" for men to be dominant over women? Or perhaps we're getting ahead of ourselves. *Are* men dominant over women? If not, where did the idea come from?

This business of "natural" brings us to another question, one that has plagued philosophers for years. It is sometimes called the "is-ought" problem. Essentially it is this: Just because something exists in nature, *ought* it to exist? Is "natural" the same as "good"? Perhaps it is if you're selling bread or corn oil, but what if you're dealing with matters than can affect entire cultures? Maybe things exist in cultures that are not good. Perhaps those things that exist in human culture should be evaluated by thinking people, and those things that are harmful to society should be methodically erased. Sociobiologists have been accused of saying that what *is* exists because it works, and therefore it *ought* to be. But sociobiologists have been wrongly accused in a number of instances, and this is one. Everyone realizes that social changes are in order (a delicate phrase as we march resolutely toward blowing ourselves into oblivion). The sociobiologist, however (if there is such a thing as "the" sociobiologist), would approach the problem of molding our culture to make it more compatible with modern man in quite a different manner than would, say, the Marxist ("the" Marxist?). Sociobiology, in fact, is the new kid on the block and is meeting intense resistance from some of the old hands. These old hands are the "social sciences" and include anthropology, psychology, sociology, political science, and philosophy. Their turf is being invaded, and they are accutely aware of it. But sociobiology is also drawing surprising support from among their ranks, and a powerful, emotional, vitriolic debate has begun. We will soon see why.

Let's ask another seemingly innocent question. How does aggression arise? The question is an important one because, as the numbers of human populations swell, we are brought into more frequent contact with other people. Thus, if a certain proportion of our interaction is aggressive, we are increasingly dangerous to each other. So, we ask, is the aggression innate or taught? Does it have a role in our lives? Why haven't we been able to reduce aggression through cultural programs? Should we stop trying to reduce aggression, admit it exists in almost all of us, and simply try to rechannel it?

I have deliberately used several "red flag" words, so you are probably already squinting suspiciously at these pages. "What is he getting at?" But I'm not afraid. Because at this point I disclaim everything. I am saying nothing, taking no stand. I'm just showing how easy it is, if we admit that our present efforts at cultural modeling have some basic flaw (while also admitting notable individual successes), to find ourselves left with an unappealing alternative—one that has been horribly abused in the past. It seems, however, that if our social programs have failed, we must begin to search for alternatives in order to change society in any real way. The search means we must ask new or refurbished questions. Basically, it seems, the questions can be condensed into one: To what degree is our behavior evolutionarily (genetically) determined? That, then, is the question we will ask here. We will approach the answer from various directions, and we will unabashedly rely on a measure of circumstantial evidence, extrapolation, intuition, and common sense. Any conclusions must, of course, be viewed in the most tentative of lights. We do not experiment on each other, and virtually any generalization about "the human condition" throws open the doors to impassioned argument. So, even though my argument may best be considered a mental exercise, it should explain a bit better the stance of the "alternative position." It may even help us to devise better ways to live together.

Robert A. Wallace
Chapel Hill, North Carolina
June 1979

THE GENESIS FACTOR

CHAPTER ONE

A BRIEF HISTORY, OR THE NAKED WHO?

Give me a dozen healthy infants, well-formed, and my own specified world to bring them up in and I'll guarantee to take any one at random and train him to become any type of specialist I might select—doctor, lawyer, merchant, chief and yes, even beggarman and thief, regardless of his talents, peculiarities, tendencies, abilities, vocations, and race of his ancestors.

—J. B. Watson, 1930

THUS WROTE one of the earliest and most important architects of what has come to be called the "cultural" or "environmental" explanation of the development of human behavior. Watson's basic premise, that humans are infinitely malleable, almost totally at the mercy of their environment, has been rephrased and offered to us in countless forms until it seems to have become one of the foundation blocks of our culture. The result has been that we seem to believe, deep in our souls, that society somehow bears the responsibility for our flaws (although we are more reluctant to credit it for our virtues). Even at the time of Watson's famous statement, however, a new group of scientists—animal behaviorists—began to question the environmental explanation. But not many people were listening to the arguments in those days.

Then things gradually began to change. It started with a rough attempt by some Europeans to define the concept of "instinct." Of course, everyone knew what instinct meant. And strangely enough,

1

this was the problem: everyone had his own definition, and almost everyone was wrong. No bucket so malformed could hold much water. Precisely because everyone knew what instinct meant, no one knew. In fact, for years the notion was not considered a fit topic for discussion by serious scientists.

It wasn't until just before World War II that an Austrian, Konrad Lorenz, developed a highly structured instinct theory. Basically, his theory accounted for behavior that could not have been learned and that was characteristic of the species performing it. After the war the theory was modified and refined by the Dutch scientist Niko Tinbergen, working at Oxford.

Their theory gave substance and form to the rather vague notions of instinct that had previously suffered such rough treatment, usually dismissed by a casual and contemptuous wave of the critic's hand, as if returning a bottle of bad wine. The wine presented by Lorenz and Tinbergen, though, was full-bodied and could not be dismissed so easily. They argued persuasively that much of our behavior is innate; that we are born with certain tendencies and propensities that cannot be altered by learning.

In those early days, the 1950s, the argument was basically European *vs.* American, biologist *vs.* psychologist, instinct theorists *vs.* learning theorists, birdwatchers *vs.* ratrunners. The lines were clearly drawn. The Europeans, calling themselves *ethologists,* rallied behind the flamboyant Lorenz, who dismissed the Americans as "ratrunners, unprepared to ask the important questions." The ethologists stated flatly that the most important question was: How much is behavior due to instinct (genetics) and how much to learning? They suspected that instinct was far more important than anyone had previously imagined. In their model, they postulated that there are neural centers, probably in the brain, which, when unlocked by the perception of the proper environmental stimulus, cause the muscles to move in a certain way, thus producing the proper behavioral response to that stimulus. One of their favorite examples was the territorial behavior of the pugnacious little male European robin. As the days grow longer and the little bird's breeding season draws on, the increased period of sunlight causes certain hormones to be released into his blood. These hormones act on his brain, and he begins to behave differently. With the arrival of spring, he is receptive to new stimuli and feels new urges. For one thing, the little bird apparently feels like picking a fight. In fact, he feels a *need* to pick a fight, and the need grows daily until that fighting behavior can be released. Finally, he has his chance when he spots another male robin in the territory he has staked out. He attacks the intruder with a delicious fury. After the fight, the bird feels a bit less aggressive for a time, until the fighting urge builds again.

It turns out that the territorial robin does not need the sight of another male, a competitor, to release his fighting behavior. Experimenters found that placing a tuft of red feathers inside a male robin's territory will inspire him to go berserk and to pummel the unfortunate tuft into oblivion. The feathers are no threat. Why does the little brawler attack? It just so happens that for thousands of years, red feathers were generally found on the breasts of other robins—competitors. So, in time, the birds increasingly focused on this stimulus, until it alone came to elicit the entire gamut of aggressive responses.

Let's see if we can place all this into some sort of perspective. Longer days signal the onset of the breeding season, compelling the robin to stake out his territory. A host of urges begin to swell within the tiny breast at this time. He has the urge to sing, the urge to mate, and the urge to fight. The singing urge is easy enough to satisfy and so he chortles away, letting females know he is available and, at the same time, advertising his presence and vigor to potential male interlopers. But he can't mate or fight without first encountering the cues that tell him "female nearby" or "male nearby." If he immediately entices a female to be his mate, his general reproductive urge will be satisfied and the urge to sing and fight will diminish. But if he remains un-mated, he will grow desperate in his search for a female and will tolerate absolutely no interference from other males. The sight of red feathers in his territory signals, in his small brain, the presence of another male. The visual cue "tuft of red" releases the block that has been holding back his aggression these past days, and his pent-up fury is focused on the target.

Keep in mind that the bird didn't have to *learn* that red feathers are associated with competitors; these could be the first red feathers he has. ever seen in his entire adult life. He doesn't even have to be aware that competitors can deprive him of a mate. He was simply born with the propensity to attack a certain cue (red feathers) at a certain time of year—nothing more. Because he behaves in such a way, however, he is likely to leave offspring. If his aggression does drive off a competitor and he wins the girl, then he will successfully propel his genes into the next generation. His behavior, then, may give the impression that he understands the causal relationships involved when, actually, he does no such thing. He simply behaves *as if* he knows what he is doing. A man catching a baseball acts *as if* he has solved all the mathematical equations of the ball's trajectory, but actually he's responding almost reflexively. This point, by the way, is deceptively simple. In fact, in this paragraph lies the nugget of my entire argument. But let's go on.

The ethological explanation of fighting in European robins probably doesn't arouse anyone's passions. So far, so good. Nice idea, but who cares? The problem is, the ethologists were not content to talk about robins. The controversies arose when they attempted to blanket all animals, from insects up, with their great ethological explanations. Peering from under their blanket was a host of species, and some of them had hair. That did it. Hairy animals, mammals, had already been claimed by the psychologists as "their" animals. The ethologists were free to deal with anything up to and including birds, but mammals were reserved. They were different because they were smarter. With their intelligence they did not have to rely on "genetic learning" or the evolutionary encoding of appropriate responses. They could learn whatever they needed to know. And besides, humans are mammals, and was anyone going to have the temerity to suggest that humans blindly obey the calling of their heritage? Nonsense!

While the ethologists were developing their arguments, the noted psychologist B. F. Skinner was defining his own paradigms. Humans, he announced, are infinitely malleable and subject to environmental conditioning. He elegantly presented us once more with the old idea that the minds of newborn infants are *tabulae rasae,* blank slates, ready to be filled by the sum of their experiences. Those experiences define them and direct their future responses to any given situation.

This argument, of course, is exactly opposite the ethological premise, which largely blames our behavior on our heritage, our genes being the mediators. But the ethologists were not really worried about Skinner. They were content to let him build his boxes and play with white rats, pretending, they thought, that white rats were like little people. The ethologists had a bit more to worry about from other people who were not ratrunners. They worked with many of the same species that the ethologists did, and they were willing to confront Lorenz and his group on their home turf, using data from the same kinds of animals. And they did not share Lorenz's confidence that much human behavior is innate.

The battle was mounted in earnest, and the fur flew for a number of years until each group began to learn a bit more about what the other was doing. Then grudging traces of mutual respect began to develop. Those traces never formed full-blown bonds, however, because suddenly the entire argument was somewhat arbitrarily declared over. Finished. Second-generation researchers were arriving on the scene, and they were tired of the fight. There were better things to do. Everyone seemed bored with the argument, and both sides began to say that adaptive (beneficial) behavior was the result of *both* learning and instinct. The argument was relegated to the ranks of a nonargument. One reason for the détente was that a generation of American ethologists had appeared, and animal psychologists were being welcomed in Europe. In only a few years the battle lines had become obscured by the footprints of these second-generation researchers going about their business of collecting data. The nature-nurture argument, as it had come to be called, was declared old-fashioned, unseemly, and unrealistic, and it was increasingly ignored.

One reason the battle was quit lies in the nature of the behavioral sciences; they have proven to be the most subjective and "soft" of the sciences. Traces of doubt shadow virtually every statement. Of course, one can say that an animal did this or that without fear of criticism, but the old problems remain. *Why* did the animal do it? One simply cannot describe with certainty the *source* of any behavior. Why does it occur? Whence does it spring? In the end, no one really knows. Amidst such ambiguity, then, in an atmosphere in which we can't even say what causes a dog to bite the postman, we can't expect to be too glib about the roots of *human* behavior without expecting criticism.

The absence of information, however, did not deter social scientists from developing their theories purporting to tell us how to alter our social behavior. Their various social-modeling systems were almost uniformly built on the assumption that we are programmed by experience and that genetics has very little to do with how we behave. The uniformity of their stance was interesting. Perhaps they were atoning for the fact that so many of their predecessors had too quickly adopted the concept of "social Darwinism," a theoretical system in which Darwin's notion of the "survival of the fittest" was twisted and grotesquely misapplied to social and economic systems, thereby rationalizing the bad treatment of those in the lower socioeconomic levels. The result was a mélange of monumental and expensive efforts to regulate experience, to *teach* people to behave in "socially acceptable" ways. The premise that our behavior is almost entirely learned was not questioned. The result was an effort that reached its zenith in the great social programs and high hopes of the sixties, a time when official attention fell ponderously on the rights of minority groups and the "socially disadvantaged." What we got was an attempt to provide those missing advantages and educational experiences so that streets and stores would be safer.

Then, suddenly, in the midst of a decade of trying to mold a better society, in the very heart of the liberal-activist era in the United States, right at the time of our Vietnam involvement/withdrawal, in the period when the social conscience of America was being sorely tried, a flurry of books appeared on the scene that rejected, or seemed to, the standard position of humanitarians everywhere. Lorenz, for example, wrote about aggression, telling us with flawed logic that our aggressiveness is instinctive, inborn. Robert Ardrey told us that we are charged with a territorial imperative, that we are compelled to defend what we regard as ours—a vestige, perhaps, of our African genesis. And then zoologist Desmond Morris capped it all by calling us naked apes. These writers might have been ignored if it weren't for the fact that they presented their arguments so attractively. And their books somehow remained popular through those critical pre-Watergate years, when people began to show a resurging interest in "law and order." Was this shift to the right, toward conservatism, encouraged by these books or simply reflected in their continued popularity? Whether the books were a cause or effect didn't matter to many people who considered themselves traditional liberals. The ideas were not new and heretical, they said; they were simply retreaded throwbacks to those same old miserable ideas that had previously permitted or encouraged so much human suffering—suffering brought on by other people who justified themselves with a shrug, saying something about the "natural way of things." Concerned humanists spotted the trend immediately and were repelled and horrified. They stiffened their necks and prepared to do battle. They could take no chances. Their target was clear: the notion that our behavior is due to an inborn nature and not to learning.

It turned out that their initial targets proved to be rather easy ones. Ardrey got it first. It was quickly pointed out that he wasn't even a scientist but a playwright—a dabbler. No real behavioral scientist would have confused predation and aggression, they said. A lion is no more aggressive toward a pig than a man is toward a hamburger, they said. And herbivores are just as aggressive toward each other as carnivores are, they said. He made too many technical errors, so it was easy to dismiss his comments about man's natural territorial instincts.

Lorenz and Morris, though, were accomplished and respected biologists. One couldn't pull rank on them. Fortunately for the critics, Lorenz seemed to have written off the top of his head, and his anecdotes just couldn't sustain such a momentous argument as the natural aggressiveness of humans. Morris, on the other hand, seemed to have written for the fun of it, and since he didn't support his contention that we are only a certain kind of animal, obeying our primitive instincts, he was particularly vulnerable to the critic's barb. Lorenz, by the way, had another problem. He suffered from the long memory of some of his critics. They recalled two of his papers published in Germany in the early forties, at the time the Nazis had ascended to power. He had applied his theory of *releasers* (stimuli that automatically elicit an instinctive response—such as red feathers on a robin's breast) to human morals and aesthetics. In these papers he argued that each race has its own releasers for moral and aesthetic behavior. He went on to say that hybridization between races would destroy these releasers and lead to breakdowns in morals and art—a ludicrous argument developed from observations on hybrid *ducks*. Thus, Lorenz's later musings on human behavior were justifiably held suspect. It is probably not coincidental that the greatest resistance to his ideas stemmed from a largely Jewish coterie at the American Museum of Natural History in New York.

The writings of Ardrey, Morris, and Lorenz were indeed soft and flawed, but they were bold and imaginative, with a distinct point of view. They had given the public a simple tune it could hum. Each writer had pounded home, directly or indirectly, the notion that human behavior is genetically programmed, and they had done it well. Some of their defenders attempted to clarify things and make the case less objectionable by suggesting that an inborn response didn't actually exist for every situation but that humans are born with a genetic foundation, and *upon this base* experience can exert its effect. But they stressed that experience can operate only within the limits set by that foundation. An analogy might be taken from home building. Once the foundation is laid, the rest of the structure can vary but only within the imposed limits. The builder doesn't have to use the entire foundation, but he can't exceed it. At least not without dire consequences.

The three books may have been strong on viewpoint, but they were disconcertingly weak on data. Each seemed to be the offhand remarks of an author with a drum to beat, and the critics came boiling out of the hills of psychology, anthropology, and sociology to mount their attack. They had one advantage: their target was not only soft, it was large—for two reasons. First Lorenz, Ardrey, and Morris had cheerfully commented on just about everything and had stepped on a lot of tender academic toes. So specialists of all stripes, feeling their private territories had been invaded, tucked their chins and pounded their typewriters, or whipped off their glasses, squinted myopically into the cameras, and proceeded to debunk this nonsense. To put us back on track.

The second reason the target was so large was that almost everyone had been exposed to the tainted idea. Millions of people were giggling about Morris's notion that women's breasts had developed cleavage so as to resemble buttocks, in order to bring men around to the front to copulate—a more "fitting" position for an animal that walks on its hind legs. The implication was that men would be blindly aroused by humps and creases just as a European robin reacts with blind aggression to an irrelevant tuft of feathers. And people were titillated by the suggestion that the lips are prominent so as to resemble the vulva (although the author coyly failed to extend the logic). These ideas were harmless enough, and even amusing, but the errant books also included grains of more threatening ideas—ideas demanding rebuttal. Is man to be viewed as a naked ape, lusting for the blood of his own kind? Are we born with an aggressive spirit, a mood just as genetically encoded as the shape of our nose? If so, some were beginning to dimly wonder, what good are our expensive social programs? You can't teach a nose to be straighter and you can't teach a man to be peaceful.

And what about the other behavioral patterns that many people had been trying to eliminate from our social repertoire? If we are innately aggressive, are we also innately xenophobic (fearful of strangers), racist, and sexist? And if we are, does this mean we can't change? Many of us recoil at the idea because we know that we *must* change!

To many people, however, the great need to change meant that we must continue to strengthen our existing social programs—that we must improve society. Others argued that if our behavior is genetically influenced, then our chances of changing grow ever more remote—at least if we continue to try to change things with our present techniques. But rather than admit flaws in present techniques, and in lieu of conceding defeat, the defenders of the status quo attacked!

However, they quickly learned that it is one thing to score an intellectual point among one's academic peers and quite another to penetrate the hearts and minds of the voting public. And most people were going about their business, arguing with their spouses and fretting over the home team; they weren't really aware that the battle had been mounted, much less who was winning. The detractors of the evolutionary argument may have brought seriousness, expertise, and data to bear, but the few people who caught them doing an occasional four-minute segment on the "Today" show didn't really understand the rebuttal anyway. So even after the arena had long been cleared and the dead corpses of ideas dragged away, most people remained unaware that there had ever been a fray. Thus the old ideas of Lorenz, Ardrey, and Morris continued to pervade the public consciousness. Besides, the idea about lips had attracted a lot of public attention. That was a good one.

After some more ado, the whole argument was relegated to the back burner, and there it stayed through much of the sixties. This is not to say that there were not occasional localized eruptions and flareups. For example, one was brought on by two anthropologists at Rutgers University, Lionel Tiger and Robin Fox (they met at the London Zoo, by the way). They wrote about men in groups and said that the fact that prehistoric men had banded together to bring down large game resulted in the political arena being largely a male domain, in secret societies having been traditionally reserved for males, and in stronger bonding between men than between women. Fortunately for the environmentalists, this was a serious, heavily documented book and didn't work its way into the budding groundswell of what we now call pop psychology. The voting public didn't read it. Nevertheless, because some of the humanistic energy that had fueled the antiwar effort was now being channeled into the feminist movement, Tiger and Fox undoubtedly contributed to making enragedfeminist one word.

But in spite of such outbursts things were relatively quiet on the nature-nurture front. The late sixties and early seventies had seen the birth of large-scale feminism and, paradoxically, a shift toward conservatism—or at least away from radicalism. Students were quiet now and pursuing job-related studies. Fraternities and sororities were gaining strength on American campuses. Even Watergate seemed to be more of an exercise of the media than a mandate of the people (although it certainly increased public cynicism). No one seemed to be looking for trouble, with perhaps the exception of some feminists who were dedicated to raising the collective consciousness at whatever cost.

Then in the mid-seventies a dedicated and greatly respected scientist at Harvard published a book, the product of having worked ninety hours a week for three years. It was a massive tome titled *Sociobiology: The New Synthesis.* The scientist was the bespectacled and greatly respected Edward O. Wilson, and his field was the behavior of the social insects, such as ants and bees. However, the book covered the entire spectrum of animal social behavior and was an excellent example of scholarly work. In the opinion of many, it was, quite simply, one of the most important scientific works of the century. It was eagerly received, and kudos poured in from around the world.

Then the trouble started. It was triggered by a discussion that began on page 547 of Wilson's book. The book was 700 pages long, and Wilson had reserved only about 28 pages for humans, but that meager discourse initiated one of the most lively and unfortunate debates in recent biology (rivaled in its intensity only by the recombinant DNA argument). It seemed that Wilson could write all he wanted to about how evolution shaped the social behavior of bees or penguins or goats, or whatever. He could even write about the natural selection of social patterns in chimpanzees. But how dare he seek to shade man under the Darwinian umbrella? We are *intelligent* creatures. Our social

systems are shaped by learning! By cultural influences! We are infinitely malleable!

The outcries had a familiar ring, sounding a bit like the anti-
Lorenzian theme. They would only have caused embarrassed glances,
shrugs, and shuffles as people tried to shy away from this sticky old
dead-end argument, but this time there was a new twist to it all. This
time the noise was coming from down the hall; in fact, from the
cubicle of Richard Lewontin.

The owlish Lewontin possesses one of the finest minds and independent spirits in biology today. He has time and again broken new
ground, leaving lesser souls to till the soil, and then has moved on to
new horizons. He can fill a room with professional biologists waiting to
hear him talk, appear late, and be sure no one will leave. While others
work diligently and hopefully to be elected to the National Academy
of Sciences, Lewontin resigned in protest of the Academy's role in
defense research.

Lewontin's resignation from the Academy tells something about
the man. He, and a few other young and respected colleagues, dramat-
ically pulled out amid great fanfare about the time of the Vietnam
war. Obviously, he is bold, committed, and political. At one time
someone would have shouted, "He's a Communist!" These days,
though, the term is viewed as indelicate, so one is obliged to accede to
the scientist's own "Marxist" label. But so what? The halls of academe are filled with Marxists of all persuasions. (There's no stigma
attached to that these days, unless you drink your beer at places with
names like the Split Rail. But Marxists drink beer in places with
names like Irishes, so there is no problem. These days, in fact, you can
find good company whether you are a Young Republican or a Wobbly.
No one cares much.)

However, ideally a scientist's political persuasions are not supposed
to influence his science. Ideally. But it turns out that where science
departs from the doldrums and gadgetry of technology, the scientist's
biases, political or otherwise, certainly do taint his or her findings. Just
as two cooks using the same recipe turn out bread with distinctive

tastes because of differences in the flora inhabiting their hands, so, too, does the scientist put some of his own essence into his work. His prejudices, of course, may not be conscious, and they are rarely admitted, but any thoughtful scientist knows they exist.

Wilson, then, submitted his statement on human sociobiology, and it admittedly bore his essence. His basic statement was actually quite simple. He said that human social patterns are undoubtedly shaped by evolutionary processes acting through genes. He did not say that our genes drive us by remote control or that we are compelled to blindly follow whatever dictates they impose upon us. Rather, he said that our behavior can be *influenced* by our genetic makeup; he also said that behavior can be the subject of natural selection and that it can evolve just as our physical makeup does.

The statement seemed innocuous enough and, in fact, the premise that genes influence behavior has been taken for granted by behavioral geneticists working mainly on other species. But when Wilson applied the principles to humans, it provoked a surprising attack. The detractors argued that if our behavior is genetically controlled to any degree, then we lack freedom of choice to precisely that same degree. If our freedom of choice is limited, we are, by definition, to some extent unchangeable; human society, it follows, cannot be altered very much by cultural programs or by changing the social environment. And if this is true, then where does this leave the Marxist ideology, with its social-modeling schemes, its belief in the "perfectibility" of man, its assumption that the improvement of society is dependent upon a fundamental change in the individual?

Lewontin and two or three equally formidable colleagues decided, for some reason, that Wilson's statement was worthy of attack and that they had better do it before things got out of hand. They had brushed off the earlier musings of the pop-ethology writers, but Wilson's argument was so sound, so solid, that it was undoubtedly going to receive serious attention from all quarters. (The work was of such import and magnitude that one insider was even compelled to say, a bit effusively, that Darwin would one day be known as the nineteenth-century Wilson.) So an ad hoc "study group" was hastily formed around the nucleus of Lewontin and his colleagues. Its leaders were respected Harvard faculty men. Its members were drawn largely from the ranks of Harvard and Radcliffe students, some other professors, and assorted hangers-on. It met regularly, and its posture was one of sheer indignation.

Wilson and Lewontin were so well known in academic circles that their argument received all the publicity it could stand. Support for the "study group" formed on other campuses, but Wilson's supporters never organized or, in fact, saw the need. A lot of professional biologists were standing around scratching their heads and wondering what the argument was about. What was *really* being said? What was *really* at stake? Why was Wilson being attacked? Maybe they were missing something. Perhaps something was going on, the details of which were not public knowledge. The disagreement provided material for endless hours of cocktail conversation, a lot of hands on mantelpieces, eyes staring into the fireplace, and sentences that began, "As I see it . . ." But everyone remained a bit puzzled.

In the meantime, Wilson was met with organized resistance wherever he broached the subject. He was publicly derided by a vocal few on those occasions when he dared speak. Still, professional biologists did not come to his rescue in any dramatic way. He was rarely defended in any public forum. For one thing, to do so would have subjected his defenders to suspicions of racism/sexism because of the shrill, and often erroneous, charges that had been levied against him.

As the positions of the people involved became clearer, however, scientists began making up their minds, individually, as quiet, unsolicited referees. And their collective weight came down solidly on Wilson's side. In fact, some scientists were incensed. Others felt duped by having given Lewontin's argument the benefit of doubt until that position revealed itself as so patently absurd that it fell under the weight of its own, to use Lewontin's word, bullshit. In many cases Wilson's words had been taken out of context; in other cases his detractors had lied or had not read the book. The Sociobiology Study Group was flailing at a straw man.

Wilson, in the meantime, never very gregarious to begin with, had withdrawn from the unseemly fray. The Sociobiology Study Group was still shaking its collective fist, but the voices were thinner now and fewer were listening. The group had failed in its attempt to beat down this germ of an idea, this ideological herpes that never seemed to die out but lay dormant, sporadically erupting in the minds of men. It was as if they had tried to beat out a grass fire with a broom—the more they hit it the faster it spread. Lewontin would have been well advised to clam up. Sociobiology was getting press. After all, when a topic makes the cover of *Time* magazine, the next step is Household Word.

One must ask again, at this point, *why* was Wilson attacked? Lewontin is certainly smart enough to see anything that his critics can see. Also, Wilson and Lewontin had always been friendly enough, and there are rumors that, earlier, Wilson had actually helped to advance Lewontin's career by acting behind the scenes. So why was the Sociobiology Study Group formed, and why did it seek to lead so many people down the garden path? The answers may become clearer in following discussions when we trace the basic sociobiological assumption to its logical conclusions. You may come to see what they were afraid of. You may well feel that much of the material I will present does in fact violate your sensibilities. We shall see.

Perhaps these people saw, early on, where the argument could lead. It *could,* in fact, be used to bolster racist or sexist argument; it *could* foster a rebirth of "social Darwinism"—the idea that society benefits by the stronger prevailing over the weaker. Ultimately, and misused, it *could* help support a number of positions that any humanist would find distasteful or even abhorrent. Perhaps sociobiological descriptions would be self-fulfilling. If, for example, aggression were assumed to be innate, then it would come to be accepted as the "normal" condition, and such acceptance can obviously be dangerous. After all, Ardrey's book about a territorial "instinct" in humans had helped make blind nationalism more respectable in the minds of some people. This being the case, perhaps the study group was simply guilty of embracing the adage that the end justifies the means. They may have been exceedingly well intentioned as they fought to head off what they regarded as an idea that would ultimately be detrimental to society. But they chose to fight in the wrong arena. They should never have taken a "scientific" posture, nor should they have tried to cloak their arguments in the guise of rationality. Their position was based on a political view, and it didn't take long to unmask it as such.

But one may also question the scientific validity of the sociobiological position itself, especially in its efforts to make grand assumptions on such meager and "soft" data. Perhaps its greatest strength, at this point, is simply that it attempts to let the chips fall where they may. Its charge is now to proceed carefully so that those chips cannot be used to fuel the fires of bigotry, bias, and hatred. But proceed it must.

One hopes that the fears of the detractors will not be realized. Instead, one would wish that the sociobiology paradigm will simply provide our introspective species with one more window into itself. After all, we need all the windows we can get. We are altering our world with dizzying and accelerating rapidity. And we are placing ourselves in the peculiar position of having to adapt to what we have made. Yet we know so little about ourselves, our motivations, our goals, our heritage. You can't even predict what *you* will do under this or that circumstance. If we are ignorant about ourselves individually, how little we must know about our species. Our efforts to understand the human condition have been met too often with abysmal failure. Perhaps we need a fresh approach. Sociobiology can provide such an approach. But take a deep breath, because it may not be what you think it is.

CHAPTER TWO

THE REPRODUCTIVE IMPERATIVE— OR WHY YOU REALLY LOVE YOUR CHILDREN

WHEN A BIOLOGIST, a person who studies living things, begins a sentence, "All life . . ." you can almost be sure he or she is going to say something wrong. There are very few ways you could end that sentence and be correct, because life is so varied that we find exceptions to almost every rule. However, that said, I would now like to say: All life must obey the Reproductive Imperative. I have an advantage in making this statement because, since I made up the term, I have the privilege of defining it. The Reproductive Imperative, as we will consider it, is: *Reproduce, and leave as many offspring as possible.* We will see that the most successful living things are, quite simply, the best reproducers. Another way to say the same thing is that the most successful individuals are those with the greatest reproductive success.

This is such a simple idea that you may wonder, why all the fuss? However, from this simple beginning will spring ideas that will cause great dismay among many people who would rather not follow the statement to its logical conclusions. Many of those conclusions, you will see, are unpleasant. They lead us to places we would rather not find ourselves. They go against the grain of the humanistic spirit. But "going against the grain" is not the same as "wrong." Perhaps the grain has been shifted around to the extent that it now lies crossways to the truth.

17

In this chapter, I set up the foundation for all the discussions that follow, and, simply, that foundation is the Reproductive Imperative. We will, of course, discuss such topics as why you love your children, but you may not be prepared to deal with the ideas as they are presented here. However, this is just the beginning. We will repeatedly leave the comfortable ruts of well-worn ideas and seek out new roads. It is not a particularly easy task, because untraveled roads can be rocky indeed. But before we go on, we need to review some of the basic principles of reproduction.

In the jargon of biology, *fitness* is not a measure of strength, vigor, intelligence, agility, health, or any other quality to which we often aspire. Fitness, biologically, is simply a measure of one's *reproductive* success. Your neutered dog may be fat and sleek and in prime condition, but his fitness is zero. His genes will disappear from the gene pool with his death. The next generation of dogs may be largely the offspring of clearly inferior animals, but at least those scruffy souls got around to copulating. Tomorrow's dogs may not be very beautiful, but they will exist. *The traits of an individual animal that do not help it to reproduce are biologically irrelevant.* This will be important to everything that follows. Read it again.

Consider an example. Jonathan Livingston Seagull was a remarkable soul, perhaps the most splendid bird that ever lived. He was a fast and acrobatic flier and a philosopher of profound dimension. But he did not mate. He spent his days flying ever faster and entering new dimensions of the mind, but when he died, his genes died with him. So you won't find Jonathan's descendants on our beaches today. Instead, you will find the offspring of smaller-minded gulls—those who, while Jonathan was off philosophizing, were occupying their meager little minds by mating, building nests, catching fish, rearing their young, and putting in a humdrum, uninspired, tunnel-visioned, unromantic, middle-class 9-to-5 day. So when Jonathan's generation passed on, what was left? The descendants of those dreary gulls. We can see them today, standing around and squabbling at the water's edge.

Perhaps the greatest loss to our own species was the genes of

Leonardo da Vinci. He was, by any standard, perhaps the most re-markable man who ever lived. But in spite of his great physical beauty and strength, he had little to do with women. He was obsessed with his art, his science, his music. He may have been homosexual, but in any case, history gives us no reason to believe that he fathered any children. So his kinds of genes have been lost, replaced by the fecund offspring of peasants—responsible, child-loving peasants. It is hard to think of Leonardo, of all men, as having zero fitness, but he failed in the charge given to every individual: Reproduce!

The corollary of the charge to reproduce has already been implied: Among animals that compete with each other, each individual must not only reproduce but must out-reproduce its competitors. Maximum reproduction, then, is an imperative to the individual, *not* to the species. Keep in mind that the more similar two individuals are, the more likely they are to be after the same resources. Thus, any animal's strongest competitor is likely to be of the same species, and the successful animal will be one that tends to out-reproduce its own kind.

"Reproduction," by the way, is not a particularly accurate term for what goes on. It implies that an individual produces another individual just like itself, but of course it does no such thing. In fact, an individual may make offspring that are quite different from itself. Actually, when you get right down to it, the individual doesn't even really make offspring; it just makes copies of its genes. But let's not confuse things. For now, let's just see what offspring are.

Offspring, of course, are descendants. We call our offspring "children," and we are usually pleased when they are like us. "Oh, look! He has his mother's eyes," is a compliment to his mother. Of course, children look like us because they spring from us. But they are not formed from great masses of doughlike protoplasm, molded and sculpted by magical hands. Instead, they are like us because they bear our genes. I will ignore the protestations of narrow-minded geneticists who tell us that technically there is no such thing as a gene, and I will define *gene* as a particular kind of molecule that forms long chains called chromosomes, which are found in the nucleus of all cells. Every human body, and almost every other kind of body you can think of, is composed of billions of cells. Within each cell is a nucleus, and it is within the nucleus that the chromosomes (or genes) work their magic. Basically, what chromosomes (or genes) do is direct the formation of other kinds of molecules, and they do so with dazzling speed and precision. In particular, they orchestrate the formation of certain proteins called enzymes. These enzymes produce certain kinds of chemical reactions, and it is the sum of these reactions that determines the nature of the cell. Thus, because of the kinds of chemical reactions within them, some cells become muscle, some nerve, and some bone. The surprising thing is that virtually all an individual's cells have identical chromosomes.

This may seem paradoxical at first. How could the same chromosomes cause chemical reactions that produce both muscle and nerve? The answer is that the chromosomes are enormously long and only certain segments along their length are activated in any cell. Thus, while a segment will be merrily making muscle enzymes in a muscle cell, that same section will be lying dormant in a nerve cell.

Chromosomes always come in pairs. One chromosome of each pair came from the father, one from the mother. Furthermore, if a gene for, say, eye color is located at a certain place on one chromosome, an eye-color gene will be found at exactly the same place on the matching chromosome.

There are twenty-three pairs, or forty-six chromosomes, in any human cell—with certain exceptions. Among the exceptions are some of the cells that lie deep in your gonads. These cells in your ovaries or testicles change in ways that are impossible for any other kind of cell. After a period of rather complicated shuffling and rearrangement of their chromosomes, these cells and their chromosomes neatly divide in half. It works out that one member of each chromosome pair ends up in each "halved" cell. If we continue to watch such cells, we soon see what they are up to. They are becoming eggs or sperm. Since each egg and sperm has only half the normal complement of chromosomes, when they join at fertilization, they will restore the normal chromosome number to the embryo. After fertilization, the chromosomes simply duplicate themselves each time the cell divides. Thus, from a single cell (the fertilized egg) grows an enormous body composed of billions of cells, each with identical chromosomes. As the body develops, the chromosomes activate and shut down various segments along their length in a harmonious concert of development until, in our species, the embryo takes on the rough figure of a human. Finally, the refined body is ready to be born, carrying the genes of its parents (now its own genes) out into the cold world. Of course, within each of these infant bodies lie the gonads, waiting, biding their time, until they, too, begin halving their chromosomes so that these infants will one day be able to discharge their responsibilities to those chromosomes.

And so it is with almost every living thing that reproduces sexually. Those that skip the complexities of sex duplicate their genes in other ways, but the important point is that everything that survives duplicates its genes.

You can visualize genes as the beads that make up the key chain of the chromosome. Because genes control the chemical reactions that occur inside cells, they ultimately direct the fate of those cells as the cells form tissues and organs. The differences in the tissues found in different people are likely to be due to the differences in the genes within the cells of those tissues. Thus, because the genes that code for eye color are not identical in everyone, different biochemical pathways are initiated, some of which lead to blue eyes, some to brown eyes. No matter what the eye color, though, the trait is directed by genes.

There are only a few traits, such as eye color, that are directed by a single pair of genes. But most traits are directed by a group. Another example of a single-gene trait in humans is the hair on the part of the finger nearest the knuckle. If you have the single gene that codes for hair, there it will be. If that gene codes for no hair, you'll have bald fingers. Hair on the knuckles, of course, has no redeeming social value, nor does another single-gene trait—the ability to roll one's tongue. (Some may wish to argue this latter point.) Most traits, however, are controlled by many genes. For example, height in humans is a multiple-gene effect, and a person is tall if, among his genes that control height, more code for tallness than for shortness. Thus, people are not simply "tall" or "short" but come in a wide range of heights, depending on the ratio of their tallness genes and shortness genes—*and* depending on their diet. People with a lot of tallness genes who don't get enough to eat may end up short. This point should be kept in mind as we proceed, since I will be stressing the importance of genes in human behavior. The example of height should remind us that we are the sum of our genes *and* our experience.

Genes are clearly responsible for producing physical traits, but what about the idea that genes can code for behavior as well as for height? Is there any evidence to support this notion? The evidence, it turns out, is abundant and includes experiments that have produced strains of animals with peculiar behavioral traits. For example, a group of fruit flies may include both fast and slow breeders along with the more common flies that reproduce at the more normal rate. If fast-breeding flies are artificially bred with each other, and slow-breeding flies are also interbred, two distinct strains of fast- and slow-breeding flies can be produced in only a few generations. There are also a number of studies showing that some human behavior, such as the tendency toward schizophrenia, is also inherited.

So let me see if I can collapse the preceding paragraphs to justify why I went through all this. Reproduction, we now see, refers to the reproduction of chromosomes, or genes, and, since we are but temporary sojourners in this world, these precious molecules are placed for safekeeping in our offspring (a chilling thought). Genes direct the formation of enzymes, and enzymes control the chemical reactions that occur inside any cell. The sum of these chemical reactions controls the fate of any cell and hence influences the development of masses of cells such as tissues. Thus, genes direct the development of both bone and nerve tissue (including the brain) and, to some degree, can therefore be expected to influence both physical characteristics and behavior.

Now I would like to expand something I said earlier: successful individuals out-reproduce members of their own species. The implications of this statement are far-reaching, even though the idea seems basically simple. It means that any population will be made up of the descendants of the best reproducers of previous generations. Consider an example. Suppose there are ten gene-bearing individuals living in a limited system such as this rectangle:

1	2	3	4	5	6	7	8	9	10

Because there is natural variation in any population, we can expect some of these individuals to be better reproducers than others. So if we follow their offspring through the generations, we will see the genes of some dwindle in the population while the genes of others increase. The trend, in fact, may be evident only one generation later:

Genes of generation A
Genes of generation B

1	2	3	4	5	6	7	8	9	10

You can see that because of differences in their reproductive success, some individuals in generation A have contributed more genes to generation B than have others. Individuals 2, 5, 7, and 8 have managed to increase their kinds of genes in the gene pool; 3, 4, and 9 have held their own; 1 has lost ground; and 6 and 10 have died out, suffering a genetic death. Keep in mind that 6 and 10 may have been superior to the other individuals in every way, but if they didn't devote their attention to reproduction, their superiority was for naught; it was irrelevant on the evolutionary scale of things.

Here we have covered only two generations, but already the enormous power of such a system is apparent. The genes of nonreproducers have vanished, and those of the best reproducers are increasing; they are well on their way to dominating the population. The logical extension of all this is, of course, that when many generations have passed, the genes of the best reproducers will have become magnified. Any species that has been around for a long time, therefore, will be composed of individuals who are the descendants of the best reproducers of previous generations. We can expect them, then, to be compelled, above all else, to obey nature's Reproductive Impera-tive. They, after all, are the result of a system that rewards *only* reproduction.

The two arguments that may immediately come to mind are, first, that animals do other things besides reproduce, and second, that hu-mans are exempt from any such system by virtue of sheer intelligence and the ability to make conscious decisions. This second argument is the central dogma of the anti-sociobiology camp, and I would ask you to defer your judgment on that one for a while. Answering the first one, though, is easy.

It *is* true that animals spend a great deal of time and energy in nonreproductive activities. At any point in time you may find them eating, fighting, grooming, sunning, or just poking around their neigh-borhood. But each of these activities can ultimately contribute to reproductive success. For example, an animal must eat if it is to have the strength to reproduce. Breeding birds, as a case in point, must have the energy to attract a mate and then to copulate. Female birds must have the energy to produce the eggs and to care for the young. The male may help care for the young in some species, such as sparrows, but in other species, such as chickens, the male may immediately abandon the lady he has just inseminated and search out yet another willing partner. So whether a male stays or goes, he needs energy.

Fighting also can be considered a reproductive activity. In nature, almost all fighting occurs between competitors—for food, mates, or territory. The reproductive advantage of fighting for food and mates is obvious. But what about fighting for territories? A territory, it turns out, is usually a place reserved for rearing young or for attracting mates—perhaps a place where food is stored. Thus, territorial fighting is a reproductive activity.

How about grooming? Again, this behavior can be considered a reproductive activity, for two reasons. First, a cleaner animal is a healthier animal and thus is more likely to live through more breeding seasons. (Besides, who wants to copulate with a dirty partner?) Sec-ond, mate grooming may help form bonds. Touch can be reassuring among animals. So birds or mammals that clean or groom each other can be building social bonds and enhancing the probability of reacting positively toward each other at a later date, thus increasing the likelihood of successful reproduction.

But how about animals that just sit in the sun or mosey around their environment? How can these activities be reproductive? We'll ignore the fact that some lizards sunbathe to rid themselves of parasites, because that falls under the category of grooming. But other cold-blooded animals may be warming up so they will be able to move faster and thus to feed, fight, or mate better. Other animals, though, may simply be resting. Resting, it turns out, can be reproductive in that energy is not being expended at inopportune times. Thus, the animal conserves its energy so as to be able to behave appropriately when the time comes; in this way it increases its efficiency. Efficient animals are likely to make better parents.

And as for moseying around, animals learn about their environment from simple exploring. They learn where the best food is and they learn where hiding places are to be found. The fruits of their learning may not be apparent until they become hungry or are forced to flee a predator, but suddenly it becomes clear that in their aimless wanderings they have been familiarizing themselves with their habitat. Thus, they increase the likelihood that they will live to reproduce. The point is, virtually everything that is self-protective is gene-protective.

Just as genes can be protected in a number of ways, genetic death can be brought about in countless ways. For example, a little aggression may be good if it helps one to chase away competitors. But if that aggressive spirit swells too mightily, it could also turn away prospective mates. In addition, an animal that spends all its time fighting has little time left for copulating. For some species, appearance or cleanliness might be important in attracting a mate, but if one spends too much time grooming, opportunities for copulation may be lost. And then genetic death could also be brought about because an animal is just too stupid or eccentric to attract a mate or rear young successfully. The point is, no matter what the reason, failure to breed is a kind of death. The genes of reproducers live on; those of nonreproducers disappear when the animal dies.

Failure to reproduce, then, can be the result of many obscure or unexpected factors, but the key to *successful* reproduction is better known. Put simply, a reproducer is an individual who follows the rules. His or her aggression, sociality, fears, anxieties, and general behavior are usually rather predictable. One can watch a pair of nesting wrens and can be sure they will flee if approached (with a certain probability that the parent sitting on eggs will simply crouch and thereby become inconspicuous). One can also be sure that the male will attack another male that enters its territory and that the female will behave belligerently toward other females. One can be sure that the parents will dutifully exchange places on the eggs and that each will make numerous visits each day to stuff insect parts down the gullets of the gaping young. Parental behavior is predictable. And we are familiar with it because *it is the norm.*

A moment's reflection will indicate why it is the norm. Keep in mind that any generation is, by definition, made up of the offspring of the most successful reproducers of previous generations. Thus, as we look around us, we see the progeny of good reproducers. Now, it doesn't matter whether good parental behavior is encoded in genes or whether each generation learns parenting from its elders, the result is the same: We can expect most of the individuals in a population to be good reproducers. So as we look around us we see animals being good parents. Any deviation is considered, well, deviant.

There is probably a wider range of parental behavior in humans than in any other species, and, of course, this variation has produced endless debate over the "proper" way to rear children. Most parents feel proud of their behavior toward their offspring because they feel they are rearing them well. The neighbors and the children themselves may disagree, and, in fact, some parents do a terrible job, loading their wide-eyed kids with countless hangups. But the important point is that most parents try to be *good* parents.

Good parental behavior is highly prized in our society. Our values are such that we are aghast when we read what Evelyn Waugh, the great cynic and satirist, wrote of his six offspring: "My children weary me. I can only see them as defective adults; feckless, destructive, frivolous, sensual, humourless." And, when a day-old daughter died, he said, dispassionately, "I saw her when she was dead—a blue slatey colour. Poor little girl, she was not wanted." You probably don't know his children, yet you may notice that you harbor some hostility and resentment toward Waugh because of his words. Why? He could easily have spoken that way of adults without necessarily arousing your ire. So why is it taboo to speak of children in such a way—even children you don't know or who stand a very good chance of growing into adults you won't like? Waugh's feelings were unusual. They went, as much of his life did, against the norm. One would normally predict quite different behavior of a family man like Waugh, with so many children. Most fathers spring from a different mold, and although they may have all manner of philosophies regarding parenting, we expect most fathers to have a certain love of children, especially their own.

One may ask, why is there so much variation in parental behavior among humans and so little variation among wrens, gulls, or bees? The evolutionist at the back of the room would eagerly raise his hand and blurt, "Because of low selection on humans." His proud glances around the room would be met by quizzical stares until he explained himself. He would probably begin by saying that, in many ways, natural selection doesn't operate very strongly on modern humans. Wrens have to be alert or they will be caught by the falcon. Nonalert wrens generally don't live long enough to pass on their genes, so natural selection, the process of ensuring the success of the best reproducers, selects for alert wrens. Humans don't have to be very alert because most of our predators are gone. If we see a lion in the yard, we call the police; we don't have to be able to deal with lions. Thus there is reduced selection for alertness in humans. Dull, unalert, and rather helpless humans are able to reproduce.

But even a dull human is pretty smart in comparison to other animals on the planet. Our intelligence enables us to *decide* how we will rear our children. We are not genetically programmed to respond in stereotyped ways to every situation that arises. As we make up our own minds, we come to all kinds of decisions. Some of us decide to spare the rod; others have house guests.

Another difference between wrens and humans is the rigidity of the specifications for successful reproduction. Because a wren must carefully shield its eggs throughout the day, a parent can't leave for too long. The time limits are narrowly fixed. In addition, once the eggs hatch, the parent *must* carry the shells away so they do not attract predators and it *must* feed the young high-protein insects. There are a lot of musts, and if they are not met, the young will die.

In contrast, human infants can survive a wide range of caretaking techniques; they can thrive on rigid schedules or loose ones, lots of attention or not much, and they can eat all kinds of foods. Babies may be fragile, but they are born with their tiny bodies already dominated by an enormous convoluted brain. Because of this brain, almost any regimen, with certain minimal requirements, will do. Children are helpless but they are smart, and unless they are grossly mistreated, they will adapt to about anything. They may not grow into very happy people, but they tend to survive, hangups and all. Some human infants grow up to be indomitable and expansive, while others retreat solemnly into the recesses of their own minds. But most of them, no matter what their outlook and life style, will live to reproduce. So, as an evolutionist would put it, the intelligence of humans has reduced the effects of selection in other realms. We can compensate. We have options. We are adaptable.

So, as we look around us we see children being reared under a variety of regimens. We think some methods are good and some are bad, but in most cases the parents believe they are good parents. Their weird little children will grow up to believe that they, too, are good parents. How much of human parental behavior, then, is genetically controlled and virtually inescapable? Is parenthood one of those realms where our intelligence has reduced the effects of selection? The great variation in human parental behavior is evidence that the *techniques* of parenthood are not passed along genetically. But because of the ubiquity of a very general kind of parental desire that permeates virtually all human societies, we can assume that *something* very elemental exists within us and that it is heritable, genetic. I believe that this inherited trait is simply *caring about children*. Any gene that codes for *caring about children* can be viewed as a mechanism to protect all the other genes. After all, since we must die, our children are our genetic caretakers. We must see to their welfare.

To set the record straight, caring for children is only half the story. The other half relates to sex. All any human system needs in order to perpetuate itself is a love of sex and a love of children. The sex, of course, has something to do with the children being here. Then, once they are here, they must be loved.

It shouldn't take long to see that human beings meet both criteria. We are nothing if not sex-crazed and child-oriented.

The system, as you can see, is a very simple one. An intensive interest in sex will result in children, and love of children will cause us to behave toward them in such a way that they are likely to survive to enter their own reproductive period, bearing our genes. Thus, by having children and caring for them, we tend to propagate our own kinds of genes, and this, as we know, is the name of the game.

We can also ask why parents so readily sacrifice the quality of their own lives for what they assume to be the needs of their children. The family may live in a dismal place that the father hates, but he'll live out his days there so his children won't have to leave their friends or undergo the trauma of changing schools. Or a man and a woman who care little for each other will sentence themselves to spending their lives together "for the sake of the children." Some parents who have substantial amounts of money will forego vacations and exciting times because they feel guilty about spending money on themselves that could have gone to their children. Their wonderful, deserving children, so full of promise, raw talent, and insight.

This business of love of children is interesting. Have you ever sat in a movie theater and witnessed the cooing of the audience when a baby's face was shown on the screen? When a TV sitcom is played before a "live audience," why does the whole place chuckle and coo when Little Joey's face is shown? Perhaps you have seen women (rarely men) on a subway playing with a baby peering over its mother's shoulder. The same mother without the baby would probably have been ignored or even treated brusquely; even with the child, the smiles are reserved for it, not the parent. Why is this scenario so prevalent? Is it true that we love children—any children?

Sometimes in my classes I ask how many people love children. Among college students these days, a few from any class will inevitably profess not to like children very much. (We can discount a few who are after the shock value.) There are usually a few "mature" students in the class—those going back to school after having raised a family— and they will almost invariably say, "Ah, but wait until you have your own." And this makes sense. One need not love other people's children in order to reproduce—only one's own, those bearing one's own genes. The Reproductive Imperative is thus fulfilled, and all is well.

But still, most women do like children, anybody's children, and although some men feel the same way, not as many do. There are some fascinating data to support this argument. Eckhard Hess, at the University of Chicago, found that the size of the pupil of the eye is a rather dependable indicator of interest and appeal. Basically, he found that the pupil tends to increase in diameter when a person sees something appealing. It is as if the pupil were opening to let more light in so that the subject of interest could be seen more clearly. Furthermore, the pupil will constrict at the sight of something unappealing, as if it were blocking out the image. I have tested students rather informally by picking a blue-eyed person whose pupil could be easily seen and then watching his pupil as he looked at a sequence of photographs. Sure enough, pupil size would constrict at the sight of a photo of a dog dropping or a laughing old crone. I also found, as did Hess, that the pupils of most men widened when a picture of a nude woman was shown and that women's pupils widened at the sight of a nude man. It had been assumed for years that women were not interested in viewing a nude male body. Eckhard Hess had discovered what Burt Reynolds knew all along.

But we're interested in whether men and women react differently to babies. And it turns out they do. Hess found that the pupil size of most people will change at the sight of a baby, but the direction of the change depends on sex and parental status. The pupils of women dilate at the sight of a baby, whether the woman is single, married but childless, or a mother. In contrast, the pupils of single men and married-but-childless men constrict when they see a baby; only fathers show increased pupil size.

The findings indicate that women are generally more receptive to infants than are men and that men's interests in children increase with fatherhood. It would be interesting to discover whether men showing constricted pupils claim to like children. A cynic, of course, would suggest that single men might profess, untruthfully, to like children in order to avoid appearing aberrant or to keep from repelling women. It would also be interesting to find out what causes the change in men who become fathers. Do they learn to love children through associating with their own, or does fatherhood alter their hormonal constitution, thus causing an unconscious but compelling change in behavior? In any case, it seems that the childless man who coos over someone else's baby is merely being polite or bowing to what he hopes is normal and natural but that a cooing woman means it.

Why the difference? Let's consider the answer in evolutionary terms. Women have traditionally remained in closer association with children than have men for the simple and mundane reason that they are the milk producers, and thus they could be expected to feel more strongly attracted to infants. But perhaps men should, in fact, be less attracted to babies, because in their traditional role as hunters, they would have had to be able to range widely, unencumbered by strong ties to home and hearth. That tie would have had to strengthen with fatherhood, however, if a man's offspring were to have any chance of succeeding. He had to stay close enough to offer protection and he had to be drawn homeward in order to yield his catch to his offspring and to the woman who was assisting in rearing his offspring. We will say more about all this in the next chapter, but the point here is that there do seem to be differences in the love that men and women have for babies.

I have often asked my classes at various universities *why* they liked children. (By the way, although an increasing number say they don't, most do like children or say they do.) Are children in any way deserving of love? "Is it not true," I ask, "that they are usually dirty, inarticulate, demanding, helpless, noisy, inexperienced, half the size of everyone else, and broke?" Some students laugh, some don't. I am prodding a sacred cow. So I ask again, "Why do we love them?" After what usually seems like a long pause, I begin to get responses. Then we take a closer look at each one.

Innocence! "Children are innocent," someone says. Innocence, I point out, may simply indicate the lack of opportunity. And do we really love innocence? A dove is innocent, but each autumn they tumble from the sky by the millions under the polished guns of child-loving clerks. So if innocence is only appealing when it is attached to children, then we are back to square one: What qualities do children have that make innocence seem appealing? Answers such as "kindness," "honesty," and "straightforwardness" can be dismissed by simply watching children interact on a playground. They are just as often mean, sneaky, and manipulative. One answer that crops up fairly frequently is "needful." Children are undeniably needful, but needfulness is not universally admired. Again, it is worn best by children because we love them on some other basis. After all, needful adults can be a pain. Men do not often speak kindly of needful women, and although some women respond favorably to needful men, some do not. And if needfulness *is* desirable, doesn't it say more about us than about the children? Perhaps we need to be needed and children simply provide us with a place where we can put our care, our love.

I want to make another small point here, which I will expand later: If our love of children fulfills our needs in any way, then adults' love of children may be largely selfish. We care for them because they make us feel good or because our *caring* makes us feel good. There is an important distinction between loving children for their sake and for our own. I remember as a child watching a movie—undoubtedly a western because that was about all I ever watched—in which a little boy was hit by a falling rock. His mother rushed to him (I believe it was Katy Jurado), fell to her knees, and screamed, "What will I do?" Even at that tender age, I smelled a rat. I remember thinking, "What do *you* have to do with it, lady? The rock hit *him*." Was her love based primarily on her caring for herself in that his injury made her feel bad? Is that what love is all about?

By the way, some people say they are simply returning the child's love. They love children because children love them. But, *do* children love? *Can* children love? Or are they looking out for their own best interest by eliciting love from adults? Again, we find ourselves treading heavily on hallowed ground, but since it's hard for readers to get their hands on the throats of authors of irreverent material, we plunge ahead.

There is some evidence that the infant smiling at you so brightly has utterly no idea what it is doing but that the results of the smile are rewarding. By lengthening the margins of its lips, it causes you to care for it, perhaps to the point of sacrifice. The smile may be an important part of a baby's behavioral repertoire because it elicits such positive feelings in you at just the time when the baby is likely to be most exasperating. Just when you think you've had it with that warmness spreading across your lap, the infant looks directly at you and smiles, and all your budding hostility vanishes amid coos of delight. The infant's smile is no doubt an important bond-builder at a time when the baby is most likely to elicit rejection behavior.

But what makes the baby smile? Does it love you? An infant is able to "fixate," or look directly at, anything (such as a mother's face) as early as four or five weeks of age. It may only give the impression of seeing, however, since blind infants also stare directly ahead, where the mother's face is likely to be, as they, too, smile broadly. Infants also smile in their sleep or at other times that have nothing to do with their pleasure or love. This spontaneous smile, of course, will later be replaced by a genuine smile. A genuine smile is a response to being smiled at or an expression of pleasure.

Babies three to six months old will smile at practically anything from scarecrow faces to normal and grimacing human faces as long as those faces have "eyes." In fact, until about the second month of life, any prominent eye-sized spots drawn on a "head" (round or square) elicit more smiles than does a rectangular bar or even a painted "face" drawn on that same "head." In other words, the infant smiles at two dots (because in its world, they are usually eyes on something whose aid it needs), just as a robin attacks red feathers (because in its world they are usually on the breast of a competitor). In fact, babies a month old will smile at three dots, and it doesn't matter much how they are arranged on the head. They won't smile at one dot, though. There's no percentage there. Mothers usually have at least two eyes.

At about two months of age, the arrangement of the dots becomes more important. Dots placed horizontally get more smiles than those placed vertically. The child, by the way, is particularly attentive to the eyes; other facial features can be added in any arrangement.

A four-month-old child seems to become aware of the mouth, and experimenters find that in the fifth month, broadening the mouth (or the line representing the mouth) elicits more smiling, as if the infant were responding to a smile. At about six months, crude models of faces lose their effectiveness, and it takes more natural features to elicit smiling. By fourteen months, babies have learned more about faces and are acutely aware of the "mood" of the face they see. They smile at smiling painted faces, but, shown a face with frown wrinkles, they may cry, scream, or try to get away. In some of these face experiments the infants were institutionalized children who had never seen a "threat-frown" before. Thus, it seems that all children are born with built-in responses to certain facial cues, that such responses are gradually refined, and that these responses are the same in all cultures. Basically, then, the smiles infants produce when someone leans over them and asks, "Who do you love?" are self-protective devices. The babies must elicit loving care if they have any hope of making it through their most dependent years.

By the same token, it is to a parent's reproductive interest to respond appropriately to the love-eliciting cues of children, since those children are the repositories of the parent's chromosomes. Through carefully orchestrated mutual signaling, then, infants get themselves cared for until the disruptions brought on by adolescence signal that they are ready to leave their parents and to do the things necessary to move their own genes (actually, the genetic bequests from their parents) into yet another generation.

So, people who say they love children because children love them may not be returning a baby's love. They may be responding to a "smile" that they elicited to begin with simply by having two prominent eyes on a head of some kind.

So again, we must ask what qualifies children for our love. In my experience, as you go through the list of answers people come up with, and if you deal with the question honestly (which is difficult because the issue is charged with emotion), each answer can be dismissed in turn by simply looking at it objectively. It seems that we love children on no rational basis whatever but simply because they are children.

And doesn't this sound admirable enough? This situation is obviously as it should be. We love children simply because they are children. You could probably buy a plaque with such an inscription at Stuckey's. But stop, back up, and look again. The question remains: Why? If we agree that our love cannot be based on any quality peculiar to the children themselves, then it must swell from somewhere within us, and if it does, what is its source? Since people are notoriously poor at examining the roots of their own behavior, it might be a good idea at this point to leave introspection and look at other species. Other species can only provide us with tenuous evidence about ourselves, but they can at least provide food for thought.

Looking at other animals is, after all, one of the most tried, if not true, ways to study human behavior. Those poor white, red-eyed, inbred laboratory rats have suffered more pain and more debilitation than one cares to admit so that people can learn about themselves. It is as if we regard them as smaller, shorter-lived, and expendable human beings. Looking at ourselves in the distorted mirror of other species has its pitfalls. So, keeping in mind that the technique is imperfect, let's continue to sift through the animal lore, looking for nuggets of truth about ourselves. And the questions we now want to ask our fellow travelers on this small planet are: Do *you* love *your* children, and why?

If you have ever been threatened by a mother animal, the answer to the first question is obvious. I recall once being attacked by a ptarmigan as I stepped into an Alaskan clearing. I had been keeping an eye peeled for bears, and the sudden fluttering at my face almost did me in. I didn't have to ask why a small bird would attack a man. Even as I was trying to gain control of myself, I saw her small brood scurrying away in the forest leaves. Such defense is, of course, not unusual. Tiny nesting African groundbirds have even chased away elephants by rushing at them, feathers abristle. My cat, Mary Elizabeth, once attacked Bear, a friendly and curious German shepherd who had wandered near her weanling kittens. We have all seen mockingbirds swooping at prowling cats. And on and on the list goes. Animals, at least some species of animals, do indeed love their offspring.

I use the word "love" advisedly. It implies we know what is in the mind of the parent when, of course, we don't. Twenty years ago, however, the famous psychologist Harry F. Harlow made this kind of usage respectable when he talked about love in infant monkeys after showing that they preferred (loved) a soft, cloth surrogate mother that yielded no food to a wire one with a milk bottle attached. So we can talk about love, just keeping in mind that what we are *really* saying is that the animal behaves *as if* it loves its offspring.

I should add that we don't see much parental love outside the birds and mammals. A tapeworm lying with its head buried in your gut simply breaks off section after section at the end of its long body as it grows. Each section is a veritable sack of eggs that passes out with your feces. When the sack ruptures, the eggs are released and they are on their own. Few will make it to adulthood, because each must pass through an elaborate and precise chain of events, perhaps even inhabiting the bodies of snails and pigs, before it can again occupy a human host. It just isn't very likely that all the conditions will be met. The tapeworm's answer is to lay millions upon millions of eggs so that perhaps a few will wend their way through the incredible maze that is the tapeworm's life history. Does a tapeworm, which releases millions of unattended eggs into a hostile world, love its children? Obviously not. One might say that the tapeworm's duty is toward its own reproduction, even at the expense of most of its offspring.

We can go through the animal kingdom showing that most animals' parental behavior doesn't differ greatly from that of plants. In other words, for most species, the "love index" hovers around zero. Even among most of the vertebrates, parental care is negligible; it is found in only a few isolated species until one gets to the birds and mammals. Then it seems that virtually all the feathered and the haired creatures care for their offspring.

Why? What is it about birds and mammals that would encourage them to love their children? It turns out that *two* characteristics of these animals compel them to love. First, they are warm-blooded and, second, they are, more or less, intelligent. To see what these features have to do with love, let's look at birds.

First, birds generally fall into one of two categories, depending on how much parental care they need. For comparison, let's consider bluejays and chickens. If you have ever found a baby bluejay that fell from its nest in the spring, you know how much its parents are needed. Young bluejays are naked and helpless and cannot hope to survive without parents to feed them and to shield them with warm feathers. The young warm-blooded birds cannot tolerate great changes in their body temperature. Although they have built-in thermostats just like their parents, they lack insulating feathers. Because of their small size, they lose body heat rapidly. So even safely up in the nest, they need their parents to keep them warm, because baby birds probably cannot eat enough to keep up normal metabolic activity and maintain their body heat as well. When the adults are not sitting on the nest, they are out searching for food for their young. Bluejays are indeed attentive parents.

What about chickens? Do they love their offspring for the same reason—because the chicks are naked and cannot feed themselves? "Of course not," comes the chorus. Everyone knows that chicks hatch fully feathered and are able to run around and feed themselves within only a few minutes. So are the baby ptarmigans I almost stepped on in the Alaskan forest. Then why did their mother almost give me a coronary? Why was she even *with* them? Hens and mother ptarmigans stay with their young for different reasons than do the jays, but for good reasons all the same. These species are ground-dwellers and so the babies are likely to be caught by a predator much more readily than is a tiny jay swaying safely in its nest in the far reaches of some bough. So the mother stays with the young and watches for danger. When she spots it, she either confronts it directly or gives a warning cluck. The young are genetically programmed to take evasive action as soon as they hear that cluck. At the sound they scatter and "freeze." When the danger has passed, the mother gives the "come" call, and the chicks immediately return to her. By associating closely with the mother, then, they can be expected to learn the signs of danger. When no danger threatens and the chicks follow their mother as she scratches in the soil, uncovering all sorts of delicious items, they learn which objects are good to eat and which are not. So the hen's role includes giving her chicks time to learn about the environment as they grow. Chickens are undoubtedly among the stupidest of all warm-blooded animals, but they can learn a few things—and those things are important to them. Just imagine how much more important the teaching role of a mother chimpanzee is.

We see, then, that the love birds and mammals have for their young results in the young being shielded from the dangers of the environment as they gradually learn about it. The more vulnerable the young are, or the more they must learn, the greater will be the love, or attachment, of the parent.

So birds and mammals love their young in order to give the young time to learn to cope with the world. Mammals must learn more than birds, so they mature more slowly to give the brain time to accumulate sufficient information. And to carry our argument one step further, we can say that since mammals are more intelligent than birds, they should love their offspring more. To examine this point, let's consider infant love among the primates, the group that includes apes and humans.

Primates mature very slowly. One result of slow maturation is that some offspring may leave their parental protection before they are adults. Young chimpanzees, for example, may move freely among the group as they gradually cut the apron strings. But they may not breed successfully for several more years. The reason for this extended period of development is that chimpanzees are intelligent creatures. They are born with large brains, but their brains are not already preprogrammed as, say, a cockroach's is. They need time to *learn* before they go out entirely on their own. So they mature slowly, not straying very far from mother (paternity is an open question in this promiscuous species) but gradually branching out on their own and accumulating information all the while.

Young chimpanzees continue to associate with their mother even as new brothers and sisters come along. In the years that they remain attached to her, she offers protection and education. For example, she can teach them what to eat by giving them food or by letting them take food from her. Since chimpanzees are opportunistic and eat all sorts of things, it is unlikely that they are genetically programmed to search out particular food items. So they watch, try, and learn—sometimes by bitter experience. The mother can also socialize them. She can teach them to fear the large, dominant males and to recognize the meaning of threat and appeasement gestures. Her job, then, is to offer what protection she can, especially at first, and to fill the large brains of her children with useful information—information that will help them to survive and to carry her genes into subsequent generations, just as she has faithfully discharged her responsibility to her forebears by perpetuating *their* genes.

Another point can be added here. Mother love may be different from father love. Let's compare the chicken and the bluejay again. The father and mother bluejay look exactly alike and have very similar responsibilities once the eggs are laid. They both protect and feed their doddering young. They behave like loyal, devoted parents—both of them. Why? We know the mother is intimately tied to the eggs, having borne them in her body, but the father isn't. So why isn't he out increasing his fitness by inseminating other females? It turns out that insects are not very easy to catch and that he is needed to help bring home the bacon. If he were to wander off looking for other females, his offspring might starve. His best reproductive bet, then, is to stay at home tending the offspring of one mating and to see that they carry his genes into the next generation.

But while Mr. Bluejay is dutifully carrying out his chores, where is the rooster that mated beneath his tree only yesterday? Gone. Seeds are easier to find than insects, and since chicks can run around and find their own food, the rooster's family does not need him. In fact, he is so noisy and bright that he might help draw a predator's attention to his brood. So it's better for everyone if he leaves. The hen can raise their offspring just as well without him, and he can increase his genetic output by seeking out other females; the more females he copulates with, the greater his reproductive success. To him, then, falls the role of Master Seducer. He must dazzle and conquer every hen he encounters. A Master Seducer can't run around looking like a chicken, though, so natural selection has draped him in colorful long feathers, a bountiful chest, and a long comb and wattles. He also has sharp spurs to convince other males of his virility. By his appearance he persuades any females he might meet that he is indeed a splendid specimen and that their genes would do well to mix with his. Obviously, so magnificent a creature can't be a family man. No indeed. He loves not his children, but the hens don't care. They don't really need him, and besides, isn't he gorgeous?

Let's back up a second and take stock of what's been said. We see that tapeworms don't love their young at all and that they share this trait with almost all the other animals. A young insect that has just completed its metamorphosis looks like all the other adults and is simply treated as one of the group, even by its own parents, who have no way of recognizing it. Young crocodiles are not showered with affection and may even end up on their parents' menu. But they are born with teeth, a predatory instinct, and a deep suspicion of anything bigger than they are. So when it comes to eggs and the opposite sex, most animals lay them and leave them. Birds and mammals depart from this pattern by caring for their young, and we have seen some of the advantages of their care. In fact, without care, most of these young would die, and the parents' chromosomes would be lost to future generations. Thus, loving children is just another way to increase one's fitness.

We can make predictions about how much a parent loves its off-spring by examining the parents' longevity. I recall watching a film of a group of African hunting dogs trying to kill a baby wildebeest. The mother fought valiantly for a time, and if Hollywood had written the script, she would have driven away the ravenous dogs. But evolution was the author, and so the mother, after fending off the voracious predators for a time and feeling herself tiring, suddenly turned and loped away to leave her baby to its fate. Even as a biologist I was horrified. I didn't expect it. Then it dawned on me that by fleeing she was increasing her fitness. She was increasing her probability of leaving other offspring by saving herself to breed again another day. Wildebeest live several years, and if they can reproduce in most of those years, they are successful. If they put too much effort into any one offspring, they decrease their likelihood of having more. On the other side of the coin, if an animal has only one shot at reproduction, it can be expected to defend its young to the death. All the chips would be on the table. It would be the mother's only chance at perpetuating her chromosomes. By the same token we could expect animals near the end of their reproductive years to be more protective of their offspring than younger parents would be. The younger ones have less to lose. These two ideas, however, are at this point purely conjecture. We don't have any data to support arguments one way or the other, but we can ask ourselves: Do older parents put more of their encrgy into their offspring than younger parents do? Are they more protective?

I now wish to make another peculiar statement: The more a species is forced to compete, the more love the young will receive. I don't mean to imply the maudlin notion that parents love their "poor little competitors" out of some sense of pity. I mean that animals born into a competitive milieu will have a better chance of making it if they have had careful preparation for the competition ahead.

In this sense, tapeworms receive no love because they don't need it. Their mortality is so high that they are not likely to ever reach a host, much less compete for one. A parent tapeworm has very little investment in any egg and certainly does not waste a second in loving it. The eggs leave their anonymous mother with only the bare necessities for survival, and the rest is left to the winds of chance.

Bluejays and chimpanzees, however, live in a competitive environment. For example, members of both groups must seasonally compete with members of their own species for dwindling food. They may even compete with each other for nest sites or sleeping places. Bluejays, like other birds, certainly must compete with each other for mates, and chimpanzees must compete for higher rank within the group. Because birds and mammals live in a competitive world, then, we cannot expect them to discharge their young willy-nilly into the environment. Any ill-prepared offspring would fail before more carefully trained ones from other parents. Thus, a parent's best bet is to keep its young around, attending to them as they grow and develop, until they are prepared to face the competition. So whereas the tapeworm leaves thousands of ill-prepared eggs, birds and mammals leave only a few carefully attended offspring—offspring that, because of parental attention, will be likely to survive among others of their kind when times are hard. Some animals, then, are in the numbers game, while others are interested in quality. But, the point is, everyone is trying to maximize his or her reproductive success.

Now that I've said how carefully some animals prepare their young for the rigors that lie ahead, I would like to make a point that may seem surprising, or at least inconsistent. It may be in an animal's best reproductive interest not to prepare the offspring *too* well. This point has not yet been demonstrated in the animal world, but animals may have evolved ways to send their young out into the world ill-prepared and half-cocked. In other words, they may produce "faulty" young as a means of increasing their reproductive output. In another book, I have referred to these faulty and ill-prepared young as "genetic emissaries." Keep in mind that the world is a variable and changeable place and that every opportunity for success must be explored. Now, a parent has discovered a life style that works, or he or she wouldn't be there. But perhaps there are other, untested, ways and places to live. The parents might not want to risk their personal well-being to explore such places, so they produce adventuresome or ignorant young. Let's take some examples. Some migratory birds move vast distances each year; the older birds tend to make the trip more safely than younger ones. The first-year birds are more likely to be blown off course and thus to invade new places. They may succeed or fail in these new places, but the parents wouldn't want to take that risk themselves, especially if they stand a good chance of producing more young at a later time if they continue to live the way that works best for them. Thus, they allow the young to begin the trip ill-prepared because they may benefit if the young happen to end up somewhere where food is more abundant or competition is lower.

Of course, a bird has too much invested in its young to just send them on some hopeless journey, so the young are somewhat prepared to deal with the world they encounter. But for another example, let's return to our friend the tapeworm. The tapeworm has very little invested in any egg, so the eggs are simply given a tough coat and scattered over the earth—most of them to a certain death. That's OK; the tapeworm just makes more and disperses them into every nook and cranny of the planet. The point begins to come clear: The more a parent has invested in its offspring, the less it will allow the offspring to depart from the safe and traditional mode of life for the species.

So let's test the idea by looking at a group with a very large parental investment: the chimpanzees. A mother chimpanzee does not go through months of pregnancy to bear a single young just to allow it to wander off and be killed. Instead, she carefully cares for it. *But* if we watch this prized offspring, we will see that it is an adventuresome and fearless little tyke—up to a point. Thus it goes places where its mother wouldn't go, and it puts all sorts of things into its mouth, in a sense testing new places and new food. It even plays with baboons, and it shows a great deal of curiosity about everything. In a sense it may be exploring an environment on behalf of its more cautious parents. But because the mother has so much invested in it, she still watches it rather closely, takes some things away from it, and keeps it from wandering too far. The idea is that by producing adventuresome, reckless, and curious offspring, the mother is producing genetic emissaries, bearing her chromosomes, who will cheerfully attempt to exploit the environment in ways she wouldn't dare. Also, the examples of tapeworms, birds, and chimpanzees show that the greater the parental investment, the better prepared (or monitored) will be the young. So we see that this, too, is just another way of leaving one's genes.

Let me emphasize that I am not saying that animal parents *wish* to leave their kinds of genes or that parents are actually interested in numbers or quality. But it turns out that the genes comprising any generation are those from parents who acted *as if* they wanted to leave their genes and *as if* they had some particular reproductive "strategy" in mind. One day I stood on a grassy beach in Bermuda and watched thousands of tiny fish arch their sparkling bodies clear of the water in wave after wave as they fled before a feeding school of mackerel. Probably many of these darting, jewel-like little fish were only a few days or weeks old. Perhaps this was, for many, the first encounter with their voracious predators. But they all fled in terror. Terror? I call it terror because if I were a fry I would have been terrified. But could it really have been terror? Were they frightened? Of what? Death? A two-week-old fish frightened of the prospect of dying? Maybe we'd best back up and look for a better explanation—one that we don't have to inflate with human motive in order to make it float.

Perhaps a better explanation of the behavior of these fish is that when a dark form of a certain size moves across the tiny fish's field of vision at a certain rate, impulses are sent from the eye to the brain and back out to the swimming muscles. When these muscles contract, they rapidly propel the fish through the water. But these fish didn't move blindly; they were coordinated. Once those muscles were activated, their precise movements would have been directed by the position of the other fish. Thus the tiny prey would have clustered together and leaped clear of the water in synchronous waves, driven not by fear but by an image on their retinas. By banding together, they would have had a "confusing" effect on their predators, which wouldn't have been able to single out any of them until almost all had escaped. It all sounds like a rather mechanical explanation of a complex behavior, but it is, nonetheless, a simpler explanation than one invoking terror. Fish that behave in such a way leave their genes. Those that don't, don't. And people who behave *as if* they love their children leave their genes; those who don't, don't.

We tend to say that the mother hen "loves" her children because we see her taking such good care of them. But we can now reject this explanation in favor of another one: the mother hen is a descendant of animals that maximized their genetic output, so she tends to behave in such a way as to maximize *her* genetic output. The vehicles by which she must propel her genes into the next generation are her offspring, so she does everything she can to increase the likelihood of survival for those vehicles. To put it even more bluntly, her children are merely receptacles for her genes.

This whole point is distressingly driven home when one observes parental love among gulls. Both parents care for the young, dutifully defending them from predators and spending virtually the entire day searching the sea for morsels of food that they will regurgitate into the gullets of their fuzzy children. The parents are alert, protective, and attentive, showing all the signs of parental love at the sight of their fluffy little chicks. The chicks may doze in the sun, jump up and run around a bit, peck at things, and beg for food when a parent appears. They are indeed lovable little creatures. However, should a gull chick stop sending the proper signals to the parent's eyes and ears, signals that say, "I'm a healthy chick," a terrible thing happens. If a gull chick should fall sick and lie unresponsively in the nest or if it should die, the "loving" parental behavior is no longer elicited. The receptors in the eyes and ears of the adult are not properly stimulated, and love therefore disappears. The parent may then take one look at the immobile youngster, give it a couple of tentative pecks, and then toss it into the air and gulp it down. In spite of our shattered sensibilities, this is precisely what one would expect of an efficient reproducer. No use tending a sick child or mourning a dead one. Better to use its tissue to form new and healthy young.

I should add that primates usually do not behave so callously. A female baboon may carry her dead infant for days before she abandons it. Is her love greater? Not in the unemotional arithmetic of evolution. She *should* make a greater effort to salvage any existing young because she has more invested in it. She has undergone a long pregnancy, has suffered the trauma of giving birth, and has had her physiology altered for milk production. She can't afford to discard her young so easily. It is doubtful that she understands the one-way nature of death, and it probably takes a great amount of "incorrect" signaling from her limp baby to persuade her to abandon it.

By now you can see why the sociobiological position so easily arouses antagonism. Most people are willing to talk freely about birds and to speculate about their motivations, but they grow increasingly uneasy as the conversation extends to mammals, and especially to primates. One problem here is that *we're* primates. To see the nature of the problem, ask a mother if she loves her baby. Watch her snatch it closer to her breast; be prepared to withstand her glare and hear her say indignantly, "Of course!" Then ask her *why* she loves her baby. You can be prepared for circular reasoning ("Because it's *my* baby.") and irrational responses ("Because! I just *do.*"). At this point you touch the baby at your own risk until she calms down. Of course, you can try explaining to her that she is compelled to love the receptacle of her own genes if she has any hope of leaving those genes in the next generation. You can say that all her sacrifice is just her way of maximizing her reproductive output and that her protectiveness and care are important to the future of those peculiar, coiled molecules. You can even explain that she herself is the descendant of successful reproducers and so she bears genes that compel her to behave that way—that, in effect, *her love is a device employed by her genes to look after themselves.* But keep two things in mind: you had better say it carefully, and it won't make a damn bit of difference to her. She knows what she feels. You just can't expect her to pull up in front of the kindergarten and announce that she is there to pick up her genetic repositories.

I don't want to beat a dead horse here, but unless this one point is made clearly, none of the rest of what I have to say will hold together. Animals *appear* to love their young because they treat their children just as we treat our children, and we love our children—although we can't say why. Possibly, however, love is a term that is only operational. In other words, it explains nothing; it simply *describes* a set of behavioral patterns. Those patterns have one evolutionary use: to help us propel our genes into the next generation. Individuals who do not reproduce, no matter what their personal successes, suffer genetic death. In species in which the genetic recipients (or children) are harder to produce and need more protection or more opportunity to learn, parental care, or "love," will be accordingly more intense.

So now you know why you *really* love your children. You are simply the descendant of generation after generation of people who loved theirs. From the platform of the Reproductive Imperative, we will now fearlessly dive into a number of discussions: We will see, for example, why Mr. and Mrs. America hate homosexuals and why the sexual double standard has been so important. We will consider a host of topics, and the conclusions I will ask you to accept may well dismay, if not infuriate, you. And though I'm actually quite a nice fellow, I have to admit that I don't care. In fact, in our rapidly changing and increasingly dangerous world, a world in which we are continually forced to reevaluate our directions, it seems to me to be high time that we stopped contentedly grooming our sacred cows and stepped back for a long, hard look at them. They may never seem quite the same to us again.

CHAPTER THREE

THE GENETICS OF MORALITY

O NE MORNING when I was teaching in Germany, my ritual morning coffee was interrupted by a colleague, who asked me to lecture to one of his classes. We were both teaching in the psychology department, but we had a history of disagreeing on just about everything. Perhaps to show me what he thought of my ideas, he asked me at 9:00 to lecture at 1:00 the same day. To show him what I thought about his ideas, I accepted. Furthermore, I decided to title my lecture "The Genetics of Morality"—all this amidst much giggling, table slapping, snorting, and snuffling from a student who had joined me for coffee and who generally shared my opinion of my colleague.

The afternoon lecture suitably enraged the good professor, but I probably did no great service to science that day. I understand he was kept busy untying knots and smoothing ruffled feathers for days afterward, his students being convinced that I was some sort of madman, if not a direct descendant of Attila the Hun. In essence, all I had done was to try to describe the Reproductive Imperative and to follow that description with essentially what I have to say in this chapter. Of course, this topic can't be covered in a 50-minute lecture, and the main reason seems to be that anyone who wishes to talk about humans from a sociobiological viewpoint will not easily be allowed the premises on which to build a case. In the lecture, time after time I would suggest something that obviously went against the traditional grain, and the troops would reflexively fall back to the familiar positions and begin confidently and loudly to mouth the standard cliches, in almost any order. The premises of the Reproductive Imperative would wearily have to be reestablished each time I wished to make a new point.

In any case, the discussion finished well after the usual hour, and in my search for something outrageous to say, I had stumbled across new material for thought. As I played with some of these ideas in the days afterward, I came to believe that the primary advantage of the sociobiological argument lies in its being so malleable and ductile. It can be stretched to cover practically everything. Of course, as it is stretched it must grow thinner, and holes may appear. But in the best tradition of science, any encompassing theory can be expected to have holes. To the pessimist they may appear as dark abysses of ignorance, but to the optimist they are openings through which light can shine. Darwin provided us with an umbrella that shaded virtually all living things, and its "holes"—its inability to explain special cases—led, not to its rejection, but to our focusing on those cases until we resolved the questions. Ultimately, Darwin's argument was strengthened. Already the sociobiological umbrella is revealing its weaknesses as we try to use it to explain more and more of what we see. But it seems that the ribs will hold secure in the winds of criticism and that the holes may one day be filled. Perhaps the result will be that the umbrella will be barely recognizable as the device we see today, but I suspect that, in essence, it will survive. So let's gradually open our new umbrella and see how large a shadow it casts. In particular, let's see whether it covers "morality."

I am compelled to place the word in quotes because of its subjective nature. It's a word like "love," which defies definition and whose essence exists in the eye of the beholder. It is important here, however, to define it as it is *usually* defined, relying on the definition of the man in the street. We're interested in "conventional wisdom" because it is, by definition, what most people believe. Even those who don't subscribe to it are well aware of what it is because they were probably forced to escape from it somewhere along the way. So, then, what does conventional wisdom tell us? Just ask Mr. or Ms. America what morality is, or better yet, what *immorality* is, and for some reason you will receive your answer in sexual terms.

I recall being asked to participate in a lunchtime student-faculty seminar in Virginia in the mid-sixties. The topic was to be "Morality on the American Campus." I pretended to be very surprised that the discussion was centered on sex, exclaiming that I must have come on the wrong day and that I was unprepared to discuss this new topic. I asked at one point what condoms had to do with cheating on an exam (and didn't receive the obvious retort that it had to do with what one was doing to his fellow students). In any case, my point was not well taken, and the discussion could not be budged from its sexual track. Of course, I knew that we were going to talk about sex. But why? Why is right and wrong defined in terms of plumbing? Does it simply reflect a preoccupation with sex (as was expressed in the old joke about a Rorschach test in which every ink blot reminded the examinee of sex—a puzzle until he explained that *everything* reminded him of sex)? Or can it be that our concepts of right and wrong are basically derived from *what is right and wrong for reproduction?* Are our moral codes based on the Reproductive Imperative? The idea seems ludicrous at first, but perhaps its greatest problem is its simplicity. Let's see.

I once asked a class to help me make a list of immoral acts, immoral in the conventional sense of the word. I believe I asked them to give me the words that might appear on their *parents'* list. We didn't know each other very well, so there was a pause before someone said, "adultery." I wrote it on the board. "Fornication," someone said. I kept writing. The list was expanded as the students warmed to the task. "Pederasty!" someone shouted. Everyone laughed. "Necrophilia!" they cheered. They were having a fine time, except for a few who were unsure of what some of the words meant. Finally, they were out of words. I stepped back and we looked at our list of immoral behaviors. It was apparent that it was a compendium of sexual transgressions.

I then asked the class if it was possible to justify the presence of each word on the list in terms of the Reproductive Imperative. That is, were these acts considered immoral because they interfere with successful reproduction? Could a case be made? We started down our list, considering each entry in this new light. Some were easy. Masturbation, necrophilia, and pederasty obviously earned the right to be there because they were patently unreproductive, but how about the others? Were they also guilty of interfering with successful reproduction? The answer, as I see it, is an emphatic yes, but before we consider each act separately, let's see how unreproductiveness could come to be confused with immorality.

I would like to suggest a two-part answer. First, I would argue that "moral" behavior is related to the historical *norm,* and second, that the norm itself is a function of the Reproductive Imperative. Normality, then, is that which is reproductively effective.

To make any sense of this, we must step back and view the human condition over the long run. As a species, we have been around a few million years, but, in the spirit of delicacy, we might not care to claim kinship to those first people. Anthropologists quibble about where to draw the line separating prehumans and humans, but even if we picked the most recent line, we would be left with thousands of generations of true humans. Using this time frame, then, we can assume that anything that has happened in the last few decades, or perhaps in the last few hundred or even thousand years, has not yet had much evolutionary impact. This absolves us of any responsibility to account for the effects of recent social changes; they simply haven't had time to mold our genetic constitution. (But if we manage to survive, they may come to have enormous influence in coming generations.)

We must keep in mind that conditions have changed at a dizzying pace since the agricultural revolution some 10,000 years ago. Before that, and throughout most of our history, humans ambled over the earth in small bands of perhaps 200 people, the groups rarely exceeding 500. Basically they were hunters and gatherers, which means they lived off the land by killing game and searching for edible parts of wild plants. They didn't raise anything. This type of subsistence is so undependable and inefficient that even 8,000 years ago, after millions of years of evolution, the earth harbored no more humans than presently reside in three of New York City's five boroughs. The bands were small and didn't have much impact on this great planet, but they were successful. They persisted. Because they represent such a large part of human history, our genetic constitution—and perhaps our traditions and moral values—developed largely in these shabby bands. *They* are the representative humans. Not us. We are only an embellishment on their sturdy constitution. *They* are the real *us*. Thus, we cannot deny the roots of our heritage by pointing to any modern trend, belief, value, or development. Instead we must grope through the fog of prehistory to learn what the archetypal human was like. Our task is to try to deduce what life must have been like for humans through *most* of our tenure on the planet, to learn what pressures they faced and how they might have confronted them. We may have no hope of unveiling the truth, but we will at least be looking in the right place. We can only be sure that these people did indeed survive for a long time on the earth and that they were subject to natural selection and that we bear the genes of the most successful reproducers among them.

Keeping in mind, then, that we are primarily interested in what has transpired over the long run, let's see how our morals might have evolved. We shall see that while our intelligence has been our salvation, it has also led to our confusion. The impact of this confusion has not been small, and it may well lead to some of humankind's most resounding errors. We are presently being forced into making decisions of incredible moment, for ourselves and those sharing this small planet, and unless we have considered all our options, we may be setting the stage for years of grief. We may even be sealing our fate.

The problem arises because of our great faith in a recent addition to our anatomy, the cerebral cortex. The great convoluted mass of gray that we usually think of as the "brain" is actually only a part of the brain. Furthermore, it is the newest part. Deep inside its shallow folds, we find that the old elements—the ones we share with lizards and birds and shrews and frogs—are still there, largely unheralded, mostly ignored. (We will see later how these fibrous, unpublicized structures alter our behavior in specific ways and cause impulses to swell within us that cannot be overcome by even the most concerted effort of the famed cerebrum.)

But, as I said, the cerebrum is both our blessing and our bane. Our blessing because of its enormous versatility and ability to help us cope with a complex world by giving us options. Our bane because we have come to depend on it too much, to revere it, to swell with pride as we worship at its great gray altar.

The problem is that it is a limited god. One can argue that a person with an IQ of 80 is not much worse off than one with 160. Both can drive a car. Neither can explain death. Both have trouble making free throws. This god, at its best, offers too little. Also, in some respects it is only a figurehead; we will see that it is secretly compelled to respond to certain dictates of the old brain. But the brain's bearer continually rises to its defense and swears that, in his or her case, the *cerebrum* is in charge and that it alone ultimately holds the solutions to our problems, needing only the proper encouragement to produce pure, undiluted wisdom. And so we spend time and money and energy trying to provide that encouragement. And, strangely enough, even while we tout our intelligence, we bemoan our stupidity—our lack of wisdom (usually while discussing war, whales, or pure water).

Our intelligence has let us down in one case in particular. Paradoxically, it has failed us by allowing us to communicate. Those first animated grunts and mumblings probably stemmed from the stirrings of a primitive cerebrum indeed. But the cerebrum grew and developed. As our communicative abilities grew more sophisticated, they enabled us not only to communicate better with people within our group but to reach those outside our immediate group, for example, by our writings. But worse, we've been able to communicate between the generations. This may sound fine, but perhaps our present social problems are exacerbated by the fact that each generation can saddle the next with its values. How many times have we heard it said, "The founding fathers of this great country intended for us to . . ." (complete the sentence). Furthermore, we are taught to try to live up to their expectations—as we dutifully ignore their greed, racism, and debaucheries. Even in illiterate societies, as was perhaps the case in our own prehistory, ideas can rather effectively be passed through the generations in a number of ways, such as by word of mouth or by imitation. But however it is done, our intelligence enables us to easily pass along our values.

Now that I've labeled intelligence and communication abusive, let's see how they abuse us. Again we must step back to view ourselves over geologic times—a way of keeping in mind that even our own species has been molded by natural selection. Basically we are interested in the social systems of our ancestors. Of course, it is pretentious and dishonest to claim that we know anything about the social systems of prehistoric people, or that we can do much better than guess at the nature of the societies of our preliterate ancestors. What we *can* be sure of is that those early populations were rather variable, both physically and mentally, and that some individuals, through sheer reproductive prowess, had inordinate input into the genetic constitution of subsequent generations. As thousands of generations passed, then, those traits that led to successful reproduction would have been magnified in each population. Of course, the stupid brutes who were our ancestors probably didn't waste time analyzing their behavior. They were too busy reproducing and doing whatever led to it. Nevertheless, natural selection was relentlessly having its way. Because the tough, rigorous world of early man would have blindly obliterated the genes of any individual who failed to behave reproductively, aberrant genes would have disappeared about as quickly as they were produced.

As time passed, and as the cerebral cortex grew, those early populations would have grown more variable in their behavior, as some individuals "decided" to be different from the rest. And then there were others, those who couldn't help themselves, who were just . . . different. But no matter what the individual proclivities of any of these people, they were all subject to the Reproductive Imperative, a blind, unretributive, and unforgiving god. If an individual's peculiarities interfered with his or her reproduction, that difference tended to die out either genetically or culturally. The unreproductive individual wouldn't have been able to transfer the peculiar trait through his genes *or* by teaching it. People in each generation would have tended to learn most of their social patterns from their parents, so individuals who were not parents would have had a negligible social impact.

Eventually, those pre-men gave rise to *Homo sapiens,* a highly intelligent species with a very pronounced self-awareness. These bright-eyed people had new options because of their intelligence and would have asked, "What manner of creature am I, and how do I behave?" To find their answers, they would have simply looked around (thus, perhaps, sociology was born). They would have seen that their parents behaved in such a way as to leave offspring and that most of the people around them were busy tending to their children. There was, in effect, a *proper* (or "normal") way to behave, and it resulted in children, whether these people made the connection or not.

As time passed and intelligence increased, busy little minds would have developed newer and stranger behavior. Thus, people with all sorts of behavioral patterns were scrambling over the earth. Of course, people were free to be as weird as they chose *as long as* it didn't interfere with their breeding. If an individual was so peculiar that no one would mate with him, that peculiarity died out or was forced to arise anew each time it appeared; it couldn't be transmitted. If an individual had itchy feet and roamed too far from the protection of the group, he could carry his "itchy" genes to his grave. Super-aggressive individuals would chase away potential mates or spend too much time and energy fighting. Super-docile individuals would not compete successfully for mates or for food for their family. Always, then, behavior was kept within the limits set by the rules of reproduction, because the genes of those who drifted outside those limits were swept into the dustbin of oblivion. These rules were the norm. Most people followed them because they were the offspring of people who followed them.

As time went on, our newly intelligent species was growing increasingly introspective. It was watching itself. And what it saw was a standard of behavior that resulted in children. Everywhere one looked, people were following the rules of reproduction. Now, as people became increasingly cerebrated and communicative, these rules became codified—set in stone. How things *were* suddenly became how things *should* be. It was probably one of the most important developments in the history of our species—the word "should." (For one thing, it enabled us to formulate the word "guilt.")

The early codes could have arisen by parents simply communicating with their children, keeping them in line, ensuring that their children didn't behave in such a way as to shorten their life span or impede their reproduction. Remember that it is to the parents' reproductive advantage to see that their children reproduce. After all, simply *having* children is not enough if those children fail to obey the Reproductive Imperative. So codes of behavior arose as parents sought to ensure their own reproductive success by keeping their genetic repositories— their children—in line. And the point I wish to make here is that *those early codes are virtually the same ones that were transmitted to my students by their own parents.* It all becomes increasingly apparent as we look at the list of "immoral" behavior my students generated in class that day.

Just as those early parents could not afford to have a homosexual child, they could also not afford to have homosexuality arise among the population. What if it were accepted and their children became involved? They could not tolerate any condition that might lower the reproductive success of their descendants. Homosexuality, then, was against the reproductive norm and was labeled undesirable. Where are the descendants today of groups that encouraged wholesale homosexuality? Perhaps those groups were right, but they are also gone—so how right could they have been? It has been suggested that perhaps homosexuality would have been tolerated whenever it arose anew because the homosexuals could have contributed to rearing other people's children. The strong bias against homosexuality in most cultures, however, suggests that people believed that its threat outweighed its promise.

As successfully reproducing populations began to find the interest, time, and ability to analyze themselves, they recognized a whole gamut of behavioral traits that appeared as constant themes in their societies. The pervasive themes were regarded as common and normal. Generations came and went but the same themes continued. Finally these persistent themes were not only embraced but named. Any antithetical themes undoubtedly met resistance. In essence, then, people were making their first lists of immoral acts. Child-loving, they said, is admirable. Child-hating is abominable. Heterosexuality was encouraged. Homosexuality was discouraged. In time, of course, those things that were perpetually present in successfully reproducing societies, those things that made up the norm, came to be formally encoded in all manner of tradition, laws, religion, codes, and ethics.

As generation after generation followed, and as our societies grew ever more complex and increasingly dependent on the written word, an individual didn't have to rely on a gut response or a vague dictate to know whether something was moral or immoral. He had a list. That list is a monument to immutability. It has been handed down virtually intact through our history until today a class of university students can recite it without a second thought.

Now let's return to that list of "immoral" behavior and see how each entry is justified simply by the fact that it does not fall into line with the best traditions of good reproductive behavior. We've just mentioned one: homosexuality. And then we only need be reminded that many state legislatures, in their infinite wisdom and while mumbling through their Cheezits, have labeled oral and anal sex as *illegal*—against the norm. In fact, these deeds have been called Crimes Against Nature by those with no earthly idea of how right they are. Of course, *we* know that the law should read, "Crimes against the Reproductive Imperative."

There are those other activities on our list that can be explained away intuitively, such as necrophilia and pederasty, as we saw earlier. My class disagreed about masturbation until I asked how many had ever been warned about its dangers, whereupon it was quickly added to the list. Of course, it's easy to see how it got there. Our parents cannot have us relieving our reproductive urges with a flick of the wrist; that's reproductively wasteful, and besides, who wants to go blind?

How about child sex? In many cultures sex play between children is encouraged, permitted, or at least ignored. After all, it's a natural tendency and may be viewed as an expression of good healthy curiosity. As children in those cultures reach puberty, however, they seem to become increasingly modest and shy, and their sex play may stop entirely for a time. Parenthood is now possible. It's no longer a game, and their parents approve of their restraint.

Why do children become more discriminating as they enter adolescence? Why do adults consider sex between 12-year-olds a more serious matter than sex between 8-year-olds? One reason, of course, is that the younger crowd is not likely to do it right to begin with. They don't quite have the equipment or the hang of it, so their sex play is likely to be, in fact, innocent. And even if they do figure out the mechanics and are able to carry out copulation, no real harm is done because they are not fertile. But 12-year-olds are entering their period of fertility, so sex among borderline pubescents is viewed with more seriousness. It is here, for the first time, that the old double standard descends with its full weight. The heaviest "moral" burden falls on the girl, and it is on her that parental protectiveness is focused.

An old joke has it that when a young girl confessed to her father that she was pregnant, he countered, "Don't worry, it's probably not even yours." The humor stems from the fact that this is the first line of defense for *boys*. Boys have an out. They can deny everything or leave town. A pregnant girl can't deny a thing, and if she leaves town, she leaves with the baby.

It is important to the girl and to the reproductive hopes of her parents that she be sufficiently mature before attempting reproduction. If she is very young, she is not likely to be able to bear the baby, much less rear it. Her hips will be too narrow to provide an adequate birth canal. The milk-producing tissues of her breasts will be undeveloped and unable to produce enough milk to sustain an infant. If she mates under the handicap of these physical inadequacies, her parents will suffer reproductively as a result of the reproductive failure of their daughter. Therefore, they must try to see to it that she doesn't become pregnant before she is physically able to bear a child and to care for it. Furthermore, if she is too young, she will not have accumulated the knowledge necessary to be a parent in the complex world of the human animal. Therefore, young girls must be protected, and they are.

A young girl is protected not only by her parents—particularly by her formidable father—but by society as a whole. Virtually everyone frowns on fertile males having sex with adolescent girls. At a recent international convention held in Australia to discuss the subject of love among humans, a lecturer began by announcing his proclivity for sex with children and then attempted to be more specific in extolling its virtues. He probably thought that in an academic forum, where any idea is theoretically welcome, he would be free to develop his argument and discuss it in rational terms. He was wrong. The intellectual matrix of the meeting disintegrated as soon as he announced his subject, and he was hooted from the auditorium. The room was filled with sociologists, so they would have had precisely as many explanations for their behavior as there were conferees, and all the responses would have been couched in cultural terms. But no one could have really explained why, with their varied backgrounds, experience, training, and parentage, they rose up together in total outrage. A biologist could have told them, though.

Later that evening this unfortunate fellow encountered a female sociologist in a bar and promptly received a punch in the nose that required hospital treatment. "Good," you say, "good for her." But why? You didn't actually know any of the children involved, so it couldn't have been for their sake. Could it be for yours? Is it to your advantage to discourage sex with children, particularly little girls, because you are a descendant of efficient reproducers who had winnowed such unreproductive behavior out of their social repertoire? Is your distaste for such permissiveness a reflection of your need to protect your own daughters from being inseminated before they can successfully carry on your genes? Or did you think your response had a loftier motivation?

We are often less concerned about the sexual behavior of young boys, not just because they can deny everything but also because they need not endure the hazards of pregnancy, childbirth, and child care. In fact, if a young boy casually inseminates a girl, there is a slim chance that she will be able to successfully bear and rear the child, especially with help from her family, so his reproductive output, and that of his parents, is increased at little cost to himself. With the burden on her, his parents are less concerned about his behavior than her parents are about hers. We frown on young boys actually getting married, of course, because they are not yet able to successfully provide for and protect a family, and they might suffer a lower net reproductive output if they tried.

Of course, I don't write about all this unaware of the reaction it will generate. Throughout this book we will be picking up the most cherished pearls of human culture from where they have been lying unmolested for years. Our task here is to turn the pearls over, to look at them from new angles, to examine them as rationally as possible in order to learn about their real nature. Some of these precious items will have had their value set by our emotion, a property that is, by definition, irrational. But here "irrationality" takes a strange twist. I am trying to show that even irrational emotions are eminently rational when considered in evolutionary terms.

So, sex with children appears on our list and now we know why. Some of the other items on the list require even more explanation. For example, adultery and rape. We can put adultery and rape under one heading by considering how important the family unit is to successful reproduction. Families, after all, are not arbitrary groups. They consist, in almost all societies, of a man, a woman, and their children. Of course, there are the exceptions, such as harems, but they are precisely that: exceptions. Most women have one husband and most men in the world have only one wife. Some chieftains or long-haul truck drivers may have two or more, but we are interested in the *usual* condition—the norm.

Traditionally, the roles of the sexes have been quite distinct. Women are usually smaller, weaker, and slower than men, and their role has been that of a gatherer of high-carbohydrate plant food. A woman has traditionally been forced to remain with the child, feeding it, and to rely on a male for high-protein game and for protection. A man has traditionally concentrated his efforts on one woman and her (and his) children. If a man were to attempt to spread himself too thin, perhaps by attending to another woman in the cave across the hill, his original mate and their children would suffer. Since he is not likely to be able to attend to both families successfully, he risks both families dying out, and his genes with them. His best reproductive bet, then, is to attend mainly to the original family.

Not coincidentally, this is precisely what the woman wants if she is to successfully reproduce. She needs a "loyal" male, and if he is not naturally sexually "loyal," she needs one that can be intimidated—by herself or by society. She would have her greatest reproductive success by choosing a male who has demonstrated a low tendency to wander or by forcing a potential wanderer to attend strictly to business at home. Even today, a man who would rather be somewhere else stays home to keep the peace. Paradoxically, his wife may not even like him much; she just knows that she wants that sucker at home, and she is probably not really able to say why. Historically, of course, a man with the qualities of docile loyalty and malleability may have lacked other important traits such as imagination, courage, and indomitability. The ideal male probably would have possessed elements from both columns to some degree.

The reproductive man may have another reason to stay close to home. It would be important to his interests to see that he not be cuckolded. If he were to be careless so that the female he is feeding and protecting is, unbeknownst to him, inseminated by some other male, his genes would be lost. All his effort would go into perpetuating the chromosomes of another individual. He might be a perfect husband and father but his fitness would be zero.

Thus we see the strong reproductive advantages of mate jealousy. It is so pervasive and reliable an emotion that it can be used as a ploy or tool in human courtship. A person can almost always stimulate the interest of someone by showing interest in someone else. The feeling of jealousy, though hard to describe, is even harder to change. (How often have you heard, "I *try* not to be jealous, I just am"?) We must realize that, on an evolutionary basis, jealousy is important. Women must see to it that they and their offspring are the sole recipients of a male's services. The male must see to it that he does not raise someone else's chromosomes.

In nature, some males go to rather extreme lengths to see that they do not expend their energy caring for another male's offspring. Perhaps the most gruesome case arises among the langur monkeys of India. In this species a single dominant male "owns" a harem of females. The females are a rather stable group, but there is quite a high turnover rate in harem-masters. New males are constantly challenging, and occasionally one wins and drives the old male away. Of course, all the infants in the troop taken over by the new male are the offspring of the old male. If the new male were to consort with a troop of mothers who were already nursing, he would lose opportunities to breed until the infants left and the females became sexually receptive again. But he faces a constant stream of challengers for his new harem, so he doesn't have the time to waste. He therefore adopts the terrible strategy of infanticide. A new harem-master tears infants from their mothers, bites them fatally, and then runs away before the mother can defend her baby. Systematically, he purges the troop of its infants. Thus, the childless females, no longer lactating, become sexually receptive again. One might think that the murderous behavior of adult males could quickly be weeded out if the females simply refused to mate with a male who has killed their children. However, there is no room for spite in nature. It is to the females' own reproductive advantage to become pregnant again as soon as possible, so they yield to the child killer. Besides, half their children will be males, and it is to a mother's reproductive advantage to produce male child killers. As their adult sons slaughter infants, they ensure the success of their mothers' genes. Fortunately for our sensibilities, most male animals do not deal with the offspring of other males so harshly. Human males, though not so harsh, nevertheless tend to be jealous, suspicious, and protective of "their" females so as to discourage their insemination by foreign males. Now it becomes clear why adultery is immoral.

Rape, strangely enough, appears on the list for the same reason as adultery. A raped woman is likely to bear offspring that are not those of her attendant male (which *he* resents) or offspring of a male who will not stay and help her rear them (which *she* resents).

And that brings us to another immoral act: fornication. If I correctly recall my religious training as a good southern Protestant, fornication is copulation by unmarried individuals. In most societies, especially those with a strong religious influence (in other words, those in which The List is specific and legible and plays a powerful role), fornication is *out,* aside from a little fooling around by children. The reason? It's reproductively inefficient. Unless he is somehow constrained, the male who has casually inseminated a woman is likely to go his own way, leaving her alone to bear a child that she will not be able to feed and protect. The price of fornication, then, is particularly severe for women. Parents cannot afford to encourage it, even among their sons, because if it catches on in the society, their female children will suffer, thus lowering the parents' fecundity. So, since most of the people in any population are not the offspring of fornicators, fornication falls outside the reproductive norm and is labeled immoral.

Perhaps you are bothered that our discussion of morality has centered on sex. You may, quite correctly, point out that morality may have nothing to do with sex. That may well be true, but that doesn't alter the fact that *most* people view morality in sexual terms, and we are interested here in what *most* people do. We're trying to get at the common denominators of human behavior. The thoughtful and/or aberrant person has, time and again, upset our penchant for bold generalizations about the human condition, but we're not about to allow that to happen here.

In token gesture to these disruptive souls, however, let's consider a few cases in which immorality may not be viewed as a sexual phenomenon. Two such behaviors are the double cross and cheating.

The double cross is simply a betrayal of trust. In the small bands in which humans evolved, people were most likely to interact with those they were related to or depended upon, and so trust was important. It would not have been in one's self-interest to betray those whom he might need someday. Thus, breeching confidences or acting in bad faith could work against one's self-interest. Society in general would frown on a double-crosser since, in a small group, any individual could expect to interact with the double-crosser himself some day. Each person, then, increases the likelihood of getting a fair shake by discouraging the double cross whenever it should appear.

The immorality of cheating can be similarly explained. It is interesting that when parents try to discourage their children from cheating in class they traditionally use two arguments. One, "It's not fair to the others." (Genetic translation: those others have traditionally been in your group and so they may carry genes like yours, or you may have to rely on them someday, so don't hurt them.) Or two, "You're only hurting yourself" (a basic violation of the Reproductive Imperative). So, again, we're looking out for ourselves and our genes.

It might be very interesting to go down the list of nonsexual immoral acts and to look for the reproductive disadvantages of each one. The problem is, this list is much harder to form. If one is not going to rely on a ready-made, hand-me-down list, seeking instead to replace it with well-considered responses, the answers are going to be as varied as the thinkers. Besides, most people do not, or choose not, to think about the broader implications of morality. They prefer to simply accept what they are told. And most of what they are told relates to sex.

These very things we are talking about, by the way, help explain our incredible interest in controlling sex in our society. You can be sure that at this very minute someone somewhere is seeking to put the kibosh on someone else's sexual behavior. We see it daily in our friends, neighbors, and the media, and even the government gets into the act. When a congressman feels he might be under public pressure for being incompetent or taking bribes or bowing to the oil companies, he can always reach into his bag and drag out some well-worn pornography bill. How incensed he is. He invites the cameras in and holds "hearings." He expects great public support, and he gets it. The public is protected from nipples. The public is grateful.

Elsewhere, you can be sure that some good citizens are busy chasing homosexuals from their jobs. Others are devouring daily reports about some scandalous public figure who got caught. They're lecturing their children. They're threatening everybody's children. They're closing adult bookstores. They're writing letters of complaint. They're stopping the advertising of condoms on the radio. They're vigilant. They're fascinated and titillated. And they're afraid.

The curious thing is, they don't know *why* they're afraid. But even a discussion of homosexuality makes them nervous unless it's in an official and organized forum. They don't want to hear about it from a person standing within 23 inches of them and speaking in a low tone.

But we're still winding our way through our list of immoral acts. The next one, we find, may well be incest. Incest is obviously "immoral." Almost universally viewed as a great shame, the incest taboo pervades virtually all human societies. It may even extend into the mores of other species. For example, adult chimpanzees will rarely mate with their mother, probably a side effect of her long-term dominance over them. But why is the very idea of copulating with one's parent or sibling so distasteful, repugnant, and offensive to humans?

The biological basis of the incest taboo has traditionally been explained in genetic terms. We all harbor a multitude of deleterious genes that, if expressed, could cause us great harm or even death. But they are not expressed because genes come in pairs, one originating from the father and one from the mother. A "bad" gene, then, may have no effect if it is masked by a "good" counterpart. However, if highly related individuals breed, identical deleterious genes may end up together (a so-called double recessive), and since neither is masked by a "good" gene, the offspring suffers.

Now, it has been demonstrated that some species, such as mice, live in family groups in which incest is the rule rather than the exception. And they remain healthy. Does this example negate the genetic explanation of the incest taboo? Not at all. Perhaps mice have a very low incidence of harmful recessive genes. This low incidence could be a result of many generations of inbreeding, in which animals that had a double dose of a harmful gene appeared and then quickly died out without reproducing, carrying their bad genes with them. Mice, then, survived even with the deleterious effect of inbreeding. They survived partly as a result of their prodigious reproductive abilities and partly because of a system in which rather little reproductive effort is placed in any single offspring, thus rendering faulty offspring expendable. But we have a great investment in our children, so they are not expendable; thus we can't take the risk involved with incest.

Of course, even in human societies, a single incestuous pairing may not result in a deformed or retarded baby. However, if the practice were encouraged, the incidence of defective babies would rise. Once the correlation were discovered, incest would be discouraged. It would be labeled "immoral."

A subsidiary point is that sex is more than physically pleasurable. It is an emotional hot potato. It *is,* in fact, what makes our world go 'round, and it simply cannot be safely handled on a casual basis by most people. It is powerful and perhaps at the root of much of our behavior, albeit indirectly, as we shall see shortly. When "liberated" people choose not to have casual sex (although they can appreciate the idea intellectually) because they feel that it may not be good for them personally, they may have simply come to grips with its power. These same people usually have no truck with the book burners, but in light of the Reproductive Imperative, they should be able to understand better why these lesser souls are so upset.

Morality, then, may be viewed in biological terms. The rules, codes, traditions, and ethics that have grown up around us have not appeared in a historical vacuum. Each has taken its place in our system of values as we learned how it contributed to or hindered our *reproduction.* It is not important that intellectuals, poets, preachers, drunks, and others of bad habit have developed their own lists or have attempted to add to the existing one. We are in search of humanity's great Common Denominator, and it seems that it has something to do with sex.

CHAPTER FOUR

SEXUAL SELECTION, OR AREN'T MEN SPLENDID?

Procreation is nature's principal occupation, and every man, whether he be young or old, when meeting any woman, measures the potentiality of sex between them. Thus it has always been with me.

—Charles Chaplin

SOME TIME in the last century, Charles Darwin developed the concept of sexual selection, a term that simply refers to how an animal goes about choosing a mate. Put another way, it is about how an animal manages to be chosen as a mate. So, let's ask, how *does* a man or woman come to be chosen instead of someone else? The question seems innocuous, but at its doorstep can be laid the blame for humankind's most compelling motivations and its most horrible social ills. But, one might wonder, isn't this a bit overstated? Do we really do anything drastic just to be "chosen"? Are we so motivated by sex? Almost anyone would deny it, but we shall see that such denials, while perhaps heartfelt, mean nothing. Absolutely nothing.

But let's take our usual closer look. We can begin with some questions. Do men and women use different criteria in selecting mates? Does each sex place its specific demands on the other? Do men behave differently from women because different things are expected of them? Are those differences mediated culturally or genetically? What *are* our sometimes unspoken codes and rules for choosing a mate?

These days we are finding some of our most venerable codes to also be the most vulnerable. For example, consider the old "double standard." It is one of the easiest and most common targets for the broad-side attacks of feminists. Why are some things OK for men but not for women? Why do mothers tell their daughters going out on a date, "Now, I'm *trusting* you." This statement is always made with the head tilted down, staring meaningfully with upraised brow. All the girls in my family in Arkansas received the same baleful admonition, and they always left the house with jaws set, *determined* to be trust-worthy. But when I was growing up, no one ever said that to me—perhaps because no one ever trusted me, perhaps because they were sure I didn't have a prayer anyway, but also because I'm male. An indiscretion by me or any of my male cousins would have been met with disappointed clucking but with no great surprise.

No one told us, "Girls won't respect you." In fact, around school the greatest respect was reserved for those guys who had "done it!" The rest of us wondered what it was like, but we never asked. We wanted everyone to think we knew.

But! Once a *girl* had done it, she was marked—forever! She was viewed with a kind of awe, but she wasn't respected. Her parents were right.

Looking back, I *hated* the double standard. It turned out that I could have been trusted completely. I never got anywhere—with any-one. I couldn't have made out in Laredo with a handful of fifty-dollar bills. But I was expected to at least try. And I did, but I failed. All the girls I knew were "trusted," and I was afraid of the other kind.

In any case, my generation, the one portrayed in *American Graffiti,* was perhaps the last one to feel the full and terrible impact of the double standard. The direction of our evolution and our culture may now change, but we still need to know what it was that carried us this far. Perhaps it will help us to alter our course in the future.

What I'm going to say here is that the double standard is not a male device to keep women suppressed. Instead, it has been an important factor in our evolution. It is a critical part of the Reproductive Impera-tive. I will admit, however, that the double standard is a result of a continuing evolutionary battle of the sexes. In other words, as a man seeks to spread his own genes in the population, he may behave in a manner that is not conducive to the best reproductive interests of females, and vice versa. I will also say that men and women employ fundamentally different strategies in perpetuating their genes. So let's take a closer look at the old ogre.

Basically, the question is simply: Why has promiscuity been more acceptable for males than for females? Some reasons are obvious. If a male spreads his sperm widely among females while remaining un-mated or while attending mainly to his primary family, there is a chance that some of the females he has impregnated will be able to rear his young, either alone or with the help of an unsuspecting and cuckolded male. It really makes little difference to the Masked Insem-inator whether these females are successful, because each dalliance consumes little of his time and energy and is undoubtedly pleasurable. If a female somehow succeeds in rearing these offspring, so much the better; he has increased his reproductive success. So it is to his advan-tage to stray as widely as possible without taking himself away from his own family too much. This has been a highly successful reproduc-tive scheme for the male. His promiscuity works for him, if not for most of the females he seduces. Thus, because male promiscuity is more beneficial to one segment of the population than another, it has received mixed reviews among moralists.

Females, on the other hand, don't like sex. We know this because of the frequency with which they reject male advances. The phenomenon has long been a linchpin of our society. We can expect males to come on to females, and we can expect that most of the time they will be rejected. Thus, because they reject it so often, we have developed the notion that women are not "supposed" to like sex. I once facetiously suggested that my students in an "adult" class perform an experiment in which members of a pair (man and wife) would enter a crowded bar and see which sex could persuade a stranger to copulate with them first. We decided that the success of most women could be measured with a stopwatch but that the men might well require a calendar.

Now, are we to believe that women are, in fact, less interested in sex than men? Archaic. But, for most women, it may well be true. They really may be less interested in sex. (Feel your hackles rise? That's because when humans had fur, anger would make the hair stand on end so that one would appear more formidable. You see, *everything* can be explained by evolution.) But as I was saying, women may well be less interested in sex than men. The reason is, they must be more discriminating. Consider what would happen if they weren't. An undiscriminating woman might end up bearing the child of a clearly inferior male. He might be cuddly and lovable, but he also might be a failure at providing the protection and food that she and her offspring will need. Furthermore, if he is genetically debilitated in some way, perhaps weak or stupid, she may go through months of pregnancy, finally risking her life at childbirth, only to bear a weak or stupid child. Such a child could not be expected to survive in the traditionally rigorous world of the human animal, and thus her enormous reproductive effort would have been wasted. It is not important that she is happy with her weak husband or retarded child. There are no points given for happiness. If that child dies, her genes die with it. Her only hope is to attempt to reproduce again, but now she has less time left.

Through the generations, then, the women who had the greatest reproductive success, the ones who gave rise to *us,* were those who were the most discriminating. When a leering male showed up at the door, the woman's best bet was to hesitate, to wait until she had a chance to size him up. Along with his broad shoulders and keen hunter's eyes, he would be particularly attractive to her if he were not already mated or if he gave indications that he could be won away from his mate. These traits would make him interesting because she would stand a better chance of gaining *all* his benefits. Of course, she could only do so if she could manage to curtail his wanderings once she accepted him.

So here is the point at which friction arose. *His* tendency may have been to put his sperm in as many receptacles as possible because it paid off with children and took so little time or energy. *Her* tendency, however, was to resent being treated merely as a receptacle and to demand to be treated as a long-term mate. In order to help ensure the success of her children, she would permit him to leave his sperm only if he left his heart as well.

With males wandering all over the place ready to copulate at the drop of a bearskin, then, a female had to become discriminating. A woman didn't have to be very perceptive to see that some males were simply "better" than others, so it was up to her to choose the best male possible. After all, if her child were to be strong and healthy, it must bear the best possible combination of genes.

Keep in mind that a woman can't improve upon her own genes; she can only add to those the best that she can attract. If she has a number of suitors, her task is to look them over and choose the one that seems the best. This means that most suitors will be rejected. The rejectees then shuffle away, mumbling something about women being fickle and unresponsive, not interested in sex. They gather on corners and confirm each other's suspicions. Thus the rumor grows: Women don't (and therefore "shouldn't") like sex.

Fifteen nays and one yes prove it—except to the guy who got the nod. He may have a different story to tell. And, in fact, he may be in for a bit of a surprise. He may soon come to believe he's found too much of a good thing. He may find her sexual responsiveness rather impressive, even imposing. What's going on here? Has he been laboring under an illusion? Was he wrong about women?

Actually, he may not know too much about "women" because once he has made his choice to remain with a particular female, he won't get around much any more. There are a number of reasons for this. For one thing, if the woman is bearing his child, he must provide for her and the developing infant if he is going to leave any offspring. Also, since she is physiologically ready to copulate at any time, he must remain vigilant lest a better male come by and seduce her, leaving him to rear a child that is not his. In addition, he may have lost his position in the sexual marketplace. He has a mate whom he must watch and who watches him, so he is less desirable to other women. He may try to sneak one under the fence now and then, but his success rate will have dropped markedly. His biceps may still ripple and his teeth may still glint in the sun, but now he is treated differently, a fact he will bemoan for years. He now loses to males who may be clearly inferior but who are chosen over him simply because they are "free."

What about this question of whether women are less interested in sex than men are? On an evolutionary basis women have undoubtedly been less interested in *casual* sex. They have had too much to lose. A male can make up the energy expended in a sexual episode by eating a grape. His cost is low, and—who knows?—perhaps it will result in a child for him. For her, though, the potential costs are enormous. She is weighted, contorted, and slowed with pregnancy as the embryo grows parasitically within her body. (A parent doesn't normally like to think of offspring as parasites until they're in their late teens.) Late in pregnancy much of her diet will go toward maintaining the fetus that is her genetic repository. Finally she will literally risk her life to give birth to it. Should she survive, she will continue in intimate association with it as she nurses it, forming an ever-stronger attachment. With all this in store for her as the result of a single copulation, you can *bet* she's going to be careful who she mates with! She will have to live with the fruit of that interlude. If the child is defective, she loses.

We can apply our deadly post facto reasoning once again and see that, in general, casual sex would be more appealing for men than for women and that a woman would become sexually very active, once mated, as a means of keeping the chosen male around, sated, and suspicious. So even though a female may appear less interested in sex in the early stages of a romance, her lasciviousness may sharply increase should a male stay around long enough to make her believe that he will be of assistance in rearing her offspring.

Therefore, we see that differences in the sex roles have left us with a codified and rather rigid double standard. So that explains that. On to other great questions.

I was once told by a very wise 23-year-old pool shark that if a couple were to put a dime in a jar for each time they had sex over their first six months of marriage and then to take a dime out each time they had sex after that, they would never go broke. I believed it, because at 17 I believed everything. As the years pass, however, I am beginning to question a few more things, and I think that that is one.

But is there an element of truth there? Does frequency of sex diminish? Of course, another pearl of pool-hall wisdom is that sex improves with time; but this is a statement about quality, not quantity. I think this last is partly a function of the era. In my era, sexuality was suppressed. Because of our inexperience, our techniques were undoubtedly so abominable that anything was an improvement. But how about quantity? Do couples in fact have sex less frequently as time goes by? Is there an initial burst of wild sexual activity that later levels off to fluctuate around the Suburban Mean of two or three times a week? If so, why?

At this point we must remind ourselves of a fact that we have been assiduously ignoring: people form bonds. Some call it love. It seems also that bonds do not develop overnight (unless people desperately wish them to—and then they usually live to regret it if the mettle of that bond is ever tested). If bonding takes time, then, there must be some way to keep the sexes together long enough for the bond to form—and pure, raw sex is one way. Once the bond has formed, copulation becomes less important and often does decrease in frequency.

Copulation, then, has roles other than a means of insemination. Certain church doctrines, by the way, hold that sex might rightfully be reserved purely for insemination because this is the natural, God-given way of things. As evidence, church fathers like to point to the other animals, saying, "In nature, sex is for reproduction." Balderdash! They know not whereof they speak, having apparently spent more time with beatitudes than with beetles. Animals, particularly the primates, have sex for about as many reasons as the heathen do. For example, a female chimpanzee in heat will copulate with just about any male who waves at her. She will even stoop low to service tiny adolescent males. Adult males, it turns out, are not particularly easy to entice by the blatant posturing of a female, often ignoring the temptress. (It is hard to know what turns male chimps on. Some females who may be truly ugly by human standards are considered sexual prizes and receive much more attention than other, healthier, younger females that seem "prettier.") In any case, sex among chimpanzees is a free-for-all, and it is believed to be an important bond-builder. It helps keep the troop together by sensory reinforcement. Other animals, such as baboons, are also highly promiscuous. So are gorillas, although these animals, in spite of their appearance and the injustices of Hollywood, are not very interested in sex.

Although female baboons may have sex with a number of individuals, they show that they are quite able to discriminate among males when the occasion arises. For example, a female in heat is usually accompanied by a "consort," an adult male who walks at her side as the troop moves along. He copulates with her more frequently than other males, but not necessarily because of his dazzling personality. He may be the greatest recipient of her favors simply because of his proximity. His proximity may not help him much later on, however. It turns out that at the beginning of her period of "heat," the female baboon is sexually receptive but not very likely to become pregnant. At this time she copulates with practically everyone. A few days later, however, when she is likely to become pregnant, she presents herself to only the higher-ranking males, thus seeing to it that her offspring will bear "good" genes. So she promotes group harmony by satisfying all the males, at the same time increasing her own fitness by selecting the best animals as fathers.

Monkeys and other animals use sex in yet another way: to express dominance. A male demonstrates his dominance by mounting a subordinate male just as he would a female. In fact, a subordinate male will often turn away the wrath of a threatening dominant by "presenting" his rear end to be mounted, in the manner of a female. The dominant male mounts but rarely thrusts, usually just clasping the subordinate from behind.

So, in nature sex is used in a variety of ways—not solely for insemination. Female monkeys even present their rears to males to divert their attention so that they can swipe their bananas. Although this is also a "natural" act, we rarely hear clergymen encouraging it from the pulpit.

What I'm saying is, sex may also have multiple functions in human society. For example, it may help to keep couples together during difficult periods. But keep in mind that even though insemination may not be the only function of sex, in the long run reproduction is. To illustrate, if sex among primates facilitates bond-building, then it helps keep the group together. Animals in groups are often safer than animals alone; it is harder for a predator to sneak up on a group because there are more eyes watching. So if a female produces harmony through promiscuity, she not only keeps potential mates and protectors around, but she is less vulnerable to predators. So she increases her likelihood of living a long reproductive life by promoting casual sex. She also promotes a more harmonious environment in which to bear her genetic repositories, her children. So we see once again that everything is done in accordance with the Reproductive Imperative. Even when reproduction isn't the goal, it is.

One might wonder, if reproduction is so important, then why is it so often suspected that sexual activity decreases once bonds are formed? Why are the dimes removed so slowly? Wouldn't frequent copulation not only promote harmony and reinforce social bonds but increase the probability of producing more children as well? Are we the only animals that suffer this diminished libido? If we are, it would be safe to rummage for the answers among our cultural patterns and ignore our evolutionary heritage. But we aren't. Interestingly enough, it turns out that many other animals are also likely to keep a reserve of dimes. For example, stud bulls who have regularly serviced certain cows may stop copulating with their usual partners. It doesn't matter whether the cows are actually the bull's sexual partners or whether they are simply used to excite him to the point that he will mount a large frame and ejaculate into a receptacle so that his sperm can be stored for artificial insemination. If the same cows are used over and over, his interest wanes. They finally fail to arouse him at all. He won't mount anything. In fact, he gives the appearance of being sexually exhausted. One might well believe he is if it were not for the fact that when he is introduced to a strange female, all signs of fatigue disappear and he's ready to go again—and again. He will remain potent and enraptured with her until she, too, grows familiar.

Such callous behavior is not restricted to bulls. The same phenomenon has been observed in such diverse male animals as flies, apes, and hogs. Why is the tendency so common? The evolutionary basis for it may be that a female who is very familiar to a male is likely to already be pregnant by him, so it is to his advantage to spend his energy doing other things. A strange female, though, may not yet be pregnant, and she certainly hasn't had the pleasure of receiving *his* sperm, so she has a greater arousal effect. In any case, the Strange Female syndrome is a common one in the animal world.

Among humans, we've already considered one reason why frequency of sex may decrease: After those bonds we call love are formed, frequent copulation is not necessary to keep a couple together. They may, in some instances, like each other, or need each other, or reassure each other enough to stay together. There may also be another reason for the decline. Once a woman is pregnant, there is little direct reproductive advantage in copulating. Sex after pregnancy is solely a means of sustaining (or expressing) the bond, at least until that pregnancy is terminated. Infrequent copulation between an established pair, then, is probably adequate to ensure repeated pregnancies and to maintain the bond.

Unfortunately, some people tend to view this reduced rate of sexual activity as an indication of waning interest or a weakened bond, and they may become alarmed. If a member of a pair measures the strength of the bond in terms of frequency of sexual interaction, he or she will be in constant distress, and this can lead to problems. The fears can generate a self-fulfilling prophecy as the individual seeks desperately to strengthen the bond. This attempt at "strengthening" can take many forms, most of them ill-fated. The threatened individual may play on sympathy, use children as levers, become increasingly dependent, try to invoke feelings of guilt in the mate, or use a number of other means, perhaps unconsciously, to try to increase the strength of the bond, if not the love. Another ploy, of course, is to throw up defenses in anticipation of being hurt, to barricade oneself, perhaps to press attacks. Such unfortunate devices can only weaken the existing bond and eventually confirm what was suspected.

Of course, there *is* another explanation for waning sexual interest. Perhaps one mate is, in fact, no longer as interested in the relationship. Among human beings, a relationship can be weakened by any number of factors. One is a simple shift in priorities: A dentist friend of mine who now sees his girlfriend only on weekends told her quite frankly that his main interests in life had come to be his work and marathoning and that there was simply no more time left for her. She, an extremely attractive woman, had never expected to be replaced by partial plates and Achilles tendons. She probably would have better understood being replaced by another woman; that wouldn't have seemed so unusual. But how unusual was his change in priorities? Let's look at both kinds of replacement of affection, the nonsexual and the sexual.

Evolution is obviously not a perfect mechanism. Paradoxically, one of its weaknesses and its strengths is that it can develop a characteristic in a population that is beneficial to most of the individuals but that can be misapplied by some—expressed in ways that may not lead to reproduction. Take my dentist/runner friend, for example. How could work and running have come to take precedence over sex in his life? Admittedly, he is 35 and thus over the hill, but why hasn't his old age doused *all* his ambitions and goals? Obviously, he still has his ambitions and goals; it's just that some have gained ascendancy over mating behavior.

Or have they? His girlfriend would say yes, but he is not so sure. After all, why did he spend all those years becoming a dentist and then a professor? Why was he so concerned about his physique? Why did he become a pilot, a skydiver, a motorcycle racer, a skier? How did he come to find himself performing surgery on primitive people in the jungles of Southeast Asia? He suggests that he did all these things for the same reason that he styles his hair and unbuttons the top buttons of his shirt. He did it to make himself more desirable to women. *He did it all for sex!* He's sure enough of this to attest to it at the top of his lungs!

He's also now experienced enough to know that casual sex in the small southern town where we live often has unexpected repercussions, and thus he tries to bridle himself a bit. And he knows that sex leads to bonds, bonds that may be stronger on the part of women, who have the disconcerting habit of "falling in love" with him. In addition, he is aware of the price exacted by the formation of bonds on *anyone's* part. He has formed a few, rather intense bonds and he knows that bonds, after all, are just that. They not only hold things together, they also determine the radius of one's movement. They restrict.

At this point he is aware of the tradeoff. He is wary of bonds. He still does the things that attract women, but now the means are becoming the end. He learned to ski for sex, but he has found the net value of the relationship necessary to provide sex to be less than the enjoyment of skiing itself. The drive that compelled him to do things for sex has gotten onto the wrong evolutionary track. It now leads to a genetic dead end.

His fitness, by the way, is zero; he has no children. He is unusual in this respect, of course, His grooming "should" have provided him with a brood. Many of his male friends enhanced their desirability in much the same way he did (if a bit less spectacularly) and then employed it "correctly." They formed the bonds, paid the price, had the kids. Never mind that they have never climbed the Peruvian peaks. Ignore their dimmed spirits and rounded bellies. They are more fit. They looked after their genes.

All this, of course, makes sense only in context. One would be hard put to explain to the dentist's girlfriend that his diminished interest in sex could be traced to his reproductive drive, especially if his behavior hasn't involved other women.

The Reproductive Imperative has also been misapplied in other ways. We have all heard that super-successful, hard-driving men are "just trying to prove something" (an ominous phrase often invoked by small, coughing minds to belittle the more successful). It is obvious, of course, that these driven souls are often in positions of power and, if they chose, could tap that enormous reserve of women who are attracted to power. But often they don't. They have become interested in power for its own sake. They would rather screw a competitor.

Members of other species can also get off on the same track. In some wild animals the most dominant male may impregnate very few females because he is too busy defending his social position. The abdication of his social responsibility leaves the breeding to less ambitious, and perhaps less capable, males. It doesn't take much imagination to see how the problem could have existed among our ancestors. How about the caveman equivalent of an oil company president? If he became overly interested in the trappings of success, he might ignore the greatest fruit of that success: ensuring the survival of his genes. It might seem, then, that the Executive Problem could not be transmitted genetically, that it must arise anew, a result of individual experience, each time it appears. However, this assumption neglects certain basic principles of evolution. Let's explore this by considering any population in which we find aggression, especially in males.

A certain amount of aggressiveness in human males may be good. Perhaps it is essential. If it is essential, you can be reasonably sure that natural selection will emphasize it whenever it appears. It may be so useful that it pervades the population and is expressed in virtually every man to one degree or another. Of course, like any other characteristic present in a population, it can be expected to vary from one individual to the next, but most men, we can assume, would be fairly aggressive. At one extreme we would find very docile males whom we never hear much about, and at the other extreme would be the super-driven executive types. The docile males would be out-competed, and the executives would be too busy, so neither would leave very many offspring; yet they themselves are probably the offspring of fathers who were only fairly aggressive. This is a well-known genetic phenomenon: average parents occasionally produce offspring that are extreme in one characteristic or another. While a father with an average nose will normally give rise to sons with average noses, sometimes he may pass along a genetic mix that will result in sons with either short, pug noses or startling beaks. So even extremes, such as extremely aggressive behavior, can be inherited from a parent who himself bore a mixture of genes that led to intermediate aggressiveness. From the progeny of the mainstream, then, arises each new population, replete with its own variation and extremes. And from this group those with the "right" level of aggression will again leave most of the children. (Keep in mind that these laws may apply only to historical, not necessarily to modern, man.)

Notice, as I'm sure you have, that I've referred to men aggressively scrambling for positions from which they can tap reserves of women. "Tap," however, is not actually the right word, because the choice is basically the woman's. Men simply compete in order to be *chosen* by females. It is almost invariably the case, among backboned animals, that the female does the choosing.

The female does the choosing.

This simple phrase is so loaded that I actually hesitate to discuss it. But, girding our loins, we plunge ahead.

Again, we must ignore current events and look at our traditions. Are women really coy, shy, submissive, and retiring creatures, elevated only as high as the pedestal on which they are placed? Are men actually big, brave, dominant, brash, noisy, and hale? If not, how did these myths arise?

It has been recently fashionable to answer, "culture." Our culture did it. Little girls are told to be quiet and sit with their knees together while they pretend to make tea for their dolls. Little boys are treated more roughly, granted more freedom, and given toy pistols to shoot. With this kind of training, how could things be different? Actually, we're not so interested in the training techniques at this point; we're more interested in how those specific techniques came to be. Why dolls for girls and guns for boys? How did that come about?

The real question we want to ask is: Could it be that our "culture" is not a *determiner* of our values but a *victim*? Could it be that our culture and values merely reflect at the conscious level what evolution has forced upon us? Could the behavior of men and women be changed by altering their early experience, or do they behave according to more ancient and subliminal laws?

Perhaps the sexual differences in behavior in our society today are not some unfair hoax; perhaps they are vestiges of a time (a *long* time) when those differences were important. Perhaps each sex developed its own distinct role so as to best comply with the Reproductive Imperative. Perhaps those differences developed full-blown long before humankind began to carve pictures or form words. And perhaps the words and pictures that came later merely reflected certain things that people already knew, deep in their souls. Perhaps the sex roles were clearly defined in the bands of *Homo habilis,* our scruffy forerunners who rambled over the African plain some two million years ago. The notion is amply supported by circumstantial evidence.

We've already mentioned some such evidence in other contexts. For example, we know that women were forced into more intimate contact with children than were men by virtue of pregnancy and nursing. Men, then, were left free to do other things. It is hard to hunt with a baby on one's hip, but someone had to bring home the bacon, so to males fell the chore of hunter—bringer home of proteinaceous meat. Another male chore was protection, against both other species and other males who would seek the woman as a genetic repository. With this dual responsibility, then, it would have been to a male's advantage to be large and powerful. It would also have been to a female's advantage to choose large, powerful men.

Since humans are incredibly opportunistic and given to jury-rigging their world, it would also have been to a woman's advantage to mate with an intelligent male who was able to function under all sorts of conditions. Intelligence, of course, would be more difficult to measure than size or strength, but there were undoubtedly yardsticks. Perhaps his intelligence could be demonstrated by his rank. Other males wouldn't follow a dummy into the swamp.

It seems, then, that men have become large and strong partly because of competition among themselves—competition for women. As they became larger and stronger with each generation, they may have eventually become too large for their own good and may be suffering the consequences even today. Women are probably closer to the ideal size for a species that occupies our kind of niche and that has the inborn constraints of our evolutionary history. Men, in their mad scramble to be chosen, have been forced to outgrow the ideal human size, and the result is reflected in flashy physiques that tend to break down earlier than those of smaller and more durable women.

The life expectancy of women is three to five years longer than that of men. Furthermore, Dr. Joan Ullyot, a well-known runner, has evidence that women are more likely to survive shipwrecks, mountaineering accidents, and similar disasters, apparently because of greater tolerance of cold, exposure, and starvation. Many long-distance swimming records are held by women, and women appear to do better in ultra-marathons (50- to 100-mile races) than in marathons. All this in spite of the fact that the average female is only 23 percent muscle (by weight) versus 40 percent for the average male, and that women are 25 percent fat as opposed to 15 percent for men (that's untrained men and women—trained athletes of both sexes have 10 percent less fat). (Some psychologists have compiled long lists of ways in which women are "superior" to men, but keep in mind that superiority for some traits can only be measured *within* the sex. A small male who outlived many females would be superior on an actuary table but might well fail as hunter or protector.)

So if women are assessing men and being careful about whom they copulate with, what must men do? Obviously, they must *advertise*. Every male is saddled with the burden of trying to show that he is a better specimen than his competitors. And what is the result? Machismo. Blessed machismo.

Machismo, or "male-ism," encompasses all those endearing qualities of men that we love and admire so much. We see it at all levels. It pervades every aspect of our culture. It appears blatantly in swaggering Saturday night fights; it appears subtly in chiding put-downs over cocktails. It is more pervasive in some cultures than others, but it is a constant in the human condition.

This, of course, is the point at which some anthropologist leaps out from behind the curtain and shouts, "Wrong!" Then he or she invariably parades out some little band of newly "discovered" people, announcing that this tribe has been found in some remote area and lo! the males do not compete. *This,* then, the anthropologist tells us, is the natural way of things. Men—"natural" men—do not compete. We know this by these fourteen people.

Wonderful. But how about the other four billion people on the planet? We're seeking to make general statements here, so we must consider the condition of *most* people. Any species is variable, and if we consider any trait found among humans, it can probably be graphed as a great bell-shaped curve, with most people falling under the middle of the curve and the behavioral extremes falling under the "tails," or tapering ends of the curve. The extremes exist, but they tell us little about people in general. The very peaceful Tasaday of the Philippines tell us no more about people in general than do the horribly cruel Iks of Africa.

So we can make the general statement that males, most males, advertise. Of course, it is not only the human male that is driven to these ends; other animals are also trapped in the quagmire of the system. We see it in the whirling and strutting of the sage grouse, showing himself off on his tiny territory before all the females, trying desperately to be chosen from among the other males. We see it in blackbirds, in which the quality of the males is determined by the kind of territory they are able to acquire; females flock to those who have the best nesting area. We see it in tiny fish, whose aggressive behavior not only chases away competing males but attracts females.

So if matings are the female's choice, it is not enough for a male to be big, strong, clever, and protective. He must somehow let the females know it. A male loaded with good qualities could be passed over in favor of an inferior male who advertises. In fact, a male's very success at advertising might be an indication of drive and competitiveness—qualities that a mating female might well appreciate. Besides, if her sons turned out to be braggarts who were able to attract females, they would stand an increased chance of passing on the mother's genes. So she is, in effect, looking not only for the best hunter and protector but also the best advertiser. Whatever turns her on can be expected to attract daughters-in-law to her sons.

Thus, we find that the most reproductively successful males will be those who are not hesitant to show how "good" they are, particularly in those species in which males are promiscuous to some degree. In fact, they may lie about it. Lie? Can animals lie? Actually, they lie a lot. Lying, remember, can include sheer exaggeration. Thus, when a male chimpanzee wishes to be intimidating, he does not simply show his size by standing erect or hunching his very powerful shoulders forward. He also stands his hair on end, thus appearing to be even bulkier than he really is. Many species use the same technique. A fish approaching an opponent may swing his gill covers out so as to appear larger. Males of some species of monkeys and apes grow long hairs over their shoulders and heads, thus accenting this area of their bodies. Shoulder and head strength is important in many species of mammals, since the primary fighting muscles are located there. In humans, the apparent strength of the jaws may be accented by beards and, in fact, some studies have shown that a man is considered more formidable if he has a beard. It is well known that college professors grow beards in order to intimidate their students through fear of being bitten.

I should add a word here about lying. Probably it is easier to lie to another species than to one's own. For example, a baboon may not have associated with chimpanzees enough to know that the big male staring threateningly, hair on end, is not really as big as he seems. So the baboon may move away. He may not have been able to read the subtler signals of the chimpanzee's threat, such as the flicking hand movements, but he could read size. (Many animals, particularly carnivores, are very conscious of size. A dog shows respect only for another animal who is at least roughly his own size. A horse may ignore a small dog but bolt at the sight of a large one.) In any case, the baboon steers clear of what apparently is a big chimpanzee.

Other chimpanzees, though, may read the situation differently. After all, they have evolved together and they know each other, so they may react differently to a threatening colleague than the baboon does. A baboon may react as if it thinks, "Here is a big, dangerous animal," but another chimpanzee is more likely to read, "Leonard is trying to look big again; he must be angry." It would be to a male's advantage to be able to read other males of his species accurately. It wouldn't do to be bluffed out by a male who is actually not as large as oneself. In other words, as the mechanisms for "lying" evolved, so did the ability to read the signal correctly. This kind of lying, then, may have persisted in the population because of its advantages in dealing with *other* species.

Besides, is a male chimpanzee really lying when he stands his glistening black hair on end? He may also be transmitting another bit of information—that he is a capable animal, able to find enough food to grow the coat that is now so imposingly displayed. A chimpanzee glaring with three hairs abristle cannot be taken as seriously as one who has been able to grow a luxuriant pelt.

Male accouterments, then, may have nothing to do with accenting strength or dangerousness; they may simply be a measure of the male's general health and vigor. For example, no one has ever been beaten senseless by a peacock flailing away with his tail feathers. In fact, the feathers are likely to be an encumbrance in a fight. Yet the strutting male demonstrates his long coverlets to any female in the vicinity. Certainly, if he has the vigor to produce something like this, he must be a fine fellow indeed and worthy of mixing one's genes with. In contrast, a great mane usually means that the lion wearing it is strong and formidable. Young males have short manes; old ones are beginning to lose theirs. So, the accented head and shoulders in lions is no lie. Lions with a great head of hair are to be avoided.

Even though males accent their maleness on a number of different bases, the payoff remains the same. The name of the game is to be deemed worthy. So we can ask, how do human males show their worthiness? They can grow beards, but they can't stand them on end. Without their clothes, in fact, it is difficult for men to lie about their physiques much at all. A cursory glance will reveal the power in one's shoulders. Height can't be increased; the best a man can do is draw himself up to his full height. One can't tiptoe about. And weight is rather easy to judge. Men, then, must accent their maleness in somewhat different ways than the other animals. But keep in mind that the goal remains the same: to leave genes.

One way men can accent their maleness—or lie—is through their dress. It is interesting that in spite of the opportunities for lying in intricate ways bestowed upon us by our complex communication abilities, we often are most successful at developing variations on old and simple themes. In recent centuries men have resorted endlessly to adorning themselves so as to look larger or more powerful. The officers in Caesar's army wore sculptured breastplates resembling a muscular and well-defined human torso. The breastplates, of course, may have been covering very flabby bodies. Hats have often been used to increase one's apparent height, as we see in the domed headgear of British bobbies. Rising plumes may have the same effect. Jimmy Cagney appeared taller by wearing a high-crowned hat. His roles demanded the appearance of a "good" male.

Another common ploy is to increase apparent shoulder size. Among cowboys, physical strength is greatly prized, and men wear tight-fitting shirts whose decorations often sweep into a great Y to accent the breadth of the shoulder. Men's suits are often more-or-less subtly padded and tapered to give the same top-heavy illusion. The effect is also produced in ruffled and billowing shoulders of tunics and shirts. No one ever wrote a song about "Little John" who was "narrow at the shoulder and broad at the hip." When males wish to appear sexy or intimidating (often in one fell swoop), they accent height and upper torso.

But, as we all know, they don't stop there. After all, a male who is hesitant to *apply* his size and strength would be of no great value; so he must show he is bold and aggressive as well as big and strong. This brings us to a new realm of human interaction and, undoubtedly, one of the most unseemly of all evolutionary dictates.

As I mentioned, the goal in showing off is to intimidate other men and to attract the attention of women. You don't have to look far to see it happening, and it begins early. I recall watching children on a German playground striking a tetherball. The girls often made it soar. The boys often didn't because they didn't have the coordination necessary to hit the ball as hard as they were trying to hit it. Also, whereas the girls were making screaming (mock distress) and laughing noises, the boys' sounds were more brash and humorless. Ha! Ha! Ha! is not a laugh.

I also saw another common sight at that playground: two boys "fighting" before a group of onlooking girls. Their fight consisted of standing sideways to each other, left arm crooked, exchanging blows to the shoulder. They were both smiling intermittently. Since they weren't angry, why were they doing it? Who were they impressing? Each other? The girls? Or were they merely practicing, learning to bluff and exercise their aggressive spirits? (Of course, young boys fight more seriously at times. I was forever pulling them apart when I was teaching elementary school in New Orleans. I don't recall ever pulling two little girls apart, though. Someone might say, "That's because their parents told them *not* to fight." That may be true, but why was this probably the only parental directive ever consistently obeyed on my playground?)

It's hard to see how childhood aggression would have any direct biological value. The victor in the slugging contest didn't copulate with anyone (at least I don't *think* so). Since, however, males continue to try to prove their superiority over other males long after childhood, such mock fighting may serve as practice. If males are going to compete more seriously later, then it would be to their advantage to learn how to fight and bluff and to learn the tactics of opponents. In those rambling bands of early humans there may have been another reason. If the groups tended to remain more or less intact, the rough-and-tumble play could have been a way of establishing rank before the boys developed the ability to really hurt each other.

Among baboons and chimpanzees there is a distinct difference in the play of young males and young females. To begin with, the males are more exploratory, ranging farther from their mothers at an earlier age. They also chase each other and roughhouse a lot more than females do. Young females remain closer to their mothers and show much more interest in newborn infants than do males.

The rough-and-tumble play of males, it turns out, has a very important role in the lives of these animals. They test each other early and find out who is strongest and most determined. The resulting hierarchy is carried into adulthood. Thus, strong and potentially dangerous young males are smoothly integrated into the troop hierarchy, already knowing their place. Of course, if fighting among boys ever had any such function, it was lost when intergroup mobility became common, when people began to encounter strangers frequently. (One would have to range far and wide to find even a few childhood friends these days, and when an old friend is found, the hierarchies of youth are likely to have no meaning. The kid you used to punch is now a loan officer.)

Adolescence marks an especially crass and swaggery period for human males. Boys are reaching the stage when they must soon be mating, and so they devote enormous amounts of time and energy to gaining the respect of their comrades. Each seeks to be bolder than the other. The competition is intense, and it pays off. From the deep recesses of Arkansas, my family tells me that girls are still attracted to football players (especially the quarterback, "since he's the leader"), and I recently overheard an awed high-school girl tell another, "He drives a two-plus-two!" Vroom! And away we go, locked firmly onto our evolutionary tracks, the denials of intellectuals drowned out by the roars of cheerleaders.

But let's leave adolescents, and the sooner the better. What about later? Do grown men play these competitive games? And, more importantly, do grown women respond? You bet they do, although the technique does change somewhat. You rarely see men at cocktail parties slugging each other on the shoulder to gain the attention of women (although I really wouldn't be surprised). Instead, they take their shots more subtly. One announces, "This year my wife and I spent our vacation on the Riviera." (Nonchalant shrug.) "Needed a break, you know." The response: "Heyyy! Great! I know what you mean. We *love* the Riviera this time of year." Gotcha. Another man, not even in the discussion, may be the greatest loser if his wife over-hears all this and casts a baleful look in his direction. These wonderful men are talking about the *seasons* on the Riviera and her schmucky husband took her to Orlando. Of course, if these wonderful men can appear appealing enough and can sow enough discontent, they stand to reap a certain genetic harvest.

And here we return to a point suggested earlier. In intelligent, communicative, social animals, such as humans, for whom influence, or the ability to manipulate, is just as important as physical power, a male need not advertise shoulder muscles or height. He can just demonstrate the ability to accumulate.

Earlier I mentioned that the females of some species of blackbirds choose males on the basis of the kind of territory the males have been able to stake out. But there is an even better example, among birds, of using possessions to increase one's appeal: bowerbirds. Bowerbirds are believed to be at the leading edge of avian evolution. In general, the most primitive mating system is believed to be monogamy, when pairs form on a long-term basis and the sexes look very similar, such as we see in sparrows. Polygamy, where males become more garish and take multiple females, is believed to be evolutionarily more advanced. (Polyandry, where females are more conspicuous and stay with males just long enough to lay eggs for him to sit on before she's off seeking out another male, is very rare.) Obviously, though, there's a risk in becoming too garish, especially if one is a prey species. A garish male attracts not only females but predators as well. So male bowerbirds have taken the risk out of conspicuousness by going one step further and decorating, not themselves, but their real estate. Male bowerbirds haul in shiny leaves, shells, buttons, tinfoil, string, or what-have-you, and place them in areas they have cleared. Females immediately recognize these bowers and the fact that a splendid male, with time and energy to gather baubles, must be in the area, but predators could not be expected to recognize the clues that indicate that a healthy male bird is about.

Human beings, then, behave in some ways like bowerbirds. Men may let their acquisitions do the talking for them. In a sense, a man who has acquired a seven-car garage, a diamond ring, a Mercedes 450 SL, and a closet of $300 suits can afford to behave circumspectly. He may personally be dignified, low-key, sedate, and perhaps inconspicuous, but his possessions shout, "Look at me! I'm a successful male! See what *I've* been able to acquire! Wahoo!"

Now we're beginning to see how complex humans really are. It's hard to make general statements about ourselves. After all, even in attempting blatant generalizations, this is the third analogy I've drawn between us and other animals. I said human males are drab and monogamous, like sparrows. I also said men are conspicuous and polygamous, like peacocks. And now I'm saying that they attract females not only with physical traits but by acquisition and external trappings as well, like blackbirds and bowerbirds.

Perhaps this complexity is at the root of some of our problems. If you asked a sparrow about the nature of pair bonds, he or she might say, "One on one." If you asked a peacock or a bowerbird, the answer might be, "Males are highly promiscuous, females are very selective." But if you ask a human you must expect *any* kind of reply. So what *is* the nature of human pair bonding? Those who argue that people are innately monogamous could hold their annual conventions in a phone booth. We see monogamous marriages, that's true. But for a pair to stay together in monogamy, someone must usually bite the bullet. Our tendency to stay with one mate is often coupled with the urge to copulate with anyone who is attractive. A person who is not thus tempted, it may be said, lacks either imagination or courage. The expression of such an urge, by the way, does not always take the most blatant form. Most of us are far too "decent" in our own minds to admit to any but the strongest of such urges. Instead, we may pay compliments. "You sure look nice today," may mean, "In my frame of mind today, I would like to pounce on you." But many of us don't pounce, and, in fact, we really don't think about it. We feel good about paying someone a compliment, and we go home to our wives.

Obviously, marriages are held together by a number of factors. These factors include not only inward constraints, such as love or bullet-biting, but external influences, such as mate jealousy and social criticism. Many people would just rather not risk getting caught or being indicted by their peers. And because of the intense interest people have in the sexual patterns of others, infidelity *will* elicit indictment. (The harshest criticism invariably comes from embittered and secretly envious chalkline walkers, who tend to wrap their words in damp piety.)

I've stressed the point of male-male competition and female choice because it is very important to the understanding of human behavior. However, as any fool knows, there's another side to that coin. Females compete, and males do some choosing of their own. If men were completely promiscuous, like peacocks, our behavior would be more predictable. But men also have pronounced, if weaker, tendencies toward monogamy. They tend to form bonds with a single female and to work cooperatively with her to rear the children. A man's interludes with other females can only be brief if he is to effectively fulfill his role at home. Thus, whereas he may have any number of casual liaisons with females he would not "marry," he must be careful when it comes to selecting a mate. He must choose a broad-hipped and busty woman who indicates that she will not be promiscuous (become pregnant by another male) and who suggests that she can deliver and care for children. It is, of course, not necessary for us to dwell on those dark rumors that not all women are completely judicious and monogamous.

How about the intelligence of a prospective wife? We will consider the whole matter of intelligence later, but the argument can go both ways. Of course, basic intelligence is important to any human, and a parent would want his or her children to be bright. But intelligence has not traditionally been a highly desirable trait in prospective wives. Or so we have been told. In many societies, if a woman is bright, she had best disguise it. The reason for this may be rooted in our ancient history: Men, constantly jockeying to improve their rank in the hunting group, would have been very status-conscious and would have been quickly threatened by a smaller, weaker female showing an intellectual superiority. If she wanted to keep the peace and maintain the bond, she had best not have threatened the poor fellow.

By the way, why is it incumbent upon the female to avoid threatening the male, to be submissive? Why might she be more concerned about his frame of mind than he is of hers? Isn't marriage give and take? A fifty-fifty proposition? If it is, it's a rarity in the animal world. Some things virtually do not exist; atheists in foxholes and fifty-fifty relationships. Among social animals (at least animals that recognize each other individually—we must almost always exclude social insects from these ruminations), a lack of a definite hierarchy produces very unstable situations. Put a number of monkeys (or dogs or chickens) together for the first time and the fur (or feathers) will fly. It will continue to fly until they decide who's boss and who's not. Once the hierarchy is established, though, peace reigns, accented only by small scuffles as someone tries to climb the social ladder. Any attempt to change rank is likely to be disruptive. It is important to any social animal to know its rank. It will yield before more dominant animals and thus save itself from a thrashing. If two animals reach for the same food, the dominant animal gets it. It does the subordinate no good to try. It would only get a bloody nose and lose the food anyway. This way it only loses the food.

The attempts at maintaining equality between human couples I've observed have not been very comfortable or successful. Usually, rigid rules are arbitrarily formulated, and each person has his or her checklist. Any attempt at such an artificially imposed equality is usually to the female's advantage. Most of the time it involves the man giving up much of the privilege that "society" has traditionally bestowed upon him, privilege related to size. Among humans, as well as among all mammals in which the male is larger, he can be expected to be dominant simply because, since he is larger and stronger, he usually gets his way. So, I've argued here that hierarchies are normal among social animals and that they actually reduce aggression between the individuals involved. I also maintain that, in human pairs, a natural ranking will form and that the male will usually be dominant because of his size and his intense interest in status. Never mind the fact that you know cases to the contrary. We're talking here about what one might *expect* based on what we know about social systems, and we're talking about what worked among our ancestors to assure harmony and enhance reproduction within the group.

If an alien from another planet wanted to know the nature of the human condition, he would be best advised not to ask us anything. If he had time, his best bet would be simply to watch. What we say is not important for a number of reasons. First, we don't *know* what the human condition is. We say we abhor warfare, yet off we march with a certain regularity. We hold the family dear and spout homilies about the joys of monogamy, yet most of us are, at best, grudging monogamists. We don't know *what* we are. We say anything. We blather; we are torn. Our inconsistencies perplex us. We live in constant fear that something is wrong. And we must be reassured again and again that we're OK, that our perceptual confusion doesn't necessarily mean that something is "wrong" (heaven forbid) with us. We often look for assurance to someone who is adrift on the same raft we are but who has decided, for his own peace of mind, or for profit, to behave firmly, as if answers are in hand. We flock to anyone who seems to be able to provide firm answers. We often revere these people, who have arbitrarily picked a set of values and decided to live by them. It is *such* a pleasure to read Thoreau.

No, the spaceman would be making a big mistake to ask us anything about ourselves. He might set his own research back by hundreds of years. He should just watch. And if he or his colleagues could have watched for the last two million years, there would be no reason to talk to anyone. He would have seen our systems and our values emerge and would have seen that, by George, they work. He might have deduced the Reproductive Imperative and perhaps some of the rules about choosing sexual partners. He would have seen them incorporated into our culture and given "cultural" labels. He might have seen us try to change them by giving them new labels or denouncing them. He would have seen that we are long on philosophy and short on history. (He might learn our secrets quickly, since he would probably be the product of the same sort of system. Try to imagine a system that *didn't* work like ours.)

By the way, there is no reason to be distressed simply because we don't know what we're doing. It is not important to our biological success for us to know *why* we behave as we do. It doesn't matter one whit what we *think* we are doing or what we choose to call our behavior or motivation. That information has no value whatever. We can talk among ourselves, clucking, scolding, and reassuring each other, but our conclusions mean nothing. When all is said and done, the next generation will be made up of the most successful reproducers of this generation, and thus they can be expected to philosophize, drop out, climb up, steal, bathe, and love the mountains, but above all, they can be expected to reproduce. A person can hold the Reproductive Imperative in total and utter contempt—as long as he obeys it. If he doesn't, there will be fewer contemptuous people later. So watch what we do, not what we say.

CHAPTER FIVE

ARE THE BRAINS OF MALES AND FEMALES DIFFERENT ?

"HE'S GOT *balls*" one of my less enlightened colleagues exclaimed in rapt admiration as a woman jumper who was a friend of ours maneuvered into a skydiving rosette. We watched the group hold for a long moment and then disintegrate as the divers slowly tumbled apart. The chutes happily opened and the divers drew softly nearer to the earth, landing a bit more roughly than their peaceful suspension would have suggested.

After they gathered their chutes and walked over to us, my friend said it again. "Man, Susan, you've got *balls*!" She smiled and seemed to take it as a compliment. The hug he gave her didn't give any indication that he really believed she was physically anomalous. And, in fact, what he had really said was, "Susan, you're brave."

On another occasion, when this same fellow and I were heading out for a night on the town and I had mentioned inviting old Ted to come along, he said, "He won't go. His wife won't let him. He's a pussy." So Susan's got balls and Ted's a pussy. Meaningless, except for the underlying assumption that maleness is admirable and femaleness is not.

Not all males, of course, are admirable. Some are "better" than others. But even here we tend to identify the best ones as those bearing more of the presumably masculine traits. ("He's a real man." "He's not much of a man.")

A psychologist friend in southern California has cleared the matter up, as far as he is concerned, by dividing the world's males into "Samurai" and "Wimps." The definitions came to him one day at the

97

zoo while he was watching the baboons. He noticed that the females were busy doing all sorts of things: poking mysterious objects into their mouths, grooming each other, just sitting round, scratching, or whatever. Infants were tumbling about and chasing each other, and big males sat here and there or walked about on all fours, casting quick glances left and right. But in the midst of it all, not far from my friend, sat an enormous male, clearly the largest male in the troop. My friend noticed that the others approached the big male hesitantly and with great care, if they approached him at all, and that often two obsequious females would groom him at once. But the big male seemed to ignore it all and just sat there, like a great Buddha. My friend stood entranced by the whole scene until he was jarred to reality by the fact that the big male had turned and was looking at *him*! He reflexively gulped and looked away. In a flash he recovered himself. What is this?! He was a PhD, a psychologist at an excellent academic institution, a man of many publications, well-respected, formidable in seminars—and he had just been intimidated by a *baboon*! He decided then and there that the baboon was a Samurai and he was a Wimp. The baboon was "greater," even though he did not even have a book review to his credit.

When he told me the story, we had great fun defining the qualities of Samurai and Wimps. Samurai, we said, walked the earth with presence and abandon, took it stoically on the chin, gave as good as they got, could not be intimidated, were powerful and unafraid, and did everything with great authority (we took this last point to some rather indelicate ends). Wimps, on the other hand, were home on time, hoped not to offend anyone—particularly their wives—walked society's chalklines, and generally behaved like the men in TV commercials who are so concerned with clean collars, sparkling dishes, and the state of their cat's appetite.

But, we had to admit, not everyone fell neatly into one classification or the other. Because we were forced to admit independent variables and intermediates, we realized that we had actually constructed a graded barometer of manliness. Perhaps old Ted was afraid of his wife, but he was also a breathtaking stunt pilot. So old Ted wasn't entirely a Wimp. In spite of such problems, we sought to place each of our friends into his proper position on the Samurai Scale. Of course, we couldn't keep it to ourselves; we had to do it in their company. They loved it.

It never occurred to us to develop such a ranking for females. Why? Was it because our own sexual identity had biased us, or because females are traditionally less clearly ranked? We were giving Samurai points for selfishness, egotism, single-mindedness, and violence—but especially for bravery. The importance of bravery should have led us to include females; we were both fully aware that women, while perhaps less boisterous or less socially compelled to demonstrate it, are certainly no less brave. I might not have believed this in my youth, but the years have provided me with too many opportunities to know women braver than I. It began when my little sister accepted her tonsillectomy more stoically than I did, and it was reinforced when I scuba dived with seemingly fearless women on an expedition to the Indian Ocean. I also know that any plane I jump out of is going to have fingernail marks down the side.

Obviously, women are as brave as men. But if this is common knowledge, how could the myth of the Samurai male have arisen? Why are we generally unaware that there were Samurai women, who perhaps did not fight but who did embrace the philosophy? Why didn't my friend and I just automatically include women in our rankings? It is not surprising that we didn't, of course. In the past, men were provided with more opportunities to demonstrate their bravery; they were the hunters and warriors. Any women who fearlessly confronted danger by fighting in that very physical world of prehistory would have been decimated. And probably the ensuing years have not increased the opportunities for women to demonstrate bravery by grand gestures. (They sometimes demonstrate it more gracefully by enduring Samurai-minded men, or by childbirth—an event I'm still not sure I believe.) In fact, history records few notable women fighters at all, although they have undoubtedly become more common with the advent of technological warfare. So how is it that women can be brave but are usually not thought of as fighters? It may be because men behave more aggressively than women. In other words, they feel freer (or even obligated) to demonstrate any bravery they possess.

At this point, then, we might ask, why do men and women behave differently? For example, if men are not actually braver than women, what compels them to flaunt whatever bravery they possess? Why are women less likely to do so? Why do the sexes behave differently in so many ways? Do they *learn* to behave differently or are they inherently different? Specifically, are their brains themselves different? We will look at some interesting evidence, but first, I should say that it is reasonable to suspect there are basic physical differences in the nervous systems of the sexes. After all, is it logical that a large, powerful male, whose traditional role has been that of hunter and defender, should have the same neural constitution as a smaller female, whose role has been gathering plants and rearing children? Are the two sexes born with very different bodies and roles but the same kind of mind, which then must be programmed through experience? Or are the sexes born with different behavioral propensities to match their physiognomies? It would certainly be more efficient if men and women were born with tendencies to behave in ways commensurate with the roles they are to play.

We might ask, in what specific ways do men and women differ in their behavior? According to Stanford University neuropsychologists Diane McGuiness and Karl Pribram, some differences are very pronounced and quite unexpected. For example, men are less sensitive to extreme heat and more sensitive to extreme cold. Men have better daylight vision; women have better night vision. From childhood on, men have faster reaction times and are more interested in objects than people, showing less empathy toward others than women do. Men are better at spatial thinking than women are. For example, they can mentally rotate an object easier than women can. This ability may be related to their greater mathematical skills. Women, on the other hand, are much more verbal, talking earlier and grasping patterns of language easier. Women have more sensitive taste and are more sensitive to touch over their entire bodies than are men. They hear better, especially in the higher ranges. (In fact, at 85 decibels, sounds seem twice as loud to them as to men.) Women suffer more from repetitive sounds and are better at manual dexterity, fine coordination, and rapid choices. Thus they tend to be excellent typists. (But before you shout "Aha!" I will add that, by the same token, they should make better neurosurgeons.)

Child psychologists have recently begun to tell us that behavioral differences in the sexes are apparent even in preschool children. This is true even in cases where the children were reared under similar, even institutional, conditions. Little girls, they found, tend to confront frustrating barriers by plopping down and crying. Little boys more often try to climb the barrier and show a greater curiosity about the nature of their problem. Little girls talk to each other more than little boys do and are more likely to show a strong tendency to affiliate with adults. Little boys tend to roughhouse and wander farther from the group.

Of course, this kind of evidence shouldn't necessarily be interpreted to mean that females are sensitive and delicate crybabies while males are inventive explorers. Innate behavioral traits must mature just as physical traits do, and some patterns may simply appear later in girls than in boys. Also, while distinct differences in the sexes may continue into adulthood, or may not even be evident until then, we should remind ourselves that there is a great overlap in all these areas and that members of both sexes may be found at the extremes. For example, some girls are much bolder explorers than most boys, and some boys are much worse crybabies than most girls. But the sexual differences are numerous in any case. Girls are less distracted by sights while listening, while boys are distracted by any novel object, perhaps as a result of their greater exploratory tendencies. As infants, boys spend more time with objects other than toys and more often invent novel uses for them. Boys show better depth perception and can read maps better than girls, especially from adolescence on. Girls can sing in tune better than boys.

Our question, though, is: Do behavioral differences between males and females mean that their brains are different? In order to approach this problem, let's first determine the degree to which physical factors can influence thought patterns. The question is related to the larger problem of freedom of action: How much are our thoughts constrained by our anatomy and chemistry? Does the highly prized human mind yield before simple physiological factors? How free are we? And to what extent can we be "culturalized" past any inborn tendency?

A few years ago certain people who were seemingly unable to control their moods were receiving endless treatment from clinical psychologists. These people tended to soar from black holes of depression to dizzying heights of glee, only to crash again in the typical manic-depressive sequence. They were almost impossible to live with, and many of them sought professional help. The psychologists, of course, questioned them about their relationship with their mother; did they hate their father? They pried deeply into backgrounds and asked questions about childhood. Then the source of the problem was revealed by medical researchers, leaving many psychologists whistling softly and staring out the window.

The afflicted people, it turned out, simply had problems with blood sugar levels. Their condition was called hypoglycemia. Too little sugar in the blood made them depressed; a good dose brought on euphoria. The problem was due to a failure of those feedback mechanisms that regulate the release of sugars from storage areas in the body. Ways were found to regulate the blood sugar, such as combinations of careful dieting and insulin injections, and the symptoms disappeared. Moods stabilized. So their problem had nothing to do with their relationship with their parents after all. It had to do with the amount of $C_6H_{12}O_6$ circulating in the blood. Somehow, this simple sugar altered thought pattern and shifted a person's perception of the world he lived in. Without sugar, no matter how hard he tried, he could *not* be cheerful. The neural patterns of the brain were shifted so as to disallow it. An important question, then, is, to what extent is our behavior controlled by physiological factors that are independent of experience? The question has been brought home to many of us with horrifying emphasis.

I arrived at the University of Texas to begin my doctoral work in the summer of 1966. The University had been the focus of national headlines only days before my arrival, as a result of a terrible incident. A student had climbed to the top of the observation deck of the tower that dominated the campus in those days and, in the next 90 minutes, he shot thirty-eight people, killing fourteen.

The human tragedy was beyond belief. In the months that followed, I came to know people who were involved, both those who had been injured and the families of those who had been killed.

The student's name was Charles Whitman, and there was nothing in his background to suggest that he was capable of such a deed. He had never been violent. In fact, he was the epitome of the classic clean-cut, hard-working young college student. Something happened, though, that caused his moods to change. During the months before his death, in the course of a normal day he would suddenly and inexplicably find himself filled with a nameless rage. And, then, just as suddenly, it would disappear. He became upset and fearful about these terrible feelings and sought professional help, but he came up empty-handed. Perhaps his own words can best describe his feelings and the action they led to. On the evening of July 31 he wrote:

> I don't quite understand what it is that compels me to type this
> letter. Perhaps it is to leave some vague reason for the actions I
> have recently performed. [At this point, Whitman had harmed
> no one; his wife and mother were elsewhere in the city, still alive.]
> I don't really understand myself these days. I am supposed to be
> an average, reasonable and intelligent young man. However,
> lately (I can't recall when it started) I have been a victim of
> many unusual and irrational thoughts. These thoughts constantly
> recur, and it requires a tremendous mental effort to concentrate
> on useful and progressive tasks. In March when my parents made
> a physical break I noticed a great deal of stress. I consulted a Dr.
> Cochrum at the University Health Center and asked him to

recommend someone that I could consult with about some psychiatric disorders I felt I had. I talked with a doctor once for about two hours and tried to convey to him my fears that I felt overcome by overwhelming violent impulses. After one session I never saw the doctor again, and since then I have been fighting my mental turmoil alone, and seemingly to no avail. After my death I wish that an autopsy would be performed on me to see if there is any visible physical disorder. I have had some tremendous headaches in the past and have consumed two large bottles of Excedrin in the past three months. It was after much thought that I decided to kill my wife, Kathy, tonight after I pick her up from work. . . . I love her dearly, and she has been as fine a wife to me as any man could ever hope to have. I cannot rationally pinpoint any specific reason for doing this. I don't know whether it is selfishness, or if I don't want her to have to face the embarrassment my actions would surely cause her. At this time, though, the prominent reason in my mind is that I truly do not consider this world worth living in, and am prepared to die, and I do not want to leave her to suffer alone in it. I intend to kill her as painlessly as possible. . . .

Later in the night he did kill both his mother and wife, and then wrote:

I imagine it appears that I brutally killed both of my loved ones. I was only trying to do a good thorough job. If my life insurance policy is valid please see that all the worthless checks I wrote this weekend are made good. Please pay off all my debts. I am 25 years old and have never been financially independent. Donate the rest anonymously to a mental health foundation. Maybe research can prevent further tragedies of this type.

The next morning he carted a box of firearms, knives, food, and water to the top of the tower. Fortunately, his timing was off, and by the time he reached the deck he was ten minutes late for the change of classes. There were still students strolling on the campus below, however, and they had little chance when Whitman, a military-trained rifleman, started shooting. Some managed to flee to safety as Whitman rained down his deadly barrage, but some were felled in their tracks. The police were brought in, but they couldn't reach him, even with a helicopter, until one courageous lawman climbed through the carnage, walked onto the observation deck and, encountering Whitman face to face, shot him dead.

Why had Whitman done it? What could have persuaded him that this was an appropriate course of action under any circumstances? It turns out that even if he had received extensive psychiatric help, it probably would have done him no good. In a sense, all those people were killed by simple cells quietly dividing in the dark environs of a young man's brain. Post-mortem examination revealed a tumor (of a highly malignant type called glioblastoma) embedded in an area of the brain called the amygdaloid nucleus. It has long been known that electrical or chemical stimulation of this area can produce aggression in a wide variety of animals. Peaceful animals can be turned into raging beasts with a flick of a switch.

The amygdala area of the brain is part of what is called the "old brain" because it developed so early in the evolution of animals and because it arises early in embryonic development. Many primitive animals rely almost exclusively on the old brain, but more intelligent animals have a highly developed cerebrum, or "new brain." The old brain controls unconscious patterns, such as appetite, breathing, and perhaps drive or motivation, whereas the cerebrum, composed of the famed gray matter, is the "thinking" center. The cerebrum is involved with conscious decision and is extremely flexible and unpredictable— as witnessed by the kinds of decisions our friends make. This is also the part we are most aware of, perhaps because it is the seat of our conscious awareness (that may make no sense at all, but you're welcome to try). It makes us adaptable to a wide range of conditions and enables us to behave opportunistically in a complex and changing world. We have faith in this great gray god and it has certainly led us to whatever successes and dangers we face today.

But the vaunted cerebrum, perched atop and enveloping the unchronicled old brain, is not omnipotent. In fact, if there is any interaction between the old and new brain, it is probably almost entirely in the form of directives from the old brain to the new. The new brain, in spite of its prodigious powers, probably has little effect on its ancient predecessor. So whereas the new brain can probably influence the old brain very little, it is extremely sensitive to the neural activity emanating from below it.

Whitman, the earlier Whitman whose amygdala allowed the new brain to enable him to function socially, undoubtedly would not have opted to shoot innocent people. He would certainly have condemned such behavior. But his conscious thought processes gave way to something more primitive, more compelling, something from deeper within. He had no doubt consciously overridden those hostile urges before, but finally the message from the afflicted amygdala could be denied no longer. His new brain manufactured the rationalizations and the elaborate plans to give form to those urgent aggressive impulses coming from his afflicted old brain.

As a final example showing the relationship between the old brain and aggression, consider rabies. The dreaded disease almost always causes drastic behavioral changes, which are followed by death (although one boy, bitten by a rabid bat, developed rabies and survived in 1971). Rabies literally means "rage," and it is caused by a virus that attacks the hippocampus area of the limbic system—part of the old brain. Victims of rabies do not *decide* to become violent, and they cannot be *taught* to be peaceful. New kinds of impulses begin to emanate from the old brain and the new brain responds. Even the most gentle and agreeable of people are relentlessly transformed into terrifying souls filled with rage and violence.

Of course, usually we are merely subjected to quiet wheedling from the old brain, and if its directives are inappropriate at the moment, we can consciously override them. This is why we do not see couples copulating wildly all over the tables in romantic little restaurants. The old brain may be urging them to leap at each other, but instead they talk about their childhoods in Vermont, a trip to California, a little farm in Pennsylvania. So conscious suppression of some messages from the old brain is possible. But is it desirable? People going home alone from those restaurants may feel enormous frustration. If the normal urges from the old brain are continually denied, tension may be discharged in unexpected ways. A person who is frustrated at romance may kick his dog, take a poke at his neighbor's nose, or enter an orgy of work (to his employer's delight).

An important point here is that conscious decisions may not be so conscious after all. The cerebrum may be perniciously goaded, urged, and goosed by the old brain beneath until it makes the decisions that satisfy its ancient demigod. "I think I'll go out for a hamburger" may be a "conscious" decision, made at the directives of an old brain that has detected low levels of nutrients in the blood circulating through it. The old brain provides the urging, but it is up to the new brain to solve the problem at hand. We might expect, then, that the constant urgings from the old brain can exert a directional effect on the "conscious" decisions we make. Ask someone why he or she "decided" to be jealous of a spouse. Ask people why they love their children.

So we see that the directives from the old brain are not necessarily bad ones. In fact, they are likely to be the ones that ensured our success as a species, the ones that prompted us to do the things necessary for successful reproduction. The old brain produces the urges and leaves to the cerebrum the tasks of maneuvering the body to see that these demands are met and then of rationalizing that particular course of action. Of course, as a cerebrum goes about its task, if you were to ask it what it is doing, why it has chosen *that* course, you could expect *any* kind of answer. And that's what you would get.

By now it should be apparent that I'm going to pin at least some of our sexual differences in aggression on the old brain. I'm going to say that the old brains of men and women are different and that they send out different signals, expressed as "urges." Of course, it might be that any signal they send out is interpreted differently by the sexes, which would imply differences in the new brain. We'll look at some sexual differences in the new brain shortly. It seems, though, that the roots of some of our more elemental urges, such as aggression, should be sought in the old brain. Now obviously the old brain is not entirely responsible for our aggressiveness. We know that people can learn to be aggressive and we will see that the cerebrum can be altered so as to change the ways aggressiveness is expressed. However, the point here is, the old brain may be the seat of some aggressiveness. So, if aggression is not entirely learned, then, to that degree, it cannot be modulated or controlled by relearning. Therefore, we should not look entirely to educational programs to reduce aggression in our society.

You may have noticed that I am departing a bit from the conventional parlor wisdom that blames aggression on cultural problems. By implicating the old brain, I'm effectively saying that aggressiveness, to a degree, is inherited. At this point I should add that aggressiveness is not the same as violence. Aggressiveness is a spirit, violence is but one of its manifestations. Some of the most aggressive people I know are nonviolent. Indeed, if Mahatma Gandhi were not one of the most aggressive people who ever lived, could he have changed the course of a nation? He aggressed. He went against the tide. And he prevailed. He didn't have a retiring bone in his body.

Of course, it's hard to measure a spirit, but it's easy to see a behavior. So we will rely largely on descriptions of overt aggression, particularly violence, in forming our conclusions.

One might ask here, "Why talk about sexual differences in *aggression*? Why not some other trait?" The reason is twofold. First, aggressive differences can be expected in sexes that have traditionally played such different roles. It was incumbent upon one sex to be aggressive and the other to be more passive if a pair could hope to be successful reproducers. Second, sexual and aggressive behavior may have evolved in close association.

Sexual and aggressive centers lie very close together in the brain, and some elements of each stem from the same embryonic tissues. Scientists have been busy mapping the brain in animals, including humans, for years. For the most part, the mapping has been done by removing diseased parts of the brain or by monitoring the behavior of people who have suffered brain damage. In some cases, maps have been made when parts of the brain have been stimulated electrically or chemically. In this way scientists have located pleasure and pain centers, as well as sexual and aggressive centers. Other areas, when stimulated, bring on sleep, or irritability, or whatever. It is these kinds of experiments, then, that have shown that sexual and aggressive centers lie very close together in the brain, perhaps having evolved in unison.

But does such proximity indicate a behavioral relationship? In male monkeys it was found that the centers that bring on an erection are located within a millimeter of rage centers. In fact, stimulation of one area may bring on both an erection and rage. In humans, brain damage sometimes affects both sexual and aggressive behavior. In one case a woman was subjected to neurological testing after she had assaulted a number of people with razor blades and broken bottles. She was hard to examine because she was so aggressive and combative, and the doctors had to be very careful lest she attack them. A case history and observation revealed that she was not only hyperaggressive but hypersexual as well. She masturbated eighteen to twenty times a day (about every 45 minutes) and was extremely active in other ways. She indulged in heterosexual sex at every opportunity and frequently participated in group sex and lesbian activities. Neural examination revealed abnormal brain patterns in the temporal region. When an antiseizure medicine was administered, her aggressiveness and sexual appetite fell simultaneously.

You may have noticed that I seem to be assuming that naturally gentle people are shifted from their normal and peaceful ways by brain damage—that I'm somehow implying that their aggressiveness is not normal. We must define, however, what is natural or normal. After all, it is perfectly natural and normal to respond violently if certain parts of the brain are stimulated. The "normal" people we know are simply people whose brains are not being stimulated so as to evoke rage. When we swear that old Joe would never do anything like that, we neglect the fact that with proper neurological stimulation, old Joe is capable of *anything*. Most people probably have relatively low stimulation or high thresholds of their rage centers in the absence of some neural trauma. Nevertheless, the demon exists within us all. We can only hope that it will not be released.

Scientists have been compiling data on the effects of brain damage for years. It has been estimated that ten million American citizens have marked brain damage, a figure that could have been circumstantially verified by looking any elected congressman directly in the eye. Another five million may be brain-damaged to a less serious degree. The damage can be due to tumors, accidents, mishaps in pregnancy or at birth, prolonged reduction in blood sugar levels, drug use, oxygen deprivation, or any number of other factors. As we might have expected, changes in aggressive behavior are most likely to occur when the old brain has been damaged. Because the old brain is notoriously unresponsive to anything the cerebrum learns, the level of aggressive behavior stemming from the old brain can be analyzed without worrying too much about how experience may have biased the results. Of course, learning is usually very important in the *expression* of aggressive urges, and we are actually measuring this expression. (Whitman, for example, expressed his aggression through the military tools he had learned to operate; a man without any experience with guns would most likely have used some other means.) So we see that learned and innate patterns, again, cannot be easily separated.

Now that we've established the critical roles of both the old and new brains in the development of aggression in humans, let's go back to our earlier question. Is aggression different in males and females? Do any such differences suggest that the brains of the sexes are different?

Such questions will form a basis for our argument, but we won't rely entirely on such circumstantial evidence. In some cases there is evidence of a much more direct sort. For example, it is known that an area of the brain called the paraformical medial forebrain is vital to sexual behavior in male mammals. If it is destroyed, so is the male's sex life. However, it has nothing to do with sex in females since a female deprived of the area continues to mate as if nothing had happened. There is also other evidence indicating sexual differences in the brain. In guinea pigs, when the part of the old brain called the hypothalamus is cut, entirely different sorts of changes in sexual behavior result for males and females. Cuts in the area just ahead of the part associated with sight completely eliminate male sexual behavior but don't change sexual patterns in females. Lesions in the front part of the hypothalamus, on the other hand, stop female sexual patterns while having little effect on males. Other studies have shown that if the two halves of the brain are separated in rats, the behavioral results are very different in males and females. Such experiments indicate a basic organizational difference in the brains of mammalian males and females.

In primate studies, Patricia S. Goldman and her research group reported that the sexes of some species of monkey not only differ in their basic reproductive behavior but also in emotionalism, aggression, play, and food preferences. In addition, the researchers found that maturation proceeds at different rates in males and females and that maturation rates affect learning ability. In one set of experiments, they removed a part of the cerebrum in eight infant monkeys (they used nine more as "controls"). When all were 10 weeks old, they were tested to see how quickly they could learn "habit reversal" (for example, if they had been trained to push a black lever for food instead of a white lever, their task would be to learn to do the opposite). It was found that the males had lost much of their ability to learn but that the females learned as well as ever. In other experiments the researchers found that up to about a year of age, damage to the gray matter impaired learning in males but not in females. After the monkeys were 15 to 18 months of age, however, any such damage affected the two sexes about equally. Apparently, then, the brains of male and female monkeys mature at different rates.

But what about humans? How good is the evidence that the brains of men and women are different? There are two kinds of evidence, direct and indirect, and some of the data can be put into either category with equal ease. But let's have a look. Evidence that is clearly indirect includes differences in the electrical activity of men's and women's brains in response to stimuli. Whereas women are more sensitive to visual stimuli, sound, and touch, they (contrary to popular opinion) may not be able to handle heavy stress as well as men do.

(They also describe disruptive experiences, such as moving or loss of job, as being more traumatic than men do, a finding that clearly *could* be related to social expectations—men aren't "supposed" to whine.)

But for more direct evidence, consider this. Spatial ability is believed to be localized primarily in the right half of the brain—the right cerebral hemisphere. Verbal ability and intuition are believed to be localized in the left half. In the 1960s a group of surgical patients had part of their right hemisphere removed. It was expected, therefore, that they would suffer reduced spatial ability. However, they didn't. They did almost as well as the population as a whole on the tests. Then they were divided according to sex, and it was found that the men who had parts of the right half of the brain removed did poorly on the spatial test while the women who had suffered the same treatment did not. Obviously, the organizations of the brains of men and women were different, but it was several years before supporting data appeared.

Some of the data were provided by Jeanette McGlone of Ontario's University Hospital. She examined eighty-five right-handed adults (the right hand is believed to be controlled by the left side of the brain while the right side of the brain dominates in most southpaws). Each of the patients had suffered brain damage in one side of the brain or the other. They were all tested for both verbal and spatial skills. It was assumed that if a mental function is located in a particular half of the brain, that function should be impaired if that hemisphere has been damaged. Thus, the researchers expected that those with damage on the right side would do poorly on the spatial tests and those with left hemisphere damage would show impairment of verbal skills. This, in fact, turned out to be the case—but only for men. The women showed far less effect, no matter which half of the brain was damaged. It seems, then, that men's abilities are more localized in the brain while women's are more diffusely spread through both halves.

This idea was further supported by Sandra Witelson, working at McMaster University in Hamilton, Ontario. She had 200 normal right-handed children between the ages of 6 and 14 feel blocks of different shapes by reaching through a curtain that blocked their vision; the children could only feel, not see, the blocks. Each child handled two of the unfamiliar blocks simultaneously, one in each hand, then was shown a number of blocks and asked to pick out the two he had just touched. (Remember, in right-handed males, the right hemisphere controls spatial ability.) It turned out that, overall, both sexes did equally well, but when scores were compared for each hand, boys did far better with their left hands, a clear sign that the right hemisphere was heavily involved. The girls did equally well with both hands and fell between the scores for the right and left hands for the boys. Again, it appeared that the spatial abilities of females are equally divided between both halves of the brain.

Interestingly, while the two halves of women's brains seem to be less specialized than men's in verbal and spatial skills, sexual differences in other skills are not as great. For example, in some tasks, women show a tendency to simply *use* one side of the brain more than the other and to employ that side in much the same pattern as men. A group at Harvard decided not to test mere perceptions but to cause subjects to *generate* responses while the electrical activity of their brains was being monitored. Subjects were asked, for example, to whistle a song, then speak the lyrics, then sing it. Some were asked to recall either a violent or a peaceful event and then to mentally compose a letter about it. The researchers found that the sexes did not always differ in their brains' electrical activity, but when they did, the brains of females showed a tendency toward greater activity on one side of the brain than the other. Furthermore, when verbal skills were called for, the left side was more active, and with spatial skills the right side showed greater activity. Thus women tended to *mobilize* one side or the other, depending on the task at hand.

It has been suggested by Deborah Waber, working at the Children's Hospital Medical Center in Boston, that the sexual differences on tests do, indeed, reflect differences in the organization of the brain but that the differences are brought about by rates of maturation in children. She found that regardless of sex, early-maturing adolescents do better on verbal scores than on spatial ones. You need only glance at a group of eighth-graders to see which sex matures faster. There we find a group of tall, curvy, and loquacious girls who can't do math discordantly sharing a classroom with undersized boys who can't compose a sentence that doesn't start with, "Uh . . ." but who will soon be able to easily handle mathematical and spatial problems. Waber also found that the late-maturers (that is, mostly boys) show greater lateralization, or sidedness, in the brain when it comes to verbal abilities. Just how maturation rates are related to such differences isn't known.

There are two major questions raised by such findings. The first has less merit. It is: Should such research be done at all? Should we look for such differences? Don't such efforts lead to sexism? One is tempted to carry such reasoning to its obvious conclusion and argue facetiously that if we study the menstrual cycle in women, we should also study it in men. Obviously, men and women *are* different, but this need not mean that we place greater value on one set of traits over the other. If we are physically different, we need to know. And if we are mentally different, we need to know. Careful interpretation of clear-minded investigations is better than reciting a muffled litany with our heads stuck deep in the sand, "We are the same. We are the same." We aren't.

The next question is, since we have separate gym classes because of different abilities, strengths, and interests of boys and girls, should we also have separate educational programs? Should girls be penalized in their reading programs by being forced to tread water while the boys dog-paddle in a two-syllable pool? Also, boys and girls may respond differently to any particular teaching method. For example, the "phonics" method of teaching reading stresses the recognition of sounds, primarily a function of the left hemisphere. The "look-say" method, on the other hand, involves recognizing words on sight and, here, both hemispheres are involved. Since girls are likely to have spatial skills on both sides of the brain, they can learn to read either way, but because the spatial and verbal skills of boys are localized in different parts of the brain, they may need a combination of "phonics" and "look-say" instruction to help them integrate their verbal and spatial skills. Are such suggestions sexist? They are if sexism is an admission of sexual differences.

It has been argued that the brains of the sexes are not really different, that the perceived differences are caused by the brains' responding to different hormones. (Hormones are chemicals that are formed in one part of the body and transported via the bloodstream to help direct activities in another part of the body. Sex hormones are produced by the testicles and the ovaries.)

The influence of sex hormones on behavior is well known. A person who rides a stallion can feel quietly superior to someone riding a gelding. Stallions are more vigorous and dangerous. Savage and bad-tempered bulls can be reduced to plodding oxen by a simple stroke of the knife. A "fixed" dog is easier to handle, and an ex-tomcat stays closer to home and gets in far fewer fights. Our knowledge of the importance of sex hormones on behavior has also been applied to humans. In earlier times choirboys were castrated so that their bell-like voices wouldn't change and they could continue to sing for royalty. Eunuchs, we've been told, could be trusted in the harem. Recently a judge suggested castration for a sex offender (but couldn't order it), harking back to the days when U.S. prison convicts were legally castrated. Other countries, including Germany, Switzerland, and Denmark, have also legalized the operation for criminals. One result of castration, by the way, is a general pacifism and a low incidence of recidivism. In any case, the evidence clearly implicates the testicles as a source of aggression. And testicles belong to males.

Testicles are blamed because the sex hormone most directly responsible for aggression seems to be testosterone, which is produced in the testicles (ovaries of females produce very small amounts). This hormone directs the sexual changes that appear at puberty, a time that, in males, marks sexual maturation and increased aggression. In rats, for example, young males don't fight much until puberty, but if young rats are prematurely injected with testosterone, they will begin fighting earlier.

So what about female sex hormones? Female hormones have indeed been implicated in some changes in aggression. For example, the premenstrual period is often accompanied by heightened irritability and aggressiveness. In fact, most crimes by women are committed just before their period. The change seems to be due to a drop in the level of progesterone (one of the two main female hormones). In general, however, the behavioral changes associated with changes in sex hormone levels for females seem to be far less drastic than those for males.

If hormones influence behavior by acting on the brain, it may seem that the person who wishes to argue for innate sexual differences in behavior must revise the statement to say something like: the brains may be alike, but they behave differently because they are subjected to different hormones. This, of course, begs the original question. If the brains *behave* differently, they are, in all practical respects, different. It turns out, however, that one need not resort to this argument, because sex hormones can, in fact, cause basic changes in brain structure.

Consider an experiment with mice. We have known for some time that female mice are much more docile than males. However, this can all be changed. If females are given male hormones shortly after birth, their behavior is permanently altered. They may show some increase in aggression as they grow, but the real change will not be apparent until they reach breeding age. Then it becomes clear that these are not normal female mice. They come into heat as expected, but courting males are in for a surprise. The females respond to any advances so aggressively that breeding is almost impossible. Instead of humbly presenting their rear ends for the males to mount, they attack the males—sometimes crippling or killing them. It is interesting that if male hormones are administered to female mice at some later stage in life, after the brain is further developed, the results are less dramatic and aggression may not rise much at all.

In some species, however, male sex hormones may even affect adult females. If testosterone is injected into hens, they will develop the comb and plumage of a rooster, and their aggressive behavior will intensify. They may even change their status in the peck order. The term "peck order," by the way, came from studies on chickens in which it was discovered that they tend to arrange themselves hierarchically. It turns out that low-ranking hens injected with testosterone become more aggressive and often fight their way to a higher rank. There are cases where the lowest-ranking hen, treated with testosterone, fought her way to the very top. On the other hand, roosters treated with female sex hormones become more timid and lose ground in the peck order.

It turns out that the timing of the appearance of sex hormones may be critical indeed and that the hormones appear surprisingly early. Sex hormones, it has been found, permeate the embryonic body early in its development and, in fact, may actually determine the sex of the embryo. An individual beginning its long development toward becoming a male can be shunted into the female pathway if it is subjected to female hormones at the appropriate embryonic stage. When it is born, it will be a female indistinguishable, by gross examination, from any other female. Males can be produced in a like manner from genetic females. (So the sex of an individual is not "fixed" at fertilization as many people had believed previous to 1970.) The important point is that both anatomy and behavior respond to the directives of sex hormones.

At the same time that we are suggesting innate differences in the brains of men and women, we must recognize the awesome power of the human cerebrum. Men and women may have different kinds of brains, but those brains are incredibly flexible in their action. Put another way, one can pull nails with either a crowbar or a hammer; different tools can be employed to do the same task. The result of such flexibility is that even when brains are different, one can expect a great deal of behavioral overlap. Different impulses of the old brain can be overridden to a degree.

We must also keep in mind that we cannot extrapolate too freely from other species to humans. The old brain may hold less sway in humans than in other animals. In one set of experiments it was found that animals with their cerebrums removed suffered different handicaps, depending on the intelligence of the species. In rats, for example, the cerebrum is rather equipotent. That is, if one part is destroyed, another part simply takes over its function. However, destruction of certain areas of the brains of monkeys may result in permanent damage. Their brains are not able to compensate for all losses; certain abilities can be compensated for, but others can never be retrieved. In monkeys and apes, it also seems that many of the lower brain's functions are taken over by the cerebrum. Not only that, but the control of these functions is relegated to certain *parts* of the cerebrum, thus rendering compensation more difficult. One would surmise that as old-brain functions are shifted to the cerebrum, there would be more conscious control over them. This has not been demonstrated, but it's an idea which suggests that overriding old-brain impulses may be easier in more cerebrated, or brainier, creatures.

We should also remind ourselves that even if the brains of the sexes are *organized* differently, they may still have the same, or very similar, potentials. For example, it has been found that the male hypothalamus contains certain areas that, when artificially stimulated, produce female sexual patterns. On the other hand, females have centers that can evoke male sexual patterns when stimulated. Of course, the possession of a potential is not the same as the probability that it will be employed. In other words, although males possess centers for both male and female sexual behavior and may, on occasion, show either, there is a higher probability that one, the male pattern, will appear. Thus, overall, males tend to behave like males, and overall, females tend to behave like females.

We have seen, then, that eons of evolution in which each sex has become better adapted to its specific role have produced sexes that are behaviorally and physically different. Physical differences in the nervous systems may contribute to differences in the behavior of the sexes. On the other hand, the vast compensatory abilities of the cerebrum can cause certain impulses to be consciously overridden, thus producing identical behavior in the sexes. We should be aware, however, that, historically, identical behavior of the sexes would have been detrimental to child-rearing. We should also be aware that overriding an urge does not negate the urge. The urge may emanate from deep in our subconscious, untouched by what the conscious mind is doing—a subconscious that continues to send its directives into one's mind, only to be rejected or redirected or otherwise handled in some socially acceptable way. The question is, does the brain, particularly the old brain, urge men and women to do different things? Although either sex *can* perform a given behavior, it may be more difficult or unlikely, even slightly so, for one sex than for the other. The constant, if gentle, wheedling by the old brain can be expected to cause any act mediated by it to appear with greater frequency in one sex than the other. The expression of any urge can be pounded, beaten, and molded so that it is virtually unrecognizable. Nevertheless, its roots remain the same.

CHAPTER SIX

THE IQ QUAGMIRE

OW, WE'RE GOING to settle this business of IQ once and for all. Everyone who believes that, put a twenty-dollar bill in an envelope and send it along to Uncle Bob. Then I want to talk to you about some real estate in Arizona.

I don't expect to find many envelopes in the morning mail and I'm not likely to sell much land. The reason is that anyone who has any interest in the IQ question and has been trying to follow the arguments is fully aware that almost nothing is about to be resolved. Part of the problem is that the question of intelligence seems to serve as a beacon of misfortune, drawing all sorts of people who show a pronounced proclivity for doing truly bad research. It doesn't take long to see that many of their experimental designs are atrocious! Indeed, the IQ controversy has served as a magnet for the inept, the dreamy-minded, and outright charlatans, no matter which side of the fence they are on.

This is not to say that good scientists have not tackled the questions, heaving against them with the full weight of their great skill. They have indeed. And they continue to do so. Unfortunately, however, it seems that almost all of them approach the question hoping to support a certain conclusion, and scientists have a disconcerting way of finding what they want to find. When good scientists look at the same results and draw different conclusions, what are the rest of us to think?

If you're not aware of the IQ controversy, let me ask you a few questions. Who are smarter, men or women? Blacks or whites? What is IQ? Can it be changed? Is intelligence, in any way, correlated with reproductive output? Now you know.

We have already seen that, although men and women are intelligent in their own ways, the overlap in abilities is so great that we find some women who are better at mathematics than most men, and we see men with little spatial ability whose verbal abilities are greater than those of most women. Mark Twain, for example, was never able to understand just how it was that he could take two different routes around a certain mudhole and still get home. And Einstein was baffled by those little mechanical birds that swing back and forth, dipping their beaks into a glass of water. Lots of women could have explained the principle to him. So what, then, is intelligence?

Essentially, we're heading into a topic that will arouse all sorts of emotions. It's a quagmire that has people of various stripes firmly stuck, most of them lurching in one of two directions. Some are standing firmly in the middle as they sink deeper, many are beating drums and shouting slogans to the galleries, while others with mock sobriety imagine themselves to be in a scientific controversy. And there are a number who wonder why they're there at all and who are trying to tiptoe out, hoping no one will notice the mud on their feet.

But what is the nature of the quagmire? What are all those people doing out there? And why now? More importantly, what can we learn from their dilemma, particularly about the nature of science and scientists?

In order to come to grips with some of these questions, we must review a little history, going back to the time when the French were trying to identify the mentally incompetent among their schoolchildren. Their goal was laudable enough—it was to improve their educational system. So they hired a team of psychologists, Alfred Binet and a colleague, to devise a test of intelligence.

Binet's was by no means the first effort to get at intelligence. One of the first people to try it was none other than Charles Darwin's younger cousin, Francis Galton. Galton considered himself to be a genius, as he did Charles, and he was undoubtedly correct on both counts. (Many think Galton was brighter.) He was extremely versatile, having been a journalist, explorer, geographer, mathematician, and perhaps the first eugenist. Ten years after Darwin's *Origin of Species,* Galton published *Hereditary Genius,* in which he attempted to show that intellectual ability and excellence run in families and may therefore be inherited. He, indeed, found that people who excelled at anything, from science to rowing, tended to be related, at least as far as they could be traced in English records. On the basis of his findings, Galton suggested a systematic program of mating among humans in order to produce a higher-quality species. Not incidentally, he had noted that geniuses appear more often among the upper classes. He seemed to neglect the idea that money and connections among the higher-class Britons would have aided greatly in any effort one of them might like to make. But there was an even greater flaw in his methods. He noted that mental defectives, such as idiots and imbeciles, often suffered impaired perception, so he decided to measure perceptive abilities (sight, hearing, and so forth) as indicators of intelligence. His work stimulated discussion, and as others developed an interest in measuring intelligence, they began to test more traits, such as coordination and memory.

Then in 1895 Alfred Binet and his group entered the picture with a landmark paper in which they argued that testing the ability to sense or move was not as good as testing for the psychological processes actually thought to be involved in intelligence. Binet said intelligence operates at its own level and is independent of movement and the senses. He suggested testing memory, imagery, attentiveness, imagination, verbal comprehension, mechanical ability, suggestibility, artistic appreciation, moral sensitivity, distance-judging, and muscular endurance. He devised a set of tests, and they worked. The French were, in fact, able to identify mentally deficient children.

Binet and his group continued to revise the tests until 1911, when Binet died. One of their major contributions was to show that, up to a point, intelligence is a function of age. The tests they devised arrived at a "mental age" for each child tested.

Binet, interestingly enough, never heard of the term IQ. It was coined soon after his death by the German psychologist William Stern. Stern noted that it is not just the difference between mental age and chronological age that is important but also the *relation* between those ages. Thus a child who is one year behind at the age of 12 is brighter than someone who is one year behind at the age of 7. To get his "intelligence quotient," or IQ, Stern simply divided the mental age by the chronological age and multiplied by 100.

An IQ of 100 splits the population into two groups of equal size. This is not the way the chips happened to fall at first, however. The tests had to be juggled and changed until things worked out this way. It is interesting that the first IQ tests had to be changed in order to avoid sexual bias. Girls were doing better. The early tests were mostly verbal, and girls were scoring very high while boys were looking like dolts, until it was found that when spatial tests were added, the boys did better than girls and the scores averaged out.

Also, IQ, it was found, does not show much change after adolescence. An average 15-year-old and an average 50-year-old can both recount up to a seven-digit number. (Did the telephone company have the average IQ in mind when they gave us our seven-number link with the unseen world?) Thus, after age 15, IQ is not calculated by age (or else IQ would grow progressively lower each year, as Thoreau suspected anyway). Instead, for an adult, one is said to do better than some percentage of the population. Thus a man with an IQ of 130 does better on the tests than 90 percent of his peers.

In any case, the idea was quickly exported from France throughout Europe and to America. It was interesting that a test devised in France could also be applied to children in the United States, Italy, and Great Britain. The results were the same. With only minor adjustments, the average score was 100. Of course, these are all Western industrial societies. There is no reason to expect that children from distinctly different cultures would score the same. A Hopi child, for example, might not be able to describe what water is like. Hopis, it turns out, can talk about a drop of water but they have no name for water in general. Thus, IQ tests are valid only in the context in which they are developed. They are only useful for the kinds of populations on which they were standardized to begin with. However, if the tests compare people living within a given social unit, such as Western industrial society, then the ranking has some meaning.

Keep in mind that Binet never defined intelligence; he just tried to measure it. At first he was just sorting out mental defectives, but he found that his test also revealed brilliant students and that the rest fell somewhere along a continuum, with most in the middle. He also found that he didn't *have* to define intelligence. Everyone seemed to know what it was, or believed they did. And, besides, the tests worked. Almost all the children who were prejudged "bright" did well in school. Almost all those believed to be dull did poorly.

But there were exceptions. Some very bright children were simply rebellious and so they did poorly in school. Some dull children worked very, very hard and did as well as bright students on the material they had studied; they just couldn't puzzle out the answers in the time allotted them on Binet's test. And we need only be reminded that some students do poorly because they are not aware that they don't see or hear well. Other brilliant students may be bored (as was Einstein) or unconcerned (as was Darwin). So the test was not infallible; but most of the time it seemed to work.

Already, though, people were asking, is IQ something that can be given a single number? Aren't there "kinds" of IQ? This is the reflexive question of people (and parents of people) who didn't do well on the test. You may recall that when George Wallace was governor of Alabama he referred to "pointy-headed intellectuals who can't even park a bicycle straight," assuming, apparently, that intellectual excellence in one area does not necessarily diffuse across the spectrum of abilities.

But even as Binet was developing his tests, an Englishman named Charles Spearman resigned his army commission after the Boer War and began to work on the problem of IQ. After a great deal of work, he gave us our famous "*g*." He noted that if a person did well on one aspect of the test, he was also likely to do well on other parts. Thus, he concluded, there is a "universal" mental capacity, which he called "*g*" for "general." The *g*, he said, permeated all intellectual activity and was modulated only by several less important factors that may or may not be present in solving any particular task at hand. The *g* that

Spearman defined didn't even outlast him. He changed it himself, but in so doing he established the importance of handling such material mathematically. He also made it apparent that pointy-headed intellectuals were disconcertingly likely to be able to park a bicycle straight.

The next step was left to an electrical engineer who quit his job to work on testing intelligence. His name was L. L. Thurstone, and his contribution was to use powerful mathematics and large numbers of tests to show that Spearman's g could be divided into subunits, such as spatial abilities, perception, verbal abilities, language fluency, numerical abilities, and inductive and deductive reasoning. Since then, others have winnowed out over one hundred "components" of intelligence, and no end is in sight.

What Thurstone found was that people tended to do well in "constellations" of abilities. For example, someone who did well in verbal abilities was also likely to do well in language fluency but not necessarily in numerical abilities. So, in addition to being rather bright or rather stupid, people could be labeled verbal, numerical, imaginative, mechanical, and so on. (I recall that when I had just graduated from college and was teaching science—and biology, and art, and P.E.—in New Orleans I had an apparently dim student who was the butt of a lot of jokes and who spent much of his time puttering around with cars. His interest in the science class, and his respect from his peers, soared when I asked him to explain to the class how a voltage regulator worked. I really didn't know. He ended up teaching a short course in automotive mechanics at the age of 14. I learned a lot. The Carolina Friends School, an unusual school in Durham, near where I live, has its brighter students in any area teach the slower ones. Because of different aptitudes, almost everyone is a teacher at some point and therefore has a lot less resentment toward being taught. The system *admits* superiority in various areas and makes use of the differences in people.)

I should add that a few people can be so overloaded in one area of ability that they can excel in that area without having a high g. For example, there are idiot savants who have a very low g but who can multiply five-figure numbers in their heads or who can immediately tell you the day of the week that Christmas will fall on in the year 2207. And there are people with trick memories, called mnemonists, who can apparently recall everything they have ever experienced. For example, one normally intelligent Russian man made his living by giving demonstrations of memory. Once he memorized the formula:

$$N \cdot \sqrt{d^2 \cdot \frac{85^3}{vx}} \cdot \sqrt[3]{\frac{276^2 \cdot 86x}{n^2v \cdot 264} \cdot n^2b} = SV \cdot \frac{1624}{32^2} \cdot r^2s .$$

Then 15 years later, with no warning, he was asked if he could, by any chance, remember it. He recited it without a bobble. Although memory is one component of intelligence, total recall is not necessarily an asset. The mnemonist might look at a winter tree, look away, clearly remember its leaves from the summer before, and decide it is leafy. The bare tree and the leafy tree are equally fixed in his mind. He might also casually glance at his watch and then recall a time when he looked at his watch a year earlier; when he looks away, he might be confused about what time it is. Mnemonists may be late a lot.

Since memory is obviously a component of intelligence, why do even the most intelligent of us tend to forget? Is it because we never learned the material to begin with? Apparently not. Our minds are very peculiar, and it seems that we have tucked away in our memories virtually everything that ever happened to us. We can't consciously recall very much of it, but it's there just the same. For example, a bricklayer was once hypnotized and asked to describe the bricks in a wall that he had built 20 years earlier. He described the markings, chips, and cracks on each brick, and when researchers went out to verify his story, all the markings were there—just as he said. He hadn't paid attention to the bricks at the time, or so he thought. Yet he tucked away apparently useless information into the quiet recesses of his mind. There the memory rested, with countless other memories that normally he would have carried, unsummoned, to his grave.

Clearly, then, memory does not fail us because we fail to learn, or to record our experience. The question is, since we record so much, why can we recall so little?

We have seen the problems that a mnemonist might have by being able to recall everything. So there are obvious advantages to forgetting, but some of these advantages are not so apparent. For example, memories blur with time. I have looked out my study windows into these beautiful North Carolina woods many times and have seen the forest gray and barren as well as lush and green. But the last time I looked out, about five minutes ago, it was snowing. The snowing image is clearer in my mind. I have to work to imagine leaves on the trees. So when I go out I will wear a coat. The vagaries of the greenery, and the clarity of the snow, have signaled to me that this is wise. Thus, forgetting gives us a sense of time.

Forgetfulness also helps us to survive in a changing world. Can you tell someone precisely how many stoplights there are between you and the second shopping center from you? Probably not. You can easily get there and have traversed the route many times, yet you have forgotten many of the details. Consequently, there is a slight air of caution about you as you drive there. If you were to stalk out the door supremely confident of every bump in the road, the angle of every corner, every stop, you might notice too late the barricade erected by the city power company during the night. But, because of an apparent weakness of your memory, you don't trust it. You aren't sure of what you will encounter on your way, so you're a bit cautious, and you're better off for it.

The point is, there are advantages to forgetting, even though memory is thought to be a component of intelligence. This paradox should indicate to us that our mental abilities, in general, match our needs. And our needs, according to the idea we're developing here, are essentially those things that allow or enable us to reproduce. We will allow that idea to dangle, both ends loose, for a while as we continue our story about the search for a way to measure intelligence.

It is peculiar that we've given so much research attention to measuring intelligence without having developed an adequate definition of it. Essentially, we are left with arbitrarily defining it and its components and letting it go at that. But can we be sure that we have accounted for all the variables? We obviously must include powers of language and logic. But how about physical coordination or artistic ability or generosity or character? If intelligence is a measure of the characteristics and abilities that help us to get by (and to reproduce) in the complex world of the human animal, then isn't coordination important? Could Einstein have done a one-and-a-half off the high board? Could he have built a trap clever enough to catch a rabbit? Obviously, we haven't been interested in measuring coordination or physical dexterity, although their centers are located in the brain. And how about "character," the trait that encompasses those elusive qualities of the heart? One might argue that character is not particularly beneficial and that by being, for example, generous or altruistic, one might even lower his reproductive output, thereby allowing mean-spiritedness and tight-fistedness to come to prevail. However, as we will see in our discussion of altruism (Chapter 8), individuals of "character" may tend to elicit altruistic behavior from others in the population. Thus, altruism may well be a beneficial trait, but in any case it is one not usually measured in intelligence tests.

Part of the problem in defining intelligence arises from the fact that "smart" people devised the usual IQ tests. It is probably for this reason that such traits as memory and character aren't given much weight. In our educational system, from the time of Thomas Dewey there has been less emphasis on sheer memorization. One reason may have been that the educators themselves could excel at all sorts of mental tasks, from rote memorization to abstract reasoning to creativity. The problem was that other people, people they considered intellectually inferior, could memorize and recall as well as they could. Thus, they decided, consciously or unconsciously, that rote memorization was not an important ingredient in intelligence.

One wonders why they neglected the traits of "character." Why weren't kindness, generosity, bravery, and empathy included in their tests? These are also important traits (or were historically, when people lived in related groups). They help us to maneuver ourselves (and our genes) through the world. Could it be that the test designers were also not particularly superior in such traits and thereby deemed them to be unimportant? One could well believe such causality after dealing with some of the petty and mean-spirited souls who tread the halls of academe, where intelligence is supposedly at a premium.

And while we're on the subject of character, why haven't we given attention to a specific trait that is only now gaining research attention—a trait researchers call "invulnerability"? It refers to the ability of some children to rise above unfortunate circumstances of their childhood to become successful, happy, and well-adjusted people. This ability has been almost completely ignored. A great deal of research has gone into retracing the lives of miserable and unhappy social misfits. And sure enough, we often find them to be the product of broken homes or of neglectful or spiteful parents. But why can't we trace all, or even most, children from unhappy childhoods into the pits (or at least the doldrums) of adulthood? It turns out that our predictive abilities are extremely limited. Even if a social psychologist has all available data on a child raised under dire conditions, almost nothing can be said about how the child will turn out. Many are rather happy, even as children. Ignoring all the problems they are "supposed" to have, they wend their way merrily to the upper echelons of society, not intensely driven and grim-faced but cheerfully, loving everyone, receiving love, and not daunted in the least. They are called "invulnerables," but what makes them invulnerable? What special quality do they have? And how do we measure it? Should this mysterious trait be considered a part of intelligence?

I bring this up because intelligence tests are designed to predict one's success in school, one's suitability for various occupations, and one's intellectual achievement in life. And, in fact, the standard IQ tests do quite well in helping with such predictions. They ignore a great number of human traits, but they do quite well with what they concentrate on.

IQ, incidentally, cannot predict success, but without the ability to make a pretty high score, a person's efforts to make it in our society are doomed to failure, by most current standards. Some very bright people do fail, but the ranks of the successful are swollen by those with high IQs. In fact, there are few people with low IQs among the successful. Thus, a high IQ is necessary, but not sufficient, for success. No one knows why bright people fail—perhaps it is for emotional or motivational reasons—but their failure shows us that our tests do not yet account for everything.

In spite of the fact that we don't know all the ingredients for success and what abilities make up intelligence, you can bet your boots that *your* IQ is recorded somewhere. You may even know what it is, but you may not; and, furthermore, your parents may not know. At one time and in some places, such information was regarded as too hot to handle. IQ scores had to remain in the school's Top Secret file, to protect the children. A child given a low number might stop trying, and one with a high number might begin to hold his peers in contempt. And parents couldn't be expected to act rationally either. They might treat their child differently if they thought he or she was smart or stupid. Only teachers could be entrusted with such information—teachers, those powerful pillars of wisdom. (Two of the most frightening facts I know are that those enormous trucks one meets on the highway are driven by truckdrivers, and that children are taught by people who majored in education.) Nonetheless, our teachers probably knew our IQs. I know mine did. I was tested twice with very discrepant results. After the first test, it was suggested that I consider a trade school rather than college, and if I went to college, not to expect to do as well as the other people, but to work as hard as I could. (I didn't do nearly as well on the second test.)

Although a high IQ doesn't guarantee success in school, it is true that people with higher IQs tend to go farther in school and to make higher grades. There is a myth that educators have allowed to suffuse the public consciousness, though. It says that people who are more highly educated are smarter. The populace in general is awed by the initials PhD, which I think is unfortunate. I think the initials indicate that, at the least, the person is probably fairly bright, rather highly motivated, politically sensitive, and wasn't pressed into some occupation after college. Undoubtedly, some of the brightest people around grace our classrooms, but I have come to the conclusion that the light produced by their aura falls on their dimmer colleagues and makes them seem brighter than they are. In general, I do not believe that PhDs who have remained in academics are smarter than any other group of professionals (and that includes trackmen and basketball players). I think the brains are in business or in pure research. A lot of mechanics make a good living tuning professors' cars.

An interesting study was done on enlisted men in the Air Force in World War II in order to determine which civilian populations had the highest IQs. (I wish they had done a similar study on officers. When I worked with the military in Europe I had privileges in both enlisted men's and officers' clubs and usually preferred the former—and it was in one of these that I first heard, "If you cross an officer with an alligator you get a retarded alligator." Anyway, the study wasn't done on officers. The psychologists could probably have been accused of giving comfort to the enemy.) The research was published in 1945 and it listed correlations between IQ and seventy-four occupations. Some of the findings were:

Rank among 74 Occupations	Civilian Occupation	Average IQ (rounded off)
1	Accountant	128
5	Auditor	126
10	Draftsman	122
15	Sales manager	119
20	Clerk-typist	117
25	Radio repairman	115
30	Lab assistant	113

Rank (cont'd)	Civilian Occupation (cont'd)	Average IQ (cont'd)
35	Musician	111
40	Sales clerk	109
45	Power lineman	107
50	Riveter	104
55	Bartender	102
60	Molder	101
65	Baker	97
70	Lumberjack	95
74	Teamster (horses)	88

Interestingly, the top IQ of 149 was held by two people, one a public relations man (the group that was fourth) and one a truckdriver (the group that ranked sixty-seventh). The lowest PR man had an IQ of 100 and the lowest truckdriver registered an incredible 16, a figure that meant he had virtually no measurable intelligence at all. The latter, of course, didn't surprise me since my father was a truckdriver and he and I spent many evenings in the company of other truckers, playing poker. (I also learned that intelligence is not correlated with luck; occasionally some murky-minded character would take all our money.)

If you've heard of IQ tests, you've probably heard of the Stanford-Binet. So who was Stanford? Stanford was Stanford University, the place where a researcher named Lewis Terman and his group worked. Besides altering the procedures developed by Binet, they conducted a remarkable "longitudinal" study of people with high IQs. This means they followed one group for an extended period of time. They published their findings over a period from 1925 to 1959. It was called *Genetic Studies of Genius*. What they found was fascinating.

They began by rounding up a large group of children with very high IQs. They recorded as many pertinent facts about them as they could find, and then they watched them live their lives. They began with

1,500 California schoolchildren whose IQs averaged about 150. (Thus, about one child in 200 would have qualified.) Most were between 8 and 12, but a few were older and some were younger.

The first thing the researchers found was that it was easier to find smart boys than smart girls. And among the older children, smart girls grew increasingly hard to find. Apparently, they said, boys were maintaining their intelligence better than girls were. So in the final group of children there were 857 boys and 671 girls. They also found that the parents of most of the children were "in the professions." Very few were laborers. There were many northern and western Europeans and Jews and very few non-Jewish eastern Europeans, Latins, and Negroes. There were few Orientals in the communities the children came from, so Terman could come to no conclusions about whether Orientals were adequately represented.

One might wonder, what would a group of 1,500 so-called geniuses look like? We can easily conjure up images of spindly, owlish bookworms who absentmindedly stick their feet into buckets while they walk around working out equations, none of whom can park a bicycle straight. In fact, you might expect them to reply, squinting through thick glasses, that you're not *supposed* to park a bicycle straight, that the front wheel should be turned in the direction of the kickstand, so bicycles are supposed to be parked crooked. If this were our image of these people, we would be wrong.

In fact, such a notion suggests more about us than it does about them. Why must we compensate? Why is it so difficult to admit that we are outclassed, flatfooted? We must assume, for our own peace of mind, that if anyone is clearly superior to us in one area, he *must* be severely lacking in another. We can deal with that. But we aren't prepared to deal with your BBP. BBP is a term a friend and I made up one night, soaking up a few in a place called The Cave. (Its name wasn't an attempt to be dramatic; it was purely descriptive.) A BBP, we decided, is your Basic Better Person. To begin with, a BBP is smarter than the rest of us. And he (or she) is undoubtedly professionally more advanced. We have a friend here, in fact, who might fall into the category. He holds both a PhD and an MD. He works very hard and has a list of publications as long as your arm. He continues to turn out outstanding graduate students. He's the chairman of his department. He travels all over the world, lecturing and demonstrating techniques in neurosurgery. He's at the top, the very top of his field. "Ah!" you say, "but there are a lot of intensely driven people who are at the top of their field. But just look at their personal lives." So let me go on. This man is also the leader of a jazz combo and is a classical pianist to boot, apparently one of the best around this area. But what does that leave him time for? For organizing the local children's track club, for coaching every week, and for driving long distances to track meets every weekend. Occasionally these duties conflict with his own racing schedule because he's a national-class age-group sprinter (he's 35). He's built like a heavyweight boxer, and in physical encounters he seems to be completely fearless. He's willing to duke it out with rednecks who buzz his young runners on the road, and he recently rescued a stranded mountain climber in Germany. (He just happened to be in the area.) He has also completed several marathons (26 miles, 385 yards). And he's nice. My friend and I decided that he's nicer than we are. He's kinder, friendlier, more tolerant, the perfect husband and father. And to cap it off, he's *taller* than we are. At this point you're probably desperately searching for a fatal flaw, something at which you can beat him. But you can't. He's better than you are. He's your BBP. (By the way, he's not trying to prove anything. You have to be around him a while to learn these things.)

Our inability to admit inferiority is amusing and takes many forms. I was recently in a disco with a friend who was hoping to pick up a lady. He was having no luck that evening, but a lot of other guys were. When he would see a flash of polyester sweep out the door with yet another female, he would mumble something about those jerks who probably worked in a warehouse and couldn't form a complete sentence. I couldn't help but inform him that superimposing a new set of rules in the middle of the ballgame wasn't allowed, that verbal acumen didn't count here. He was playing in *their* ballpark and he was losing.

The fact that they were foreclosing his social activity for the night was what counted. It was time to admit that he was being outclassed, at least that night and in that setting. He had trouble with the idea because he's rarely outclassed at anything.

I also recently heard a colleague say that people may dress better than he did, but he was sure they couldn't run 20 miles. However, those are two separate events. One was a competition my colleague tended to lose at, the other was one in which he excelled. Excellence, though, is not transferrable from one arena to another. We indeed have a great deal of difficulty in admitting inferiority. "He may be able to . . . but I'll bet he can't . . ." is the chant of someone who has come out on the short end of some measurement.

But let's get back to our story. What about this group of super-bright children? Weaklings? No. Afraid not. They were as unusual physically as they were intellectually. They were taller and heavier than their classmates. They were broader of shoulder and had a much stronger hand grip. They had larger lungs and matured earlier than the other children. They were also better at sports than were their classmates; they knew the rules of more games and learned them earlier. In tests of "character" they proved to be more honest and trustworthy, less likely to exaggerate, and so on.

The question, of course, is what happened to these "special" people later in life. Did they flounder out there in the cold, cruel world? Were they simply pollyannas, unable to adjust as well as "normal" children? By now you can guess at the bad news. They did fine, just fine. In fact, by the time the group had reached their mid-forties, proportionately far fewer of them had died than had their classmates, and in particular, far fewer had been victims of fatal accidents. Fewer were alcoholics and fewer had criminal records. Minor emotional problems were not unusually rare in the bright group, with women having slightly more emotional problems than the men (it may be hard to be a very bright woman in our society). In any case, there was little difference in the level of such problems in the two groups.

So how did they do academically and professionally? About 70 percent finished college as opposed to 8 percent of their contemporaries. Only three failed to finish high school without entering a trade or professional school. Of the males who finished college, 40 percent earned professional or doctoral degrees, and over half of all the college graduates did some graduate work. Almost all did well in school, about a third graduating with honors. A large percentage also had professional licenses, such as CPAs.

Professionally, the men entered a variety of prestigious areas, the greatest number becoming lawyers, followed by college professors, engineers, physicians, schoolteachers, chemists and physicists, authors, architects, geologists, and clergymen. Only 3 percent became semiskilled laborers or farmers, and virtually none became unskilled laborers. Thus the men in the group were clumped around the top of the professions.

Most of the women in the group got married and raised children. Fewer became employed, as would be expected of women in that era, no matter how bright. But of those who did work about two-thirds held professional positions (academic, medical, journalistic, or whatever).

The bright group, by the way, also made more money. The average professional or managerial men in the bright group were making $10,500 in 1954, compared to about $6,000 for their contemporaries holding those same kinds of jobs. In general, their total family income was more than double that of other Americans in the same socioeconomic group.

A few more details about the behavior of the super-bright: At the end of the study, they were responsible for about 60 technical books, 33 novels, 2,000 scientific and technical articles, 375 short stories and plays, 230 patents, and hundreds of radio and TV scripts, newspaper articles, objects of art, and musical scores. A large proportion turned up in *Who's Who, American Men of Science,* and so on. They tended to have a lot of hobbies and an interest in community affairs.

They voted (rather conservatively) over 90 percent of the time in national elections, and they tended to marry bright spouses. They spawned about 2,500 offspring, who had an average IQ of about 130 (placing them in the top 5 percent of the population). And, in rebuttal to the argument that they excelled simply because they knew they were being watched, their performance in general matches that of people not included in the study who have an IQ of 150.

Terman's study, of course, has been criticized, but many of the criticisms have been answered by other researchers, and, in general, it stands as a landmark study—one that should give rise to similar studies if we are ever to understand the cause and effect of intelligence.

And here we find the source of one of the greatest controversies in modern science. The controversy stems from the simple question, where does intelligence come from? I hesitate, actually, to use the word "science" here since the controversy has clearly attracted a host of emissaries from the humanities, ready to do battle in ill-fitting armor. And even the most rigorous and competent of hard-nosed scientists have become so emotionally involved in the arguments that there are footprints leading everywhere through this vast quagmire. The combatants swing their broadswords at each other from such distances, and at such angles, that were the battle to suddenly stop, each would turn toward the judge and pronounce himself unscathed and victorious. It's a scene straight from Monty Python.

Terman very bluntly stated his beliefs about where intelligence comes from. He said it's largely inherited. He also said that we need to do more research to find out whether IQ can be boosted by training. If highly intelligent people cause fewer social problems, are more productive professionally and artistically, and are more innovative and creative, then we should make every effort to raise the IQs of our children, if it is possible. He made it sound as if it's our social responsibility.

No real attempt was made to respond to his challenge until 44 years later. (Now we're coming to the part you've probably heard more about.) Professor Arthur Jensen of the University of California at

Berkeley was asked to write an article on the inheritance of IQ for the *Harvard Educational Review,* a respected educational journal. He was also asked to comment on the question of race. His article was very disturbing to many people and generated a controversy of immense proportions.

Jensen began by declaring that compensatory education had been a total and dismal failure. For years the American public had been footing the bill for special programs designed to give "disadvantaged" youngsters the chance to catch up. Jensen said the programs weren't working, and his news was not welcome. These educational programs had all been started by people with great hopes that special attention to the underprivileged would raise their scholastic ability. The idea was born and nurtured in the firm belief that the environment was responsible for intellectual ability and academic achievement. Thus, in order to raise a child's performance, one merely needed to change his environment. This "environmentalist" position had been a constant assumption throughout the annals of modern psychology, anthropology, and sociology. But it remained an assumption—never tested. However, it was on this very assumption that many of the most ambitious social and educational programs (such as Head Start) had been initiated. Rarely, though, had the programs themselves been carefully evaluated. It was assumed that we were getting results, and that, in any case, we must try.

But here was Jensen saying that those programs weren't working. This was just about the last thing that the academic community wanted to hear. The alternative was unthinkable. However, Jensen *had* thought about it, and he said the reason compensatory education had failed was because it tried to raise IQs and that IQs were so strongly based on inheritance that any effort to raise them by fiddling with the environment was likely to be unfruitful. Jensen noted that the "environmentalist" must explain why a person's IQ remains so constant through his life and why high or low IQs tend to run in families. The environmentalists countered Jensen's "nativist" position by saying that IQs remain the same to the extent that the environments remain the same. They said that if a child happens to be born into an upper-class family, the careful nurturing it receives will tend to give it a high IQ. But if a child is born poor, it may be overwhelmed by its surroundings and its mental growth may be impeded. Thus, they believed they had answered both Jensen's questions, one regarding the stability of IQ, the other regarding the similarity of IQ in parents and children. From here they argued that poverty is not conducive to intellectual pursuits and that the social barriers in our supposedly "classless" society hold the underprivileged down and guard the position of the well-born. Compensatory education has failed, they said, simply because we have gone about it wrong. The theory is good; the error lies in our technique.

In any case, Jensen's findings were pure heresy. Didn't he know that all men are created equal? (Just to set the record straight, they are not.) No one believes it, apparently, but many people seem to think that we must behave *as if* we believe it. No one can trace the history of this idea in the scientific community, but it seemed to catch on about the turn of the century. It may have been fired by the social atrocities that had been instigated by what was called "social Darwinism." Social Darwinism had been an attempt to apply the notion of "survival of the fittest" to human social and economic systems. It rationalized the oppression of the underprivileged. It was a dreadful misreading of Darwin and the cause of a great deal of misery and injustice. The various social disciplines were, at first, greatly supportive of the idea, but when they saw where it was leading, they recoiled from it, firmly denounced the whole idea, and apparently swore to support the environmentalist position forever. In the decades that followed, they surged forward with their blinders firmly affixed.

Thus, when Jensen entered the picture at the end of the 1960s, he was confronted by an army of psychologists, sociologists, and anthropologists who were armed to the teeth with raised consciousnesses. The first attack was in the form of a barrage of missiles shot from the hip. These were emotional arguments, and most of them were simplistic and shrill denials and personal attacks leveled at Jensen. The logic of his arguments was ignored; they attacked him instead. What sort of man would say such things?

What things? Well, for one thing, Jensen agreed with a number of other researchers that genes account for about 80 percent of IQ and that only 20 percent comes from other factors. (These numbers shift somewhat, even among the same geneticists at different times, and the equation Jensen used to derive his percentages has been criticized as inappropriate.) Jensen's figures primarily reflected the heritability of IQ among whites of North America and western Europe, but, even though he had less data about how IQ varies within black populations, he did note that blacks scored, on the average, about 15 points lower on IQ tests than did whites. Of course, it had always been assumed that blacks' lower scores were due to their impoverished circumstances; their environment didn't permit them to live up to their full potential. However, Jensen concluded, on the basis of the results of years of compensatory education, that IQ just couldn't be raised much by any sort of program. In essence, he was saying that blacks were, on the average, a good deal less bright than whites, or at least that they learned differently. Of course, because of overlap between the two groups, he admitted that many whites were not as bright as many blacks, and that many blacks excelled at the things whites were supposed to be good at, but he was dealing with means, average IQs.

Jensen concluded that blacks were able to memorize as well as whites but that they were, in general, less able to grasp abstract ideas. He recommended that teaching methods be altered to account for these differences in abilities. If we are to raise educational levels, he said, we must account for differences in learning abilities and the way people learn, and we must adjust our teaching techniques accordingly.

Of course, the very suggestion raised spectres of classes of poor, dumb blacks sitting there memorizing rules of spelling ("i before e ...") while an elitist group of whites in the next classroom were dealing with the principles of relativity. Not a very realistic picture to anyone who knows anything about teaching. Furthermore, one could visualize such findings leading to an even more racist society, in which it would be assumed that any black one met would be somewhat dense and should be treated accordingly. In any case, almost no one in the educational establishment wanted to hear about Jensen's findings or suggestions.

Part of the problem was that many of Jensen's detractors hadn't actually read his articles. Looking back, one is struck by the disparity between what he actually said and what people *said* he said. Some of the greatest distortions were generated by the press. One often wonders whether some elements in the American press are just simple-minded or actually sinister. (I was first struck by the notion when I watched the national press beat George Romney, a presidential candidate, into the ground by picking up on his single comment that he had been "brainwashed" about Vietnam. Of course, they do sorely test the mettle of those who would lead us, so perhaps their role can be beneficial.) In any case, the press generally did Jensen no great service, and their misquotes and misinterpretations were repeated and magnified and mangled and stretched and distorted until Jensen became a swollen target for practically everyone. His colleagues denounced him, journals began to refuse to publish his material, and he was hounded relentlessly by a radical student organization called SDS (Students for a Democratic Society, if you can believe that). His classes were interrupted to the point that they were forced to meet clandestinely at a different place each time. When he was invited to speak he was heckled, and people would sometimes stand behind him with signs referring to his obvious links with Nazi Germany or whatever. Jensen didn't withdraw, however. Instead, he seemed to get his back up and to doggedly pursue the question of racial differences in IQ. He continued to test, and test, and analyze. His conclusions grew firmer, and people began to stop their shrieking personal attacks on him and to take steady aim on his science. And this is the point at which one's confidence in science and scientists becomes shaken a second time.

Our confidence in science was first shaken when a scientist with an unpopular idea was personally attacked for asking questions that other scientists thought should not be asked. Ignorance was better, they said; it was best not to know. When scientists *decide* to remain ignorant, we must begin to ask questions about the role of science in our lives. Then our confidence was shaken a second time when researchers began to attack Jensen at his own level. First, they reinterpreted many of his findings and came to different conclusions— conclusions that were more politically palatable to them. Then they ostensibly performed the same tests Jensen did, perhaps with some changes or "improvements," and came up with entirely *different* results. During the mid- to late 1970s the literature became filled with refutations of Jensen's work. Those who had been assiduously following the argument became increasingly confused. It seemed to become a question of, "Who do you believe?" Researchers kept popping up here and there in a veritable house of mirrors, each flashing a different set of conclusions. It became such a madhouse that only the most dedicated and highly trained people could keep up with events. Most people began to give up, often in total disgust. And this is about where we are left today.

But the argument about the heritability of intelligence has not ceased and, like a collapsing star, as it grows smaller it grows hotter within itself. In the white dwarf that remains, one still sees the name-calling, reinterpretations of old research, and even new and innovative efforts. The heat generated almost seems to feed on itself. For example, environmentalists like to cite a study published in 1949 by Marie Skodak and H. M. Skeels in which one hundred babies born to mothers of low IQ were adopted into upper-class homes. They reported that the infants grew up to have IQs averaging about 20 points higher than those of their mothers. This was, for years, taken as strong evidence for the environmental position. Jensen, in 1973, attacked the environmentalist interpretation of the study by noting that the increase in IQ is perfectly within the limits of probability—in other words, sheer chance. He negated the arguments, in his mind, by a technical statistical twist. This, in turn, was attacked by statisticians, who seem to speak their own language. Other statisticians came to Jensen's support. No one could understand either argument by this time. And so we begin to get a feel for the way the argument has been going. One side makes a statement, the other side produces data that seem to negate it—or gives it the Bronx cheer. It seems that virtually none of the researchers is unbiased, and each side is determined to pound the other into submission.

Then we come to one of the most surprising discoveries of all. This one shocked and horrified an already anxiety-ridden psychological community. Some of the most compelling evidence supporting the nativist view had come from the work of Sir Cyril Burt, a British educational psychologist who did well-known studies on twins. Essentially, he found that identical twins (those with the same genetic makeup) tended to have very similar IQs, no matter how they were reared. He examined many cases of identical twins who had been split up early in life, some to be reared in privileged families, some brought up by poor families. His data and analysis seemed irrefutable, and his work lent great support to the idea that IQ is inherited.

Burt was for many years the editor of a prestigious psychological journal. During this time he and a colleague published numerous articles supporting his original work. In addition, he published a number of supporting letters and statements from other scientists.

Burt died in 1971, still greatly revered for his landmark studies. But Burt's work had aroused some suspicions, and two important papers critical of his work were published in 1974, one by his friend Arthur Jensen. The argument was brought to the public's attention on October 24, 1976, when the *London Sunday Times* accused Burt of fraud. Then an attempt was made to locate one of Burt's co-authors, and it was discovered that no such person existed. Other investigators, some smelling blood, others holding their breath, began to probe his work. They found, to everyone's dismay, that the great psychologist had apparently lied. It looked as if he had made up his data, and no collaborators could be found. Many of the supportive letters published in the journal he edited had apparently been written by Burt himself, and a quick survey showed that reports by people who had submitted contrary findings were uniformly rejected for publication. This was precisely the kind of information the environmentalists needed to demolish the nativist argument, and they went for the jugular. But even armed with such a devastating exposé, they ran into trouble. It seems that other researchers had supported Burt's work with their own data, as was stated in a letter published in a September 1976 edition of *Science,* the prestigious American journal. At this point, however, there is still a great deal of disagreement over the results of studies on twins.

The motives of the environmentalists, of course, cannot be faulted. They are fighting, they believe, for the rights of another group. This is an interesting, if insignificant, point. Probably no environmentalist is defending himself. The reason is that they, of course, believe themselves to be intelligent. They are all fighting for others, those they believe to be less intelligent. The efforts of most are, as much as anything can be, altruistic. They seek to bring blacks into the fold so that they will no longer be so clear a target for xenophobic arrows. However, even though their motives may be admirable, it is possible that their premises actually interfere with our educational process. Does learning, in fact, occur in the same way for all subpopulations of humans? If not, perhaps we must account for hereditary learning differences and alter our teaching techniques accordingly. Or are we really so primitive in our mental and emotional makeup that uncovering learning differences would, in fact, fuel the fires of bigotry? Another question is, is the failure to ask such a question just another subtle form of bigotry? After all, in essence, the environmentalists are telling blacks, "You are just as white as I am." To which a black is likely to reply, "The hell I am!" Environmentalism on this basis can, after all, be a subtle form of patronization.

Many blacks, I would guess, probably do not put great stock in the Stanford-Binet test (or any of the other eighty or so IQ tests that correlate rather well with this test). If IQ is a measure of one's ability to get along in a complex world, why is there a lingering suspicion that blacks might do better than whites under more rigorous conditions?

How was it that Australian aborigines sadly watched as a group of white men who had attempted to traverse the continent with camels slowly died? After all, this was their beloved home. It was as if someone crawled into your backyard, was unable to cope with its rigors, and succumbed. Why can Kung! bushmen, who would probably test low on our examinations, live in a place where whites couldn't survive? What, after all, is IQ?

And, perhaps the most unexpected question of all, why do American middle-class whites have so little intelligence? Surprisingly, they don't really do very well on IQ tests. It is true that they score higher than blacks, but they score about the same as impoverished Mexican-Americans and well below Jews, Chinese, Japanese, and "culturally deprived" Northwest American Indians. And why didn't you already know that?

On an evolutionary basis, the importance of IQ has undoubtedly changed through the years and, in fact, it is probably today important to a relatively small segment of society. The course of human development has undoubtedly been markedly changed by the gradual increase in intelligence of our species, but a very bright primitive man probably had no marked advantage over a moderately bright one. And today the same situation prevails. Great intelligence is at a premium only in very small circles of people, and even then it has its greatest value in very restricted areas. For example, very high IQ is probably held in great esteem among the theoreticians involved in manned space-flight. But most of us encountering a very bright person would most likely have to talk to him or her at great length before that person's intellectual superiority became apparent, if it ever did. Great intelligence is probably of rather little use in general and, in fact, may be rather cumbersome baggage in a society composed largely of people who are not very bright and who do not greatly prize intelligence, although they continually give lip service to it. And there are undoubtedly geniuses by the hundreds working in grocery stores in small towns across the country, amusing themselves by tinkering with ideas and living out their lives completely unheralded. The point is, our society does not demand great intelligence. Our environment presents us with problems that most of us can solve. Put another way, we are the descendants of people who solved the problems this kind of environment presents.

At the same time, however, we must admit that in an increasingly complex world, intellectual skills in various areas will gain in importance. We can expect to increasingly present ourselves with novel situations that demand creative answers, and so intelligence may rapidly become more generally prized and more readily defined and perceived. In a sense, our intelligence, by increasing the complexity of our civilization, may have created its own self-perpetuating niche in what is called a "positive feedback loop." That is, the more intelligent we become, the more complex we make things and the more intelligence is called for, which, as it develops, results in a more complex society, which . . . ad nauseam.

But in Western industrialized society, how has intelligence influenced our reproduction? Obviously, a certain level of intelligence is necessary in order to keep from getting run over—at least long enough to become a parent. And, conversely, it is easy to see that if matters stemming from high intelligence kept a person too occupied, he or she might fail to leave as many offspring as less-bright people.

The question also arises, do people tend to marry others of their own intellectual status? Probably (at least according to some studies). I would imagine that, at one time, the discrepancy was greater. It seems to me that I've seen very dull but very sexy people attract quite bright people to them on what was obviously a physical basis. Only a few years ago, though, if one wished to avail oneself of someone else's physical charms, it was necessary to either marry him or her or to pretend that the thought had crossed one's mind. Thus, some rather surprising marriages resulted.

If, in fact, we are becoming increasingly sexually liberated, such constraints may not be as strong. Thus, one need not marry a stupid person for sexual reasons. Maybe one need only tolerate a bit of incredibly banal conversation.

If this is the case, we are in the position of having our cake and eating it too, as it were. The result, it seems to me, will be an increasing stratification of IQ across our society. One can elect to spend most of one's time with (or marry) someone whose conversation is interesting and understandable. Thus, people will tend to aggregate according to their abilities and interests, and children will be raised in more homogeneous environments, straying only from that social structure for brief interludes. Such stratification, by the way, has long been a fear of the environmentalist. Paradoxically, the environmentalists are usually considered more "liberal," so their very liberality could conceivably lead to the social stratification they fear. It's just an idea, but one that would also generate concern among some anthropologists since, as Margaret Mead maintained, mixing of the strata is desirable in a stable and functioning society.

So, at least we've seen some of the problems involved in even considering IQ and in applying what we know about intelligence to our society. Now, let's leave this morbid subject and discuss something more cheerful, like growing old and dying.

CHAPTER SEVEN

THE ADVANTAGE OF GROWING OLD AND UGLY AND WHY DEATH IS GOOD FOR YOU

ONSIDER TWO WORDS: (1) firm, (2) flabby. One of these words is sexy, the other is decidedly unsexy. Why should this be? Why is the word "firm" so often used by those who are trying to arouse our prurient interests? Why is "flabby" a derogatory term?

Obviously, "firm" describes tumescence in males, so that qualifies it for sexy right there. Attempting to have sex with a flabby penis has been equated with trying to push a dog out from under the porch with a rope. But aside from such blatant application of the word to sexual behavior, there are other reasons to consider it erotic.

Consider breasts, as I'm sure you have. Firm breasts are sexy. Again, why should this be? Why does no one say, "She has really nice flabby breasts?" Why are flabby derrieres not greatly admired? Why do fortyish people do sit-ups? Why does a man tense his arm when someone grabs it? Why are large sums spent to lift sagging faces? Sagging rears? Sagging breasts? Obviously, people want to be firm. Firm and sexy.

Firmness, of course, is associated with youth. Young tissues hold tight and are elastic. Old tissues are loose and saggy. Have you ever pinched the back of your hand to see if the skin snaps back? If you are old, it won't. If the ridge just stands there, that's bad news. That means you are old. Old is bad.

We don't like to admit that old is bad, of course. Many of the people we hold in greatest esteem are old, and it somehow seems that the admission slanders them. It also slanders the people we will become. As our own golden years (a rather pleasant, if unrealistic, euphemism) draw nearer, we become increasingly well-disposed toward the old, even as we redefine old age. We keep moving the numbers back until we hear ourselves saying something about 60 being middle age. No one wants to be thought of as old. "Why, you're not so old," is intended as a consolation. "You're not so young anymore," had best be reserved for good friends who understand how to take it.

If we are old, we try to appear young. We can simply lie ("I'm 39"), or we can wear corsets, dye our hair, wear particular kinds of clothes, be able to name five Elton John hits, or hang around with younger people. The tendency to try to appear younger is so pervasive through so many cultures that a few years ago I was surprised to see a rather pretty, twentyish Mexican woman in San Miguel d'Allende wearing the somber black garb of the elderly. Was she rushing to become a doña, or were her husband or relatives forcing her to dress in such a way so as to reduce her sexual appeal to other men? The way she clutched the black scarf to her throat indicated to me that she wanted to appear old. I thought that was unusual and made a mental note of it. I also made a note of someone I met this week who is 25 and has had a face lift. I don't know which is the more peculiar.

Why do people want to appear younger? Aren't older people wiser? Doesn't one get a better bead on The Meaning of Life with age? Aren't older people generally financially better off than younger people? If they are wiser and richer, then why do they want to appear younger?

Because young is sexy. The answer almost demands to be shouted. It's true! Young is sexy! But, of course, we can't stop there. We must ask, *why* is it sexy?

We should first remind ourselves that sexiness is in the eye of the beholder. A person is not sexy if other people disagree—no matter *what* that person thinks of himself or herself. Sexiness is a matter of attractiveness, the ability to attract potential sexual partners. Your sexiness, then, is a measure of how badly members of the opposite sex want to copulate with you, although we usually prefer not to think in such crude terms. But let's do it anyway and ask, why should people want to copulate at all? The answers are obvious: first, because it feels good and, second, because copulation is the mechanism by which children are produced. Copulators may not be thinking of children (they may even be thinking about avoiding having them), but that is of no matter as long as they copulate. The directive swells within us from our very toes, "Get out there and *do it*." Since there is some choosing and discrimination by both sexes, it is a source of pride to be chosen as one to do it with. We are aware that women have traditionally been more discriminating than men (at least the best reproducers have been), so men often take more pride in being chosen. They may even *count*, and keep track of, the number of women who have chosen them. But, strangely enough, men may be more discriminating than women when it comes to age. Both sexes, however, discriminate to some degree in favor of younger sexual partners. So we ask again, why is youth sexy?

There are a number of reasons such preferences would have evolved. After all, in the rigorous world of the human animal, sheer strength and vigor have traditionally been important. So we need a way to measure strength. If the face is sagging, perhaps the biceps are also. If the body is yielding to simple gravity, how would it do against a tiger? As the body grows old, bones become more brittle and they break more easily and heal more slowly. And the muscles themselves tend to deteriorate with age. You recall how a thirtyish Muhammad Ali was forced to replace his dazzling speed and power with intuitive savvy in the ring. Put simply, an individual grows less physically capable after about the age of 30. (I say this in the face of numerous exceptions. My own running times from the quarter mile to the marathon decreased markedly from my college track days until I turned 40, but that is of no matter. *Most* people 40 are slower, and we're interested in the *usual* condition among people.)

The signs of age, then, are a measure of general strength and vigor. But they are more than that. A person beginning to have wrinkles stares into the mirror at the harbingers of death. In fact, a very old and pallid person actually *looks* like a corpse. One can imagine that withered old man, sitting there slurping his coffee, in his coffin. It stands to reason that, as tissues break down, allowing lines to appear and flesh to sag, it is only a matter of time until the heart muscles also grow weak and fail. Thus the signs of age provide us with a yardstick of how long it will be until we are claimed by death. And, at best, it only measures our *outer* limits. It doesn't account for the fact that anyone's tenure can be cut short by mishap.

Most of us don't look forward to death, and perhaps most of us fear it. After all, we really don't know what's out there. Does it hurt? What comes after? In this matter, the world's greatest fool, when he dies, has far greater information than all the world's living philosophers. We know it's coming; it cannot be diverted; it can only be delayed in some cases and up to a point. We have spent billions of dollars trying to defer death—to hold it off a bit longer—but our abilities to do so are limited. No matter what we do, most of us don't make it much past three score and ten.

Our endless research into aging has been able to tell us little. Basically, we only know that it is a cellular phenomenon. Cells change with time, but we're not sure precisely how. We have been able to count an increase in electrically charged molecules in aging cells, but we don't know where those molecules come from. We also know that almost all cells contain tiny "suicide bags" of enzymes, bags that can rupture for some reason, releasing juices that digest the cells on the spot. Perhaps "suicide bags" in the cells of older people are more likely to rupture. Research interest at medical centers throughout the world has recently turned to cells called fibroblasts; but, in spite of all our efforts, no one has been able to stop aging, that slow but persistent march toward the inevitable.

It is apparent, in fact, that cells are *programmed* to die, that they have some sort of built-in self-destruct mechanism. It was once believed that some kinds of cells and some kinds of single-celled animals (like amoebas) never die, that they simply keep dividing again and again, with the potential of living forever as long as they receive food and oxygen and don't have to live in their own waste. But it now seems that even cells that reproduce by simply dividing can only go through the process a certain number of times before mysterious changes set in that kill them.

So we see that death is incumbent upon us all and that age is a way of measuring its probability at any point in time. Put simply, the probability of dying increases with age, and we know how to measure age. One might wonder, though, why not live a long vigorous life and then just die, just drop on the spot and be a healthy corpse? Why does old age come on so gradually, heaping upon us problem after problem as it advances? Here, when we again look for evolutionary answers, as we have throughout our discussion, we face what seems to be a puzzle.

It obviously would be better for individuals, reproductively, to remain vigorous and strong until the moment of death. We might well have expected natural selection to leave us with this kind of heritage. After all, the Reproductive Imperative leaves us with chores to perform, and we can do them better if we're strong. But our expectation simply shows that we should take a closer look at how natural selection works. To begin with, if death is somehow genetically beneficial (a point we'll get to), it is probably simpler for the chromosomes, those chainlike directors lying within each cell, to bring about death *progressively*. Keep in mind, now, how chromosomes work. Lying within the cell nuclei, they are tightly coiled and enormously long molecules composed of genes, which lie like pearls along a strand. Recall (from Chapter 2) that the genes direct the cell's activities by directing the manufacturing of enzymes, which in turn cause key chemical reactions within the cell. Since all the cells of the body spring from a single fertilized egg that duplicates itself millions of times, virtually every cell has the same chromosomal (and genetic) makeup as every other cell. Different kinds of tissue (such as nerve, muscle, or cartilage) are able to arise from cells with the same genes because not all genes along any chromosome are active within a given cell. While some genes are busily making enzymes, others are shut down. Thus, the kind of cell (muscle, nerve) that finally results from all this chemical activity depends on which genes are operating.

Now, in order for an organism to remain "young" until the end of its life and then to suddenly expire in a heap, all the cells of the body would have to deteriorate at once. Obviously, since any body is composed of innumerable kinds of cells, their simultaneous demise is not very likely. Some tend to go before others. For example, the prostate glands of men are notoriously vulnerable. They often give trouble early in life and get progressively worse with age. On the other hand, the cells that grow fingernails are very hardy. They continue doing their job through life (and perhaps for a time after). In any case, some kinds of tissue tend to break down sooner than others because of inherent weaknesses within their systems, weaknesses that are not very well understood. So aging is a gradual process.

Since some kinds of tissues begin to break down before others, we see strong men, able to lift great weights, with bags under their eyes. We see tall, commanding women wearing glasses for the first time. We see weight remaining stable while body conformation changes. What we are seeing, then, is differential aging of the tissues. Some kinds of tissues hold up and some do not. Thus one ages selectively, with the more stable tissues changing or becoming dysfunctional last. Finally, though, when critical numbers or kinds of tissues have failed, the organism dies.

So as we look around us for potential mates, we see people in all stages of deterioration. Some have about had it, but others are fresh and rosy cheeked with a softly glowing, almost neon, quality to their skin. For them, all systems are go. If these people have, in addition, the secondary sex characteristics that indicate they might be successful parents, they are sexy.

Those older people, with their wrinkles, paunches, and critical parts sagging, are less sexy. They have begun to suffer some breakdown of their component tissues. One can't be sure they aren't sexy to anyone, of course, since an infinite number of variables go into sexuality, and older people may increase their appeal on some basis other than physical traits. They may also be better manipulators and can figure out how to be chosen over a younger person. Older people, however, face an uphill battle. Younger people are basically just sexier in spite of the exceptions that may come to mind, and we are interested in learning whether there is an evolutionary basis for this. Let's see.

Why do we go to so much trouble to appear young? Why is it that youth is especially revered in sex-oriented cultures? Is there an evolutionary basis? Is it true that the person who is looking for a mate would be well-advised to choose a young one? Why? An answer is suggested when we recognize that youth not only signals strength and vigor but also suggests that an individual has good reproductive years. ahead.

Let's consider this second point. It is important to have a lot of time left in which to reproduce for two reasons. First, the more time a person has, the more offspring he or she can produce. That's simple enough. Also, and perhaps more germane to our discussion, producing even one child takes many years. Because of the extended developmental period in human beings, children are dependent on their parents for a long time. Since a parent must be committed to a child for about 15 years, it obviously wouldn't do to choose a mate who is not likely to live through the next 15 years. That much time is needed to send just the first genetic repository from a union out into the breeding population (the first child out into the world). After that, of course, these sacred caretakers of one's genes can be expelled at the rate of perhaps one per year. But each will have needed long nurturing. So, as a potential breeder casts about to find a suitable individual to tangle genes with, that person is going to be interested in age, and he or she will be very precisely attuned to the clues of age. Small wrinkles carry great meaning.

The result of age discrimination is that a person hoping to be chosen will tend to advertise (perhaps falsely) his or her own youthfulness. The irony is that even old people tend to reject other oldsters in favor of younger people. Old is out; young is in—when it comes to sex. You might hear someone congratulate another, perhaps with an undertone of envy, at having landed a young mate, but you won't hear any kudos for those who bring home an old geezer. Mating with old people is not generally as genetically beneficial and, hence, it tends to be viewed as inappropriate.

There is an interesting application of the double standard here, too. Marriages between old men and young women are decried primarily by old women, but, in general, they are much more socially (read "biologically") acceptable than are marriages between old women and young men. Although it has recently become fashionable for "mature" women in certain social circles to take young men as husbands, it's still a novel idea, and no real trend has developed. Nor, I expect, will it.

Of course, it is very likely that women have always been attracted to younger men, as well they should be, considering the young male's reproductive advantages. However, young males have traditionally been less enthusiastic about such relationships. One reason for the disinterest is that a woman's reproductive life usually spans only about 30 years (between the ages of 15 and 45). In middle age, her reproductive life is suddenly terminated by menopause. The question that immediately comes to mind is: Why would natural selection have limited a woman's reproductive period?

Actually, there are good evolutionary reasons for women to cease reproducing. After all, reproduction for women is quite trying. Pregnancy and birth are traumatic episodes and tend to drain the mother's reserves; also, those early years of motherhood are very wearing indeed. It is best that such tribulations fall on the young.

But, you might ask, wouldn't the Reproductive Imperative demand that a woman go on and risk new pregnancies at any age? After all, she might be able to rear one more child, somehow, before she died, and thereby increase her reproductive fitness. Shouldn't evolution have selected females who would continue to reproduce at all costs?

It would seem so on the surface, but the question neglects an important aspect of human biology. We are highly social animals who tend to form strong bonds. Thus, an aging woman is likely to remain a vital part of the family group and to contribute her knowledge and expertise to the rearing of *grandchildren*. She can increase her *own* fitness by ceasing to reproduce and turning her energies, instead, to assisting her reproducing children with the family responsibilities. Grandmothers, by the way, are not only helping hands around the family, they are great repositories of hard-won information gained through experience or passed along culturally—information that the rest of the family can find useful. A grandmother usually assumes this new role gladly, showing a keen interest in her grandchildren because they, after all, bear her genes. So all those years old granny was really selfishly making blueberry pies to nourish her own genes. Of course, it is just such genetic explanations that rankle the mind and wrinkle the brow of the romanticist. But let's not stop here. There are worlds to offend.

Granny is much loved, but she is rarely viewed as a sex object. A young man, after all, has no use for a postmenopausal woman. But his aversions are not necessarily shared by the woman's aging husband. He continues to love her. The old people are bonded in ways perhaps only humans understand. The old man's presence, too, can be beneficial to the grandchildren, especially if he retains some political power. So, whereas an old woman's old husband may increase his fitness by staying with her to help with the grandchildren, a young man had best build his bonds with a woman who has a lot of time left before her reproductive systems shut down. Thus he looks for rounded hips, flat bellies, firm breasts, unlined faces, and all those other traits that are equated with youth and that signal to him long reproductive years ahead.

But why is it that in May-December marriages the man is usually at the Christmas end? We must keep in mind that old men have an advantage over old women: they are fertile. Male menopause is a psychological, not a physiological, change. Technically, a younger woman could become impregnated by a man of any age; therefore, she might well choose an older man. But would that really be smart? Younger men, you say, have the advantage of strength and vigor and thus they can better perform their role as hunter and protector. Or can they? In the film *The Godfather*, Al Pacino, not a very large man, tells his errant wife, played by Diane Keaton, that he would bring all his power to bear on her to keep her from leaving with the children. Is he talking about physical power? No, he means his enormous influence over other people. Older men may actually be more powerful than younger men by virtue of influence—political clout.

Some anthropologists have suggested that all-male hunting parties were the elemental group from which politics (the art of influence) sprang. It was more efficient for several hunters to band together to bring down large game than for each to individually hunt smaller game. An elephant split eight ways is better than eight rabbits. However, large game can be dangerous, and some planning was undoubtedly necessary in order to be successful and avoid disasters. Among the hunters, some individuals would have emerged as better planners and perhaps braver than the rest, and they would have risen to the top of any hunting hierarchy. Someone must be able to say, "We will hunt here," or "You get his attention and I'll hit him with a rock." The people who could make those kinds of decisions stick were the leaders of the hunt, and they could have been expected to exert influence in other areas as well.

Once leaders developed, leadership *cliques* would have appeared. A group can hold power better than an individual can. In many species, such as baboons, chimpanzees, and lions, dominant males usually hold their position with the support of other high-ranking males. The members of these cliques tend to hang around together and to jointly attack any would-be usurpers. The emergence of leadership groups in human beings could have set the stage for political maneuverings, as individuals sought to join the group or to replace it. Finally, the maneuverings would have become an art. It would have been an art, however, primarily practiced by males—at first from need and later from custom. We see the result today.

Since males could compensate for a decline in physical power by a gain in political power, females might have been well-advised to choose such males, even long after those men had developed the tell-tale signs of age. Their leadership positions signaled good genes, and their political power suggested that their offspring would be well protected. Thus, for males there would have been less premium placed on youth, and "older men" would sometimes attract young women as mates.

We see, then, that menopause shuts down the reproductive system of women at a time when they probably won't have enough years left to be able to successfully rear a child. We also see that men remain fertile and potentially powerful throughout their lives. And so men are chosen as mates in their waning years more frequently than women are, especially if they are politically influential (a trait usually associated with wealth, by the way).

You will notice that menopause *predicts* the life expectancy of women and *assumes* the length of time necessary to rear a child. If people routinely lived to be 200 and it still took only 15 years or so to become sexually mature, menopause might well be deferred until about 180. If people usually lived to over 100 but took 30 years to mature sexually, one might expect menopause to begin at 60 to 70. But menopause assumes about 15 years for maturation and a life expectancy of about 60 to 70.

Perhaps, then, we should try thinking in terms of a *useful-life* expectancy instead of expectancy of time until death. Certainly a doddering and senile old woman would have been more hindrance than help in a family unit, and thus after 60 or 70 years of rigorous living, she would have outlived her usefulness. By this age, her reproductive system had been shut down in anticipation of her death, and she had reared whatever children she had on hand. So she spent her remaining years helping rear her offspring's children, either directly or indirectly. But when she could no longer be helpful, the economics of her genes suggested that she should die so that she wouldn't interfere with her genetic repositories.

So, the next question is, how long can a person remain intellectually useful? How long can a person's information be trusted? In part, it seems that the longer people are needed, the more useful they remain. There is some evidence that the brain deterioration traditionally associated with senility may be reduced if a person remains intellectually active. For example, it has been demonstrated that brain cells apparently die more slowly in people who continue to face intellectual challenges. Thus, if an old person were truly needed in solving problems within the group, he or she might well prove equal to the challenge. Thus, postreproductive people can continue to serve their family group in decision-making processes if the family allows them to.

An old woman, it should be noted, is likely to have a great deal of time on her hands (as we see in meddlesome mothers-in-law) because she is not very likely to have entered menopause with a lot of children on her hands. Even though she may have been sexually very active in her youth, that activity probably decreased in her later years. Of course, we are told that the sexual urges of a modern woman peak in the late thirties, just before menopause. But this surge may be a recent phenomenon, possibly due to the fact that she has finally learned that all the sexual taboos drilled into her in her youth are not necessarily valid. She has learned that coyness, shyness, humility, and reticence are a waste; they do not pay off after all. It's all been a charade. She has missed many experiences. But she has learned too late. She may intensely regret her former shyness, whether real or faked, but she must remember that it may have helped her to be an efficient reproducer.

Paradoxically, women may also become sexually more active late in life, just prior to or after menopause, because they suddenly become acutely aware of their age. They now wear coyness like a silly hat. They, and all the people around them, can read the signs of age with devastating accuracy. Menopause means they are no longer young, no longer desirable, and they resist what they know is coming. They desperately try to show that they are still attractive, still desirable, still fertile. The candle burns brightest . . .

But, as life would have it (are we the butt of some great celestial joke?), even as an older woman becomes more sexually willing, her partner may become less able. He is old, too, and, as her sexuality swells, his own peters out, as it were. Since males peak early (at age 19, we are told these days), middle-aged men do not copulate as frequently as younger ones (with some notable exceptions, to whom I offer my apologies and respect). Even the angle of elevation of an erect penis decreases as age works its wilting wonders. In particular, men show an apparent decrease in interest in their wives. Perhaps the relationship has become less sexual and more spiritual as the years have passed. (This is all rumor; in spite of a few recent studies, we really don't know much about sex among aging people. Scientists have traditionally not shown great interest in sex among the aging. After all, it is relatively unimportant reproductively, and so it is all considered a bit "unseemly.") In any case, and for whatever reasons, middle-aged couples do produce fewer children than young couples. They often begin focusing instead (and perhaps a bit anxiously) on the appearance of grandchildren.

Remember, our reproductive behavior is based upon the expectation of death at a certain age, and humans are expected to die between 60 and 70. But wait! There swells a chorus of objection! I have stressed that we must consider historical man in evolutionary terms and now it seems that I am interjecting data about modern life spans. Anyone knows that through most of our history people lived, on the average, to the ripe old age of 30. For example, there is evidence that Neanderthal man lived an average of 29.4 years; Upper Paleolithic man, 32.4 years; and Mesolithic man, 31.5 years. Bronze Age humans made it to about 38 years old, and even in classical Greece and Rome people only lived an average of 35 and 32 years, respectively. In the United States at the turn of the century people lived to about age 48. Only since 1950 have we increased our life expectancy to around 70, the three score and ten allotted by the Bible.

So was the Bible *predicting* our life span? Or was it merely recording it? Perhaps the latter. There is some evidence that we have not really increased our projected longevity in these thousands of years. Not even with modern medicine. We have merely increased our *average* life span. People over 70 were living on borrowed time in ancient Greece, and they are living on borrowed time today. The mysterious internal clock with which we are all born begins to shut down our systems right on schedule, at about 70. So if we haven't met with accident or disease along the way, when our time is up we simply wind down and fall apart. The great role of modern medicine has been to extend the life span of most of us so that we are allowed to live until our biological time is up. It is important to realize that we haven't been able to extend that time much, if at all.

In the old days, however, many people died with a lot of good years left on their biological clocks. Accident and disease claimed many of the young. Children often succumbed to childhood diseases and environmental rigors that are no threat at all today. Because a young person had a high probability of dying at any time, 30 was the *average* life span. But all this means is that just about as many people made it to 60 as died in infancy. There were old people in those ancient Spanish caves. There were old duffers limping about in the Roman senate. Human populations have *always* had a large segment of old people. In fact, perhaps there was even a greater *proportion* of old people in ancient populations than in many modern ones, since today, in developing countries, most young people now survive because of imported medicine.

Because our life expectancies are so resistant to change, so impervious to our tinkering, we can assume those limits have been rather stable for a long time—long enough for natural selection to have imposed menopause in anticipation of dying at a certain time. And long enough for humans to have become acutely attuned to the subtle clues that signal actual or reproductive death.

I recall seeing photographs of two Australian aborigines, a man and a woman. I was struck by the fact that although they looked 40 or so, each was 19. Obviously, life had been rigorous for them, and they had aged quickly. It occurred to me that perhaps this premature aging had a beneficial effect. Perhaps life was so hard in the Outback that life expectancy was short. These people may have looked old early because they were facing an early death. Perhaps it would soon be too late to call on either of them to undergo the extended rigors of parenthood. Perhaps they were growing old and ugly quickly so as to be sexually, or reproductively, unappealing. Under such conditions, they could be expected to mate early and to devote their later years to enhancing the prospects of relatives, people with whom they have genes in common.

People use age, then, as a measure of time until death. We see that it is important for both men and women to know how far along life's trail a prospective mate is, but for different reasons. It is to anyone's advantage to be able to accurately assess the age of a member of the opposite sex and, because people are obsessive about assessing each other's age, it is important to project a "young" image, especially if one is a woman. What I've said, then, is that senescence, or aging, is very important to anyone who is interested in choosing a mate. We must know the age. Age is important.

There are even some advantages in other people being able to guess *your* age. If you're young and people know it, that's good. And, on the other hand, if you're old, it might be better not to be chosen by a young person with great expectations. A young person might be bent on doing those things that directly lead to reproduction (young people are often accused of having "one thing in mind") and, in fact, he or she might be consciously attempting to reproduce, to have children. The last thing you may want at your age is the care and responsibility of young children, so you might not wish to risk attracting someone whose familial goals are so different from yours. You might prefer to do things only indirectly related to parenthood, such as aiding the family unit in some way, or attending to grandchildren. Therefore, perhaps it is best if your signs of age repel the excessively randy or ambitious and attract, instead, someone whose reproductive status is more compatible with your own.

It may have occurred to you that we have skirted a very important point in all these ruminations. We have talked about fixed lifetimes and why a person might wish to be able to assess the time left until death, for both himself and for others, but we have not mentioned the "role" of death; we have simply assumed its inevitability. So let's ask about it. Why is it inevitable? Why has it evolved? Have we evolved something bad? After all, life is obviously better than death. Ask anyone. It also seems that a longer life—perhaps an everlasting one—would be better evolutionarily; a person who lives longer has more years in which to reproduce. More years, then, could help us to better obey our Reproductive Imperative. So why does death cut us short? If life is "better" than death, why did death arise at all, or why hasn't natural selection eliminated it? Why is our existence a fixed period with a definite beginning and an inevitable end? Why is death not solely due to mishap? Why are we genetically programmed to self-destruct?

One reason we die is because of the limitations of natural selection. It *cannot* operate on longevity because of the very fact that breeding is restricted to the early years. The role of natural selection is to produce successful reproducers and, that done, it can have no further influence. Once a person has reproduced, if he or she has no further reproductive function, there is no premium on living any longer.

The inability of natural selection to affect traits that appear later in life is demonstrated in the tragedy of Huntington's disease. In 1967 folksinger Woody Guthrie died of Huntington's disease, but not before describing his ordeal, up to a point, in his autobiography, *Bound for Glory*. The tragedy was witnessed by millions of his admirers. The disease produces severe mental and physical deterioration and is marked by a spasmodic "dance"—jerky twisting movements. The brain and spinal cord deteriorate very gradually over a 10- to 15-year period, which is marked by increasing fits of depression and insanity that may lead to suicide.

The disease is inherited, but it doesn't appear until relatively late in life, usually between the ages of 30 and 45. Guthrie contracted it at 42 and lived until he was 55. Earlier in life, he had had three children, Arlo, Joady, and Nora-Lee. Arlo knows that he has a 50 percent chance of harboring the genes that will give him the disease, but he has opted to have children of his own. If it turns out that he *has* inherited the disease, each of his children has an even chance of having it. In the absence of people consciously deciding not to have children because of known probabilities of transmitting the disease, the disease cannot be acted upon very strongly by natural selection. The people who have it are likely to have already reproduced by the time it appears. By the time they are selected out of the population, their genes have already been passed along. Thus, natural selection cannot act with its full force after the child-bearing years.

Many inherited diseases, such as hemophilia, are strongly selected against because the bearer usually dies before reproducing. If the disease doesn't appear until after reproduction, however, natural selection can have little effect. If we look at death in the same light, we can see that as long as reproduction occurs early, as it must (particularly for women), we cannot expect natural selection to produce long-lived humans. And our dilemma probably meets with the "approval" of our genes. Perhaps our genes will fare better if we die.

One problem with people living forever is immediately evident: The world would quickly become too crowded. It might be argued, though, that the threat of crowding would not be enough to move natural selection toward sentencing us all to death. After all, in a very crowded world, perhaps accident and disease would be able to claim enough of us so that there would be no need for fixed life spans. We might be able to rely simply on the probability of mishap to keep our numbers low enough.

We can visualize how such a system could work by considering a group of lifeless test tubes. Test tubes, of course, show no signs of aging. They do not grow more brittle with time, for example, so age has no physiological effects. Test tubes therefore do not disappear from the "population" because of the effects of senility. An old test tube is as good as a new one. So let's devise a way of artificially removing them. Imagine that we remove test tubes by reaching into the bin where they are stored and randomly removing some and breaking them. If we start off with 100 test tubes, and every few minutes we. add four new ones and randomly remove four from the group, we will be placing ourselves in the role of Grim Reaper, the terror of the test tubes. Each time we add four new ones and remove four from the group, we will tend to take the older ones since the probability of removing one that we have just put into the group is only 4 out of 104. The odds are that the new ones will survive that first harvest. The longer a test tube remains in the population, however, the more chances it will have of being taken; thus, one can expect to find increasingly fewer old test tubes with the passage of time. Any test tube could theoretically remain in the population forever, but the odds are against it. This, then, is analogous to a human population in which an individual *could* live forever if he could escape being removed from the population by the random events of accident or disease.

So why hasn't natural selection provided us with this kind of system? Why don't we stay young and be removed randomly? Our lives *may* be ended randomly, of course, but tragedy awaits us even if we are lucky enough to escape death by accident or disease. Eventually, our systems will fail. We will grow old and die and there's not a thing we can do about it. Perhaps worse, we *know* that senility and death await us. T. S. Eliot acknowledged that grim fact when he wrote,

I grow old . . . I grow old. . . .
I shall wear the bottoms of my trousers rolled.

Perhaps Hemingway's definition of courage should have been a realist who has not become cynical.

But, back to our question. Why does so onerous—and inevitable—an end await us? Isn't there a better way? The test-tube system would certainly be a good way of ensuring the presence of wise old heads among us who could function as repositories of information. They, of course, would remain "young" and healthy until their time is up. The idea of a perpetually young population certainly has its appeal. After all, someone 80 would look and feel the same as someone 20.

But there's the catch. When you are 20 you are an adult—grown up. I didn't say someone 80 could look and feel like someone 10. That wouldn't be so good, since 10-year-olds are not physically developed. And who would want to go around looking like a 10-year-old? Who would want the demeanor and curtailed privileges of a 10-year-old (besides a 9-year-old)? The point is, humans go through a period of maturation—growing up.

And we must grow as we proceed from infancy to adulthood. It wouldn't do for a woman to give birth to a 120-pound baby, because she would have to be pregnant for about 15 years. Thus the metabolic investment in any single offspring would be enormous. Ignoring, for a moment, the trauma of giving birth to a giant baby, it would be quite a chore for a family to try to feed a 120-pounder who suddenly burst upon the scene. Small mouths are easier to feed than large ones.

No, it is to the parents' advantage to have smaller babies. They are easier to care for, and if one is defective or lost, it can be replaced without too much trouble. Also, many more smaller offspring can be produced than can larger ones. A couple can have several children since children are small. In addition, by having several children, a couple can produce offspring with a variety of characteristics, and variation is important in a variable world. Variation among offspring means that some are likely to make it, no matter what conditions arise in the environment.

Also, we know that, among humans, time is needed to develop mentally. A robust 120-pound baby may be of breeding size, but it wouldn't have been among us long enough to be able to successfully reproduce. Time is needed to learn the things necessary for reproduction and survival. Thus, children stay with their parents for extended periods, learning all the while in spite of themselves.

The developmental period, from infancy and childhood into adulthood, is obviously beneficial. But it has its price. The price is exacted because natural selection is not creative, it is opportunistic; it can only work with what it has. Thus, maturation is the slow change to adulthood, and the result is humans who change with age. Once the process is established, it is not likely to be halted at some later period.

Physiological wheels have been set in motion. It was important that we changed when we were younger. So we did. And although the time may come when we do not wish to change any further, that's too bad.

A constantly changing system has been set in motion, and we are left with it. Change continues with time, then, until the tiny orb of youth develops into the full, rounded grape of maturity, which then gives way to the withered raisin of senility, the harbinger of death. In other words, aging and senility may simply be an extension of the developmental process, a side effect of a system that permits us to have small offspring with lower demands but offspring that must therefore go through a period of change in order to be able to reproduce.

Aging, however, is more than a simple, if tragic, side effect of development. It is more than carrying the developmental process of youth to its inevitable end. It is also a grand march toward death. It may not cheer you up much to learn that although aging is bad, at least it leads to death. Whoopee! We tend to recoil at the notion of our own chromosomes, those delicate helixes that dictated our cute dimples, also sentencing us to death, because we view death as bad. It mocks us. We cannot avoid it. It awaits us and we know it. It washes us of life's small disappointments, its embarrassments, and its achievements. It is, finally, the great equalizer and we hate and fear it. We don't really know what it is or where it leads.

But is death really bad? And if so, for whom? Of course, it marks the end of the line for you and so you resent it. But, remember, you are not important. You are expendable. You are only the temporary caretaker of your genes. Your charge is to reproduce your kinds of genes and, having done that to the best of your ability, your role is finished. You may move on.

Is it really necessary to move on? To get out of the picture? Keep in mind that the best reproducers are those who leave as many genes as possible in the best possible offspring, and having done so, get out of their way—*die so as not to compete with those offspring.* After all, we live in a limited world in which competition is high. Competition is basically two individuals trying to get the same commodity, with the loser suffering in some way. Now, it wouldn't do to harm one's offspring. So, after having done everything possible to help them advance in our competitive world, dying is the only decent thing to do—and the most reproductively astute. People who die so as not to compete with their children leave more offspring than those who hang on and risk depriving them of some commodity.

Of course, few of us consciously *decide* to die to leave more room for our children. But that is of no importance. As I said before, it is not important what we consciously think, as long as we behave *as if* we are actively trying to maximize our genetic output. And by dying at the age of 70, perhaps kicking and screaming all the way, we are behaving *as if* we are trying to advance the cause of our children, our heirs to those precious coiled molecules.

In fact, in the animal world we can find cases in which parents actively commit suicide for the good of their young. For example, in certain moths, which live only one year, the female kills herself after she has laid her eggs. The advantage of suicide, in this case, is to deprive birds of a model they can use to recognize her young when they hatch. If she were to hang around until her eggs hatched, a bird might find her and then, by looking for others like her, find her children. So after laying her eggs, she launches herself into one final and bizarre flight. She whirls, dives, loops, and crashes again and again until some foraging bird spots a frayed and bedraggled specimen behaving in a most peculiar manner and devours it. But try as he might, he can't find another one like that. Not a crazy one that zooms and loops on tattered wings.

It may have occurred to you that I'm saying that *we die to ensure the success of our children.* Our death is good for them. We can smile benevolently to ourselves. Our death is good for them. Aren't we nice? At this point, some people may be tempted to rise up and shout, "To hell with *them,* I want to LIVE!" But what are they saying? Trade children for life? An interesting idea, but unfortunately natural selection won't allow it.

We are compelled to give up our lives for them, as our forebears did for us, for a very simple reason—the world changes. "I have to die for kids I may or may not have because *the world changes*?!" Yes, afraid so.

Whether or not you obey your Reproductive Imperative, your system gears you to maximal reproduction because you are a descendant of reproducers. Remember that reproduction simply involves putting your kinds of genes into the gene pool of the next generation. Those genes, of course, will be mingled with the genes from the other parent, and because of the complex gene-shuffling that occurs before fertilization, the result will be children who are different from you and your spouse. The children will also be different from each other. In fact, the odds against any two of your children (except identical twins) having identical genetic constitutions are about one in 14 trillion. With odds like that, you can count on producing a variety of children who are quite unlike yourself. In addition, because of the nature of sexual reproduction, your grandchildren will be even more variable and different from you.

Why is it important that your children be different? One way to answer that is to consider the consequences of living forever, or even a meager million years. The earth has undergone profound changes in the past million years: weather has changed, population densities have changed, the available food items have changed, rivers have changed, everything has changed. And when we look at our entire tenure on this planet, we can see that the environment for humans has changed drastically. As the environment has shifted, then, so has the premium on particular genetic traits. At one time huge forearms were more important than they are now. At one time, independent, rebellious spirits were more important than they are now (Kit Carson would probably be classified as a problem case in today's schoolrooms). At one time we needed more body hair than we do now.

Let's look at body hair as an example of a trait whose importance might change. If a great deal of body hair became important, humans would become covered with more hair. In any group of children, some will have more hair than others, and if hair is important for some reason, then those with more hair will fare better and can be expected to leave more offspring than their more sparsely haired cousins. So people would tend to become hairier with each generation. But if things should change so that hair becomes less important, or even cumbersome, hairy individuals would be at a disadvantage. Those who put their energies into metabolic activities other than hair growing would have an advantage and would leave more offspring. Hair would be out.

Now what if a hairy individual could live forever? He would do well in times when hair is important, but he would suffer when it is not. He would have to bear his hair through all the earth's periods, and sometimes it would place him at a severe disadvantage.

Clearly, his genes, instead of residing in him through all these periods, including those times when he is at a severe disadvantage, would do better to scatter themselves among his variable offspring and to let the environment do the selecting. When hair is good, the hairier children would fare better; when hair is bad, the less hirsute would prevail. So, by producing variable offspring and then dying so as not to compete with them, a person behaves in the best interests of his or her genes. And any generation will be dominated by the offspring of individuals who behaved in just such a way. It's not a matter of aesthetics, goals, or philosophy. It's simple arithmetic.

We have now dispensed with the great questions of aging and death. Aging anticipates death and is set in motion by a long developmental period. People use the signs of age to judge each other's potential reproductive status. And death, we see, keeps us from interfering with the survivors among our variable offspring. I don't expect that many of us will take great comfort in knowing that although we die, our genes live on (if we bothered to leave any). But it doesn't matter whether we are comforted or not. We are inexorably driven to die for others in that final great act of altruism—or is it?

CHAPTER EIGHT

THE MYTH OF ALTRUISM

NO ONE HAS EVER done anything for anyone else. Ever. I expect this statement to meet with howls of denial, because we've all seen cases of self-sacrifice. In fact, we ourselves often sacrifice for others, and we are fully aware of people who have sacrificed for us. So what is this patently silly statement?

It seems that such a thought could be uttered by only the most hardened and cynical of souls, but perhaps it has elements of truth that bear examination. Obviously, we're talking about altruism, and obviously I'm about to say something that goes against the grain. But before we go on, let's define our terms. Altruism, for our purposes, will involve doing good for others at some cost to oneself. In other words, the good deed hurts the one performing it, at least to some extent. The point I will make is that even when someone appears to be doing something for someone else's sake, the act may be essentially selfish.

It will soon be clear that this entire subject is a rancorous one. It involves some of our most cherished ideals. It is not easy to see a great gift of love called selfish. But undoubtedly it is sometimes that.

Some years ago when I was toying with the idea of altruism (without having a name for it), I broached the subject in a Sunday school class. It was being discussed rather loosely with the usual clichés and nodding agreement that precedes Sunday dinner. But something didn't seem quite right, so I tried to define the limits of the phenomenon by carrying it to its extremes. I devised a rather bizarre, and hopefully hypothetical, situation. I visualized a case in which one could *decide* who would go to Heaven: oneself or a loved one. (As you can see, I was a bit influenced by my upbringing as a Southern fundamentalist.) The person not chosen would burn in Hell forever. Now, in order that no one could reap hidden rewards such as the benefits of approval or the feeling of martyrdom, there were catches. Once the decision was made, the person chosen would suddenly appear in Heaven with no recollection of any decision, and the other would go to Hell with utterly no idea of how he got there. In fact, once the decision was made, the memory of all parties would be totally obliterated; no one would be able to recall the existence of anyone else. Furthermore, *God* would not remember anything about it. The prize and penalty were ultimate. There were no regrets and no consolations.

I asked, rhetorically, how many people would be altruistic under those conditions, and I have to admit some surprise at the strength and vehemence of the responses that were hurled back in one bitter chorus. One bit of information that I was able to sift out of it all was that if a person chose to go to Hell under some weird proposition like this, he wanted the solace of knowing that the loved one was in Heaven remembering he cared. The whole question was far too morbid to deserve anything but passing consideration on anyone's part, but I felt I had learned something by asking it. First, people reflexively become irrational in the defense of their sacred cows; but more importantly, I learned (from the few rational responses that were proferred) that altruism has limits and degrees. I also began to suspect that when something hurts, one wants it to hurt in his best interest.

In the years since I became interested in the question, I have discovered that almost anyone is willing to be hurt a little in order to do a great good. We see this, for example, in our willingness to tax ourselves to pay for social benefits we will probably never receive. However, the probability of an altruistic act being performed diminishes as either the cost is raised or the benefit is lowered. Finally, a point is reached where we won't do it. Of course, even then we might still harbor the *spirit* of benevolence, but we are not willing to pay the price to exercise it.

Now that we've established a few points regarding the nature of altruism, we might ask how all this relates to us biologically. Of course, we must phrase our problem in genetic terms, as we've been doing all along. I'm going to say that "good" done to others is likely to ultimately benefit *one's own* kinds of genes, and that "bad" done to others is measured in terms of the damage done to *one's own* kinds of genes. It sounds like a convoluted argument, but it isn't; it's a simple one. We need only examine altruistic acts in light of others' importance in helping us carry out our Reproductive Imperative.

In some cases the importance is obvious. After all, our children are "other" people. It behooves us to look after them because they are the direct repositories of our genes. They are so important, and our investment in them is so great, that we will suffer considerable damage to ourselves in order to protect them.

In fact, we will behave more altruistically toward our children than we will toward a mate. There is less invested in a mate. Mates are more easily acquired and do not take years of cultivation before they are functional (usually). How often have you heard a man complain that too much of the attention of the loving woman he married is now directed to the children? If you get tired of his complaining, you *might* poke him in the nose without bringing her to his defense, but you'd better not hit her kids. Her genetic investment in them is too great. She will immediately risk injury to leap to their defense.

These sorts of statements, of course, are predictions based on the principle that the greater the reproductive "investment" one has in another individual, the more likely one is to sacrifice for that person. We see the application everywhere. You can wreak havoc on tapeworm eggs without risk of being attacked by an enraged parent. At least, I haven't read of any tapeworm attacks recently. Tapeworms have very little investment in any egg, so their sacrifice and care is minimal. A lost egg is simply replaced in the next batch of eggs. But as we noted in Chapter 2, an antelope mother who has gone through pregnancy and lactation has considerable investment in her single child, so she will defend it. If marauding hyenas should attempt to catch her infant, she will stand and fight at the risk of her own life. However, once it becomes clear that the battle is lost, an antelope mother may abandon her young. Reproductive economics says that she should, so that she will live to breed later. Genes of mothers who fight too long tend to disappear from the population. Of course, so do genes of mothers who flee at the first sign of danger. The point of all this is that altruism is predictable in terms of reproductive investment. We will see shortly that altruism can be rather precisely predicted mathematically, but we will also find that the phenomenon is more complex than was once believed because animals will sacrifice for *relatives* as well as for offspring.

Biologists have summed up the complexity of altruism in a deceptively simple question. Why will a bird in a flock give a warning cry when it spots a hawk circling above? Why will it attempt to save other birds that are not mates or offspring, especially if it runs some risk of attracting attention to itself? Wouldn't it do better to simply sneak away and hope that if someone gets caught, it's someone *else*?

It turns out that it depends on whether the warning bird is likely to be related *in any way* to the birds around it. It should save relatives. They don't have to be direct offspring. They can even be distant cousins *if* there are enough of them.

You may have noticed in our earlier discussions that I said an individual must look after its *kinds* of genes. This is not the same as saying it looks after its genes. The latter statement implies that it would sacrifice only for its descendants; the former predicts that it would also sacrifice for relatives. Remember that related individuals have genes in common.

So in order to perpetuate his kinds of genes, a person must behave as if he knows how closely the people around him are related to him. Are you more closely related to your siblings (brothers and sisters) or to your parents? I used to ask my genetics classes that question, and I regretted it every time. They generated so many complex charts and convoluted explanations that it was all I could do to clear my own head. It turns out that you're equally related to a sibling and a parent. Since you received half your genes from your mother and half from your father, you obviously have half your genes in common with either parent. Since genes come in pairs (lying at the same position along those paired chromosomes that came from each parent), a sibling will share half of your mother's genes (or 1/4) and half your father's genes (or 1/4), so you share a total of 1/2 of your genes with a brother or sister. You are 1/4 related to a half-sibling (as determined by the number of genes you have in common), and 1/4 to an uncle, aunt, niece, or nephew. You have only 1/8 of your genes in common with a cousin.

So with these figures in mind, who would you die for? Let's put it another way: Who would natural selection say you *should* risk your life for in order to maximize your kinds of genes in the population? If you have a good chance of having *two more* offspring if you should live (thus duplicating your existing genes in the gene pool), you would not be well-advised to die for one or two siblings; you should hold out for at least three. You also wouldn't want to die for fewer than five half-brothers or nephews or aunts, and you wouldn't do it at all for cousins unless there were enough for a baseball team. The idea is to give up your own chances of future reproduction only when the odds are that the relatives you save would bear more of your kinds of genes than you would be able to perpetuate through your own offspring if you should live.

It is apparent, then, that the more distantly related someone is, the less likely you are to die for him. But death, after all, is asking a bit much. Perhaps you wouldn't run in front of a streetcar to save a cousin who is about to be struck, but you would certainly shout a warning. It doesn't take much to shout, so the cost is low. This brings us back to an earlier point: A person is more likely to behave altruistically if the cost is low and the benefit to others is high. As relatedness decreases, the cost must be proportionately lower and the benefits higher.

So what does the little bird do when it sees a hawk overhead? It emits a high-pitched and extended whistle. All the other birds know what it means, and they scatter. So how costly is the warning? A drawn-out *tweee*, it turns out, is hard to locate, so the alarm-giver doesn't suffer great risk to itself. One can assume that the vigilant little bird is likely to be related to those around it and that it is therefore simply warning the caretakers of its kind of genes. Since its own risk is so low, it doesn't have to be very closely related to anyone. A cousin here or there will do.

Now, you may not be inclined to accept the notion of bird brains working out all the genetic arithmetic, deciding who they'll help and who they won't. (All this at the very time we're discovering that many high school graduates can't make change for a twenty.) But, of course, by now you're so steeped in the essentials of evolutionary theory that you will immediately catch yourself and realize that birds don't have to calculate anything. Natural selection has done the calculating. The birds just behave *as if* they have; those who don't behave this way leave no genes.

Is this the only reason a bird would give a warning cry? Just to save its kinds of genes that happen to reside in the bodies of others? Maybe not. A bird in a completely anonymous flock of starlings, in which no bird is likely to be related to its neighbor, will also give a warning. This may seem like altruism, but again, the reason may be entirely selfish. The warning cry that saves others can, for example, ensure the presence of a crowd that will distract and confuse a predator. It would be easy to pick a target from among three birds but difficult from among twenty; also, a crowd of birds is harder to sneak up on because there are so many watchful eyes. Furthermore, by giving a warning, an individual may be ensuring the presence of breeding partners later. So, a warning bird may be behaving in the best interest of its own genes.

I should add that there is an even more cynical explanation for warning cries in groups of unrelated birds. It has been suggested that a bird sounds a warning in order to startle its colleagues into moving abruptly and drawing attention to themselves. Thus, the warning bird increases the probability of some other bird being taken by the hawk.

In general, however, we can expect warning cries and other acts of "altruism" when animals are related. This means that we should look for these acts in viscous species—species in which the reproductive group has a certain cohesiveness. As an example, there are species of birds in which the males of any brood tend to stay in their parents' territory. Thus, a family of birds tends to occupy a certain territory.

The young that stay on are called "helpers" because they assist the parents in defending the territory against intruders and help rear younger broods. They do all this but the older pair does not allow them to breed. Is this a selfless act? No. By helping, they increase their own reproductive fitness in two ways: first, they maximize their kinds of genes by helping to increase the reproductive output of their parents; second, they stand to inherit the territory when a parent dies, and the inheritors, of course, are then free to breed. So, in "helping" species, both relatedness and altruism are likely to be high.

I should add that there are instances where helpers may not be related to the ones they help, but they advance their own genes just the same. For example, middle-class female chimpanzees may show dogged and devoted attention to the young of higher-ranking mothers. They constantly follow the mother around and attempt to touch or play with the infant. At first they are chased away, but their persistence finally wins out and they are allowed to care for the high-born babies. They are extremely attentive "aunts" and, whereas the cohesiveness of chimpanzee groups does not preclude relatedness, the aunts reap another benefit as well. Rank rubs off and they may rise in the hierarchy by associating with the young of dominant females. Rank, of course, has its rewards, so females that promote themselves in this way will rise in rank and can be expected to increase their own overall fitness as a result. So, we see that examples of apparent altruism must be scrutinized very closely because benefits come in all shapes and sizes.

To test the assumption that, in birds, helpers are looking out after their own genes, an experiment was carried out on twenty-five pairs of nesting mountain bluebirds. One parent from each pair was removed. There were already eggs or young in the nests, and in every case the remaining bird took a new mate. The stepparents had been eager to mate with the widow or widower, but they were apparently not crazy about rearing someone else's young. Almost none helped in feeding their stepchildren, and not one uttered a warning cry when danger was clearly overhead. The stepparents were obviously waiting for this unrelated brood to die or leave the nest so that they could rear a brood containing their own genes, a brood that they *would* feed and protect.

There are a number of fascinating variations on this theme. For example, whereas both wildebeest and zebra move in great herds over the African plains, they behave quite differently toward their young. If a young wildebeest is attacked by a predator after straying from its mother, the others scatter in all directions. It turns out that wildebeest move in anonymous herds and are not likely to be related to animals nearby. But if a predator should try to attack a young zebra who has strayed, it may be met with flying hooves from all directions. Zebra tend to move in family units, and therefore an adult is likely to be related to the young and helpless animal. The adult zebra therefore move swiftly to protect their kinds of genes.

The mechanics of altruism become quite complex in some species, such as North American turkeys. Here, when two brothers grow up together, they must eventually fight each other for dominance. When one wins, the loser does not leave but stays with his brother, and together they fight other pairs of brothers who have also established dominance between themselves. Finally, one duo emerges victorious and these two brothers are then free to set about attracting females. They both strut and whirl and display their vigor, but only one, the dominant one, is likely to breed with any females they attract. The brother who lost must stand on the sidelines watching his kinds of genes being perpetuated by proxy. It's not as good as breeding, but it's better than nothing.

Perhaps the best examples of the importance of relatedness to altruism are found in the social insects, particularly in that great sexist society of the beehive. Worker bees relentlessly work themselves to their graves, and they begin as soon as they emerge from their cells. The youngest workers prepare new cells in the hive for a day or so until their brood glands develop. Then they begin to feed the larvae that will become their younger siblings. Later they will unload nectar from the field workers and pack incoming pollen into cells. Then their wax glands develop and they begin to build combs. Some of these "house bees" will become guards and patrol the area around the hive. Eventually, however, each bee becomes a field worker or forager. They now fly far afield to collect nectar, pollen, or water, according to the needs of the hive, and they will unhesitatingly die to protect the hive. In fact, bees must give their lives in order to sting. Their stingers hold fast in the flesh of an intruder; when a bee flies away after an attack, her stinger and entrails remain behind and she soon dies. When bees who have not died in such a way are worn out in their service, when their wings are so torn and frayed that they can no longer fly, they quietly die or are killed by their sisters. Self-sacrifice is the motto, the bees give their all; and the hive goes on.

The bees' lives of self-sacrifice are dictated because they are sterile. Workers cannot lay eggs, thus they have no hope of reproducing. Instead, they rely on the queen to reproduce their kinds of genes. The queen is simply a sister who was fed a special diet as a larva. She is carefully tended and lives much longer than her worker sisters, so finally she becomes the mother of all the workers in the hive. When she mated, she was fertilized by a drone carrying only half the number of chromosomes as his sisters; thus each offspring ends up with their full quota of chromosomes by receiving half their mother's chromosomes and all their father's. This means they share three-fourths of their genes in common. So any bee is more closely related to a sister than she would be to her own offspring (if she could bear them). It is better, in terms of benefiting her own kind of genes, to care for sisters than to have children, and, with the sisters' help, to tend that great sac of eggs which is the queen, since she is their only hope of perpetuating their kinds of genes. With such strong kinship, extreme altruism would be expected, and that is precisely what we find.

If the basic assumption of all this is true, then what can we say about that all-too-common statement that animals behave in a certain way "for the good of the species"? We hear it frequently—particularly in the voice-over on TV animal shows. It should be apparent by now that *nothing* is done for the good of the species. Everything is done for oneself. If an act benefits the species, it's a side effect—coincidental.

The argument was once a hot one in the world of biology. It was triggered by a rather eloquent statement by V. C. Wynne-Edwards, a British biologist, who sought to show that animals may voluntarily reduce their own reproductive output in times of overcrowding. Thus, he said, individual fitness would be sacrificed for the good of the group. It's a fine idea and certainly appeals to our moral sensibilities, but it won't work. If some animals did voluntarily cut back on their own reproduction, the genes of such altruists would soon be swamped by the selfish progeny of those who refused to cut back. Thus, any population would always tend to be composed of the descendants of selfish individuals.

It may have occurred to you that there's another way of looking at this entire question of fitness and selfishness—if not the whole sociobiological paradigm. It is triggered by the knowledge that we, ourselves, are doomed. But, looked at from the standpoint of our genes, this is no tragedy. We are expendable. Not only are we expendable, it is *essential* to the welfare of our genes that we die. The welfare of our genes? Are we really in the business of simply looking after our genes? According to the arguments I've presented, the answer is, emphatically, yes. But are we *less* than that? Are we simply unwitting *tools* of selfish genes as Richard Dawkins of Oxford University has suggested? Perhaps, in a sense, the genes *are* in the driver's seat, simply using us as temporary housing until they can compel us to provide another, younger, and more variable generation of warm bodies for them. The idea is a particularly noxious one that assaults the poetic sensibilities of each of us. Obviously, we *must* have a closer look.

It must be admitted that only our genes really have anything to gain or lose by our behavior. The ones in our bodies are—or more precisely, are replicas of—ones that were passed along from our ancestors. And they are the only physical parts of us that have the opportunity to continue when we are gone. They provide a delicate yet robust thread of life between the ephemeral generations. They are periodically reshuffled, halved, and dealt into the bodies of new generations of children. Of course, some of those children betray the trust and fail to have offspring of their own—and the assortment of genes that would permit such betrayal is thus quickly removed from the population. However, most of our children can be expected to dutifully obey the calling of their genes. They will have children and will love them. They will mistrust strangers. They will be jealous of their mates. They will make themselves attractive. They will be sex-oriented. They will ostracize perverts. They will reproduce.

So what does all this make us? Genetic caretakers? Temporary housings for chromosomes? Slaves to tiny, coiled molecules that operate us by remote control? Ponderous robots, full of rationalizations, explanations, superstitions, and excuses but blindly following the Reproductive Imperative? What about the fact that we are learning classical guitar? That we have an interest in tap dancing and may start lessons soon? That we are very tidy and responsible and hold darned good jobs? That we have read Camus and don't pronounce the "s"? That we have good, really good, friends? That we are fine people and our parents are proud of us? How about all that? Chromosomes make us do all that? "No," comes the answer from the mountain, "but they don't care if you do"—*as long as* it doesn't interfere with your reproduction. Being such a splendid person may even help you find a mate more easily and leave even *more* genes.

"They don't *care* if I do?!" you shriek. "Stupid coiled molecules don't *care*? Great! That's just great! Boy, you're *nuts*!"

But it's worse than that. The molecules aren't even stupid. They're oblivious. They don't even know they exist. They just lie there deep in your cells, blindly offering themselves as templates for the formation of enzymes. Those enzymes, in turn, produce certain chemical reactions and thus cause different cells to take on particular properties. Some enzymes will direct the formation of muscle or blood cells. Others may help form the hypothalamus or parts of the cerebrum. If the brain, then, directs our behavior, the roots of behavior can all be traced back to the genes. Genes are the devil that made you do it.

Actually, all this should not come as a surprise. It's simply another way of looking at what we've been discussing all along. And, of course, the genes need not be granted intelligence or will. It's simple arithmetic again. The genes that survive are those that help us to reproduce.

In order to illustrate some of the problems in accounting for altruism on an evolutionary basis, let's return to the idea of "genetic emissaries" mentioned earlier. People who study a wide range of animals from birds to apes have noted that younger animals behave a bit differently from older ones. We can see it for ourselves as we watch a silly kitten leap straight up into the air and then charge across the room and under the bed, from where a round little face emerges. We can see it in a frolicking puppy who may get a nose full of cactus spines. And we see it in exploratory and playful young monkeys who, even in the wild, look, poke, explore, and learn. Young animals seem to be a lot more curious and adventuresome than their elders. They may also be more innovative.

One study of Japanese macaques revealed that a very bright young female monkey had learned to separate grain from sand by picking up a handful of grain and sand and throwing it all in the water. The grain floated and could be easily retrieved. The technique apparently never occurred to the old monkeys laboriously extracting each grain from the sand on the shore. But after watching the young experimenter, they learned soon enough.

Earlier I described exploratory behavior in young birds, noting that they are more likely to invade new habitats than old birds are. Besides their propensity for exploration, young birds do not navigate quite as well as old ones and are hence more likely to fly off course in their annual migrations and get lost. This, too, can be a way to invade new habitats, even if it is a bit risky. The point is, young animals are the explorers, the innovators, and the colonizers.

This all sounds fine and we've seen it in our own species so frequently that we're not surprised. But there's a problem in exploring. It can be dangerous. There is a risk involved. Of course, one might say that youth is the time to take chances, when individuals are strong and before behavioral patterns become so rigid that adaptation is difficult. But the question arises: Why take chances at all? Why invade new habitats when the population is already well situated in the traditional area? It is undoubtedly safer to remain with the parent group. But one can argue that the parent group may be *too* well adapted to its area. The home-folks may provide such stiff competition that a newcomer does better in other areas, where there is perhaps a greater risk but less competition.

Is there another reason that young animals tend to leave the group? Do parents "deliberately" force their offspring out? And do they "deliberately" equip them with genetic dispositions that would encourage them to branch out, to explore, to take risks in the chance that it will pay off genetically for the parent? Is this the "genetic strategy" of a good parent? Is play a whimsical expression of a more evolutionarily serious tendency to do the unusual? Is the exploratory urge a behavior that has capitalized on the resilience and strength of youth? If frolicsome baby monkeys do things and eat things that their parents wouldn't, is it in *their* best interest or is it in their *parents'* best interest?

Perhaps the young animals are behaving in their parents' best interest. If they risk the unknown because their parents have genetically equipped them to do so, and if, as a result, they suffer higher mortality (mortality among most young vertebrates is high), then young animals can be viewed as "genetic emissaries" of their parents. They are stalking horses, trial balloons. Perhaps there are potential payoffs out there, but the parents may not wish to take the gamble, so they, in effect, send their genes out in the form of their children to see if there is something to be gained.

Sometimes the gains are enormous, as when invading animals colonize islands that are hard to reach and are therefore virtually free of competitors. But many would-be colonizers may be lost in making the attempt.

Since there may be high risks, a young animal may not be acting in its own best interest by taking chances, by exploring, by trying new things. It might have better luck staying with the group and behaving circumspectly. If it were acting in its own best interest, it would be expected to try to branch out into unknown arenas only when the risk

·is small and the potential payoff is high, or when the risk is higher and the potential payoff very high.

The basic question is this, then: Are young exploratory animals acting in their own best interest or in the best interest of their parents? Do they really begin to try to maximize their own genetic success as soon as they are on their own, or do they take unnecessary risks because they were not dealt a full deck by their parents? Are they out there maximizing their *parents'* success at the risk of their own? After all, the risk to the parent is a function of the parent's investment; the risk to the offspring is total. One might argue that natural selection does not immediately grant its great advantages to a new individual in the population but that these good graces are only gradually bestowed as the animal ages. The animal is at first only a more-or-less expend-able item, acting, to some degree, on behalf of its parents. Later, these exploratory/play urges will wane and the animal will become a full-fledged ward of natural selection, no longer frivolous, now acting in its *own* best interest. One would also expect that as an animal grows older, it would tend to be more careful with its genetic emissaries. It's one thing to send an ill-equipped offspring out into the world if one is pretty sure of being able to replace it later, should it fail. But it's quite another to send out what may be one's last chance at reproduction. It would be interesting to know whether older parents tend to shelter their offspring more than younger parents do. It definitely seems to be the case in human beings, the species with the greatest parental investment.

If the preceding argument—that a young animal may at first take risks on behalf of its parents—has any validity, then it could be said that some young animals behave altruistically. They may fail and be lost, but their parents will live on to reproduce again. Of course, the fruits of those reproductive efforts will be new brothers and sisters, individuals bearing genes in common with the explorer. So the ex-plorer may be seeing to his own reproductive success after all. Again, what seemed to be altruism is just a way of perpetuating one's genes by proxy, through helping relatives to reproduce.

The thrust of this entire argument (indeed, the whole chapter, if not the book) is perhaps faintly irreverent. It is, some would say, an attack on our revered qualities of love, caring, mercy, self-sacrifice. And whereas a few may find it all quite interesting, others will find it irritating. Must *everything* be viewed as a reproductive device? Is altruism really just a way in which genes multiply themselves through a network of relatives? Is it a tool whereby one keeps others around so that someone else might bear the brunt of environmental hazards? Is it a way of gaining easy access to mates? Is it just one more Darwinian enabling device? Must our most cherished traits fall under the Darwinian umbrella? One of our first lines of defense, of course, is to find exceptions. Exceptions weaken the rule.

How about the fact that strangers often help each other? How can helping a stranger contribute to one's genetic welfare? Why did I stop in the middle of a Mississippi night to help a stranger change a flat? Why did a black man stop in the rain on a bridge across the Mississippi to help me tighten a fan belt? How is it I happened to see a group of New Yorkers, of all people, follow two robbers down the street, yelling at a distance until the police came? Why did a British soldier I met in Copenhagen defend a woman against her abusive husband? Why do we daily encounter deeds of help and self-sacrifice—deeds that can have no genetic "explanation"?

You will probably not be delighted to hear that such deeds may, in fact, be accounted for on an evolutionary basis. It seems, when all is said and done, that we're at it again, looking after ourselves. Or so says the theory of reciprocal altruism. The whole idea was more or less developed in the 1970s by a bright and brash young Harvardite, Robert Trivers. (His advancement of this idea, some have suggested, led to his tenure being denied. Whether or not this is true, the reciprocal altruism idea is certainly offensive enough to many people to make the suggestion believable.)

The idea of reciprocal altruism is encompassed in a Good Samaritan parable. Suppose a drowning man is rescued by a Good Samaritan, even though the two are unrelated and total strangers. It would seem, at first, that we've found an example of pure altruism. However, it turns out that the Good Samaritan stands to gain quite a bit by his "selfless" act. Suppose the drowning man has a fifty-fifty chance of dying if he is not helped and that the Good Samaritan, being a Good Swimmer, has only one chance in twenty of dying if he helps. In our scenario we also assume that if the Good Samaritan should flail around and drown out there, the victim drowns, too. But if the Samaritan should live, so would the victim.

For purposes of illustration, let's assume that there is a strong likelihood that the Good Samaritan himself may be in need of assistance at a later time and the rescued man might reciprocate by saving him. In fact, if the drowning man should reciprocate (at the same probability of risk to each), both will receive a net benefit by having played the rescuer. In essence, each man would have traded a one-half risk of dying for about a one-tenth risk.

Earlier in our evolutionary history, a rescuer might literally have been able to count on the very man he saved to help him. Groups were small and cohesive, so the rescuer and rescuee would have been known to each other and would probably have been near each other when any crisis arose. In modern society, however, there are too many of us, and we are too mobile to expect to deal reciprocally with each other on an individual basis. Instead, we must count on establishing a behavioral pattern throughout the culture. A population of individuals who interact in this way will consist of people with increased reproductive fitness. Each individual reaps a net benefit in the trade-off.

Now, it may have occurred to you that there is a way to beat the system. Cheat. Walk around in your robes of white, with a concerned expression on your face, and if you're drowning, call for help. When help comes, appear grateful. However, should the tables be turned, why take that one-in-twenty chance of dying to rescue someone else? Let him drown. This way you have nothing to lose and everything to gain.

The problem is, we are an intelligent species with a long memory and the ability to recognize each other individually. Thus, if others see you cheating, they will come to recognize you as a cheater, to brand you as such, and to ostracize you or punish you in other ways. Perhaps they will refuse to save you.

Thus, if cheaters are identified and not saved when they get in trouble, cheating will not pay off. The risk factor in cheating will, in fact, be higher than that in altruism. If you arouse your neighbor's righteous indignation and break his moral codes, you, as an individual, will pay.

Reciprocal altruism, by the way, can account for a wide range of subtle human traits, such as sympathy, gratitude, self-righteousness, and guilt. We feel compelled to help someone else, not out of having done the arithmetic to see whether we will be benefited, but out of feelings of sympathy. We are so vulnerable to the cues that sympathy may even be evoked in situations where there is no possibility of payoff (such as we see in the faces of visitors to the Dachau museum in Germany). But it behooves us, nonetheless, to keep it in our behavioral repertoire.

Gratitude is the feeling that causes us to express our thanks, and it increases the odds that we will be helped again. ("He didn't even say thanks. See if I help *him* again.") Self-righteousness is a bit hard to define, but it might be described as that glorious feeling we get when we know, perhaps only too well, that we have behaved according to the rules. (Martyrdom can result in that equally splendid feeling we get from knowing we have behaved properly even without immediate prospects of being repaid. Martyrs may be willing to defer payment until the afterlife.) And, finally, we come to that great gray mantle of guilt.

Ah, guilt. Guilt hurts but it actually works to our advantage: When we have behaved in a socially irresponsible way that has gone unnoticed and unpunished by others, we punish ourselves. We feel rotten. We are determined to do better next time. Under the goading of guilt, we tend to rectify socially unacceptable behavior and replace our misanthropic deeds with good deeds, which others may then see and for which they will reward us. We may even behave altruistically when no one is watching so as to fuel our self-righteousness and to remove any traces of potential guilt.

Guilt, of course, may keep us in line in many ways. If we "sleep around," we are not behaving in a reproductively responsible manner. Our guilt then brings us back to the pathway of reproductive righteousness. If we treat our children poorly, we feel guilty. If we are *unable* to treat them well, we feel guilty. The crapshooter's plea, "Baby needs shoes!" probably stemmed from an effort to remove the feeling of guilt as the gambler was squandering the family's rent.

The consideration of guilt is interesting from an evolutionary standpoint. Certainly we are not born with a set of directives that say, "Don't play craps with the rent money." It seems far more likely that we are born with (1) the ability to place ourselves along a righteous-guilty spectrum, and (2) the desire to stay to the left of the spectrum. The specific behaviors along that spectrum may be innate (such as those relating very specifically to reproduction) or learned (those that society has dictated and that may or may not have reproductive rationales). Because of our ability to embrace society's dictates, many of us have crippled ourselves beyond repair by continually staggering under a load of self-imposed guilt. We feel guilty about everything. In some cases we even seem to feel self-righteous about feeling guilty, and we look at people who bear a minimal load of guilt (perhaps even, Heaven forbid, *enjoying* life), and we call them amoral. They are guilt-deficient. Strangely enough, however, some of these very people have a way of appearing when needed, perhaps with a blond on each arm, but appearing nonetheless.

Before I begin to feel guilty about chastising the amoral, let me summarize. I am fully aware of the risk of indictment suffered by those who attempt to stick pins in sacred balloons, and I'm aware that I've poked a few of those balloons in these pages. Nonetheless, it's time we took a closer look at ourselves, so I feel justified, if not self-righteous. I've noted some of our most cherished ideals and suggested that they can be explained as essentially selfish devices. I've talked of love as a way to wangle one's genes into the next gene pool. I am not saying love is bad; I'm saying that love is selfish and that selfishness is good, or at least it has been. Selfishness is the pervasive quality that percolates through the souls of living things. It is the driving force behind our behavior, the behavior that brought us to our present successes. But the world is changing. Things are different now, and perhaps it is time to change our behavior. If we are to have any hope of adapting to an altered planet, we must come to understand our motivations for what they really are, and not what we wish them to be.

CHAPTER NINE

CHANGE

A ND NOW, LADIES AND GENTLEMEN, I want to introduce a *great* entertainer and a really *marvelous* human being." How often we've heard such maudlin and effusive introductions on late-night talk shows. One might wonder what would happen if the talk-show host were to say, "And now, I would like to present a very deviant person, really abnormal, someone who has succeeded in denying vast areas of his heritage, someone who doesn't look after his chromosomes, who owns almost nothing and doesn't possess a shred of patriotism, someone who has utterly failed to respond to the calling of his heritage!"

The announcer might be describing the prototype of the kind of person that humans should become if we are to survive, but the audience wouldn't have a clue as to what he is talking about. "Was that a slur? He did call him deviant, didn't he? Unpatriotic? What's that about chromosomes? What's he talking about, anyway? What's on Channel 7?"

It is undoubtedly too early for the great messages of sociobiology to have reached society at large, and at this point most people can be expected to reject its tenets, largely out of misunderstanding. It must be admitted that even though sociobiology may present us with new insights and opportunities for social change, some of its basic premises are indeed repugnant, going directly against the grain of much of what we have been taught. After all, who wants to be told that he really loves other people as a way to advance his genes? The idea will not be met with wild applause, but in a sense it's true. It is in our genes' interest that we love other people and that we are loved. However, in some cases it is best for our genes if we dislike people, people whom we don't know or who behave in a certain way. So we do. According to sociobiological theory, we should dislike those who don't have genes like ours and who are not in a position to help our genes. We should particularly resent those who presume to threaten our genes in any way, even indirectly. But if others can help our genes along, we tend to love them. Thus, we almost invariably behave toward others in such a way as to advance our genes. And our denials mean nothing since it doesn't matter whether we are aware of the roots of our behavior as long as we obey the Reproductive Imperative.

So here we are, interacting with each other, loving, cajoling, helping, hating, building, and destroying—driven by multifarious motivations, behaving variously at different times, unable to explain ourselves, busy—very busy, introspective, and puzzled. We can't even answer the simple questions ("Why am I jealous?"). Never mind the great questions ("Why am I here?").

We choose to see ourselves in a certain kind of light, but we are continually disappointed. We value love, kindness, generosity, gentleness, and forgiveness, but we are often mean and petty and dangerous. We are uneasily aware that Christians have been known to kill.

Our history is one long contradiction, and we don't seem to be getting any closer to resolving the discrepancies. So, what I am suggesting here is yet another look at ourselves and our histories. I hope that this new look will have several effects. For one thing, perhaps it will help us stop lying to ourselves. And perhaps it will help us with our labels. We call love good and hate bad. We like to love and to promote love and we abhor hatred. However, it is important to realize that the selective application of love and hate brought us to whatever success we enjoy as a species today. Love, seen this way, is no better than hate. By the same token, food is no "better" than feces. (This may take some explanation. I'd better go on.) What I mean is that love and hate, and food and feces are simply part of the human condition.

It is currently popular to believe that people are innately good and that bad behavior must be learned, but "good" and "bad" are terms that are in sore need of revision. Love is not simply good. Hate is not just bad. Both love and hate are natural. They are important. They are part of our heritage. If we had loved our enemy, he would have defeated us, replaced our genes. If we had hated our children, we would have doomed ourselves accordingly. If we were not jealous of our mates, we would have lost genetically. If we had not been successful acquirers, we would have been replaced by those who were.

Remember that the typical human does not live next door (I probably won't get any argument there). The *typical* human was perhaps five feet, four inches tall; had large jaws, long arms, big wrists, and a small brain case; and knew the people around him—all of them. He was the raw material upon which natural selection worked, and evolutionary forces indeed molded him well to fit into the world that was at his disposal. He didn't share many genes in common with strangers, and they, in fact, competed with him for commodities. Better to hate them. Drive them away—secure the world's goods for his own group. Strangers were bad for his genes.

Millions of years of learning and evolution would have developed other traits in these representative humans. People within the group would have cooperated closely. They would have looked out for each other and each other's children. They would have hunted in coordinated groups and would have helped each other build shelters. They would have laughed together, empathized, and loved each other. Disruptions would have been temporary, often caused by someone wishing to change his status or perhaps to gain a neighbor's commodities. The in-group hostilities, however, would have been tempered by love and peer pressure. The system worked.

So people have traditionally been driven by a variety of emotions that work together to produce whole and functioning members of the species. Why, therefore, do we hear people asking whether we are essentially hostile and aggressive or really loving and cooperative at heart? The question pales into senselessness. But perhaps it is simply an appeal for simplicity. We want to know: What are we? We are distressed and confused in a world that has changed too fast. We have inherited this new world, but it is so multifaceted that we don't have many clues as to the nature of our prize. If you had asked Og the Caveman whether people were essentially loving or hating creatures, he could probably have told you that people are both. He could see the immediate advantages of both traits in his life. He loved his children. He knew that the strangers over the hill should be dealt with harshly in order to keep them from taking over. Then, as now, people both hated and loved, although the rewards of selectively applying these emotions were perhaps clearer in those days.

But things have changed. Of course, we still don't know the strangers over the hill. We know they're strange, but so are the people across the street. We don't know *their* names either. Now almost everyone's a stranger. We can't simply hate all strangers anymore; we've got to know *which* strangers. Once we hated the Japanese, but now we are told that those strangers are OK. We probably don't even hate the North Vietnamese. Perhaps we never did; we were simply told to behave as if we did. Not only are we in a quandary about *who* to hate, the *reasons* for our hatred are also obscured. Do we hate because of violations of the 200-mile coastal limit? What if we don't like fish? The point is, we have been left with a behavioral heritage that doesn't have a real place in the kind of world that we have imposed upon ourselves so devastatingly quickly. We can't see the immediate benefits of hating, if there are any. We are left with suspicious minds, but who are we supposed to suspect? Where do we *apply* these feelings?

The question of where to properly apply these feelings is a difficult one and has led to great confusion. At times, of course, there is no problem. Someone *tells* us who to hate. But there are problems here also. We could direct our hatred toward the Nazis easily enough and feel rather good about it. However, we may have had more trouble directing our hatred toward the citizens of what President Lyndon Johnson called a raggedy-ass little third-rate country. Today are we to hate the Arabs? What if they own our bank? What if we simply *like* Arabs? Could it be?

This propensity for hatred that lingers in the human spirit is so very, very predictable that it makes us extremely easy to manipulate. In order to arouse hatred, or its more benign form, dislike, all we have to do is label someone as one of *them*. Any "them" will do; it doesn't matter. When I was working with the military in Turkey, the base held Saturday-afternoon football games between the various barracks. Able barracks was playing Charlie barracks one day when a fight erupted on the field. In talking to my students later I found that the fight was only the tip of the iceberg. There was out-and-out hostility between the men of different barracks, and each soldier was keenly aware of which barracks anyone else belonged to. Never mind that we were there to monitor Russian radio transmissions. Never mind that the Turks had shut down the base because of Congressional favoritism to the Greeks. Harold was in Able barracks and therefore one of *them*. Punch Harold.

I also recall that I couldn't even beat my brother-in-law at chess after having taken his queen. That's how bad I am at the game. But I remember following Bobby Fischer's match with the Russian champion, along with millions of other Americans, and scouring the newspapers daily to make sure that Fischer, one of *ours*, had trounced one of *theirs*. I didn't know either player, but one was American and one was Russian. That was good enough for me.

The propensity of people to dislike outsiders has often been used in political maneuverings. Time after time some leader in political trouble in his own country has manufactured a problem with another country. He points to them, accuses them, identifies them, and cries for support against them. He almost invariably gets the results he wants. His countrymen rally around, forgetting their internal problems, and focus their hatred on the outsiders.

It is always best to avoid being labeled an outsider. If you are obviously different, for example, if your skin color is different from most of the people around you, you risk being continually singled out as an object of hatred. You can expect it. The whole thing is quite dependable.

We can glean two things from all this. First, we are, in fact, saddled with traits that we do not admire—either in ourselves or in others. But an honest appraisal can only lead to the conclusion that these traits are, nevertheless, there. They can be inflamed, accented, and exacerbated by bitter experience, but their presence and the course they take are far too predictable for us to believe that we each managed to learn them independently. And they are also obviously far too potentially useful, under some circumstances, for us to believe that they are not the result of natural selection.

The second thing we can see clearly is that these traits may now be of little or no use, or that they are, in fact, anachronistic and dangerous to us in today's world. This is not to say that our outmoded codes and values cannot be changed, however. But just as a diamond cutter carefully studies his rough gem before attempting to alter his prize, precisely accounting for the flawed matrix, we must also study carefully and objectively the human spirit. Wishful thinking is stupid and dangerous for both the diamond cutter and the social scientist.

Evolution flattened the human face, opposed the human thumb, and influenced the human code. We dress ourselves in tweed and ruminate endlessly about what we ought to be. But what we are is an animal that succeeds admirably in small, related groups. We bemoan the fact that we have "devolved" in so many ways. We are physically weak, or so we say. We would be unable to cope under primitive conditions, or so we say. Modern civilization has destroyed our "natural" qualities, we tell ourselves. I do not believe that these things are true. We may be physically weak, but the muscle mass is there, waiting to be strengthened. (We probably have the greatest endurance of any nonmigratory animal. A few years ago an old man in India killed a tiger that had attacked him by managing to climb onto its back and, over several hours, strangling the huge beast.) We readily store great masses of fat around our girth in anticipation of the hard, lean seasons, which never come. We tend to readily, very readily, affiliate ourselves with this group or that. When all is said and done, we are, after all, rather robust, both physically and mentally, and we come equipped with the mentality to survive—especially in small groups.

Interestingly, when we let our imaginations run wild, we frequently develop scenarios in which hate, greed, love, and altruism have clear targets. The western movie serves as a good example. We know who the good guys are, and it's OK to hate the bad guys. The new genre of realistic cinema blurs those differences and causes us to identify with all sorts of people. It's realistic because we can't completely love or hate anyone, but it certainly isn't as gratifying as watching Matt Dillon knock heads. One of the favorite themes of science fiction writers is survival after a third world war has destroyed most of the world's population and commodities. And, strangely enough, almost all scenarios depict humans surviving in small groups and suspiciously encountering other small groups, which almost always turn out to be hostile. The whole idea may have more merit than most fictional conceits in that it may depict the primal human condition, one in which our evolutionary hangover would again be adaptive.

At this point someone might ask, as the world changed, didn't we simply adapt to it? Aren't modern humans now geared to the modern world through the processes of both cultural and genetic evolution? The answer might have occurred to you during one of modern man's repeated surges toward the brink of self-destruction. There is compelling evidence that we simply haven't changed enough—that our social evolution is proceeding more slowly than the optimist might wish. The blue-sky confidence of the person who says, "We will adapt," is encouraging but unrealistic. Genetic evolution is almost always an excruciatingly slow process. Humans haven't had tails for millions of years, yet in our embryonic development tails appear, which must then be absorbed into the body. There is no reason to believe the tails are a necessary part of our development, but they aren't very energetically expensive to make, so they are still with us millions of years after they were discarded in the adult. They are on their way out, but oh so slowly.

Cultural evolution, of course, can occur much more rapidly. We can alter social patterns more easily than we can change gene frequencies in a population. Humans, after all, are highly malleable and, within limits, can behave in new ways simply by deciding to do so. Feminism, for example, has caught on in Western society with a dizzying acceleration, just as it did in Germany before the National Socialists decided it was a threat to the welfare of the Nazi system and simply put a stop to it. Social changes of all sorts occurred in the United States and in much of Europe in the 1960s. People refused to fight in Vietnam; drugs were in; alcohol was out; and sexual liberation descended with a goofy vengeance. Many of these changes were quite easily brought about, such as the de-emphasis on alcohol in favor of drugs. Other changes, however, were forged with more difficulty. It was hard to refuse to fight "for your country." And the "sexual revolution" left a lot of bewildered people in its wake. It is also interesting that it didn't "take." Sociologists now tell us that there is a revived interest in our "traditional values," that open marriages and promiscuity are losing ground, that we are returning to long-term relationships and the family unit.

We can indeed change our culture, but we'll simply not be found far outstripping our evolutionary heritage. We're like a puppy surging toward the end of its leash. Because of our intelligence, our leash may be long, but it has its limits and those last precious inches as we strain against it are extremely difficult to gain and even harder to hold for very long. We can construct any kind of social system, but unless it is compatible with the human spirit, it will not last. We are bound as inextricably to our heritage as we are to the shapes of our eyes.

Our problem of adaptation is complicated not only by the ponderous slowness of genetic evolution but by the dizzying rapidity with which we have created our new kind of world. Keep in mind that some of the trees around us are 8,000 years old, so that's a very brief period of *evolutionary* time. Today, humans tramp happily past these great relics, but when they were saplings they ran little risk of being trod upon by the foot of man. There just weren't many human feet around. The earth has historically been populated by very few people. Even as late as 1650 there were only half a billion people (one hundred times as many as there were through most of our evolution). By 1850 there were one billion; by 1950, two and one-half billion; and now we're looking at four billion. To make matters interesting, the world's human population will double in about 30 years, and then again and again every few years after that. (Unless it is checked by natural causes—a horrifying prospect.)

So today we encounter strangers continually, all day, every day. It is noteworthy if we run across even one person we know downtown. We tend to embrace those around us as being part of our group. But we look at them and see strangers. We tend not to like strangers very much, and so we are perplexed. We find that if we trust a stranger, treating him confidently as a member of our group, we will often get taken, because while we were invoking the "proximity rule" (those around us must be friends), the stranger may have been reacting to the "stranger rule" (unfamiliar people are fair game). If bitter experience teaches us to distrust strangers, we may draw the in-group line too close to ourselves, perhaps incorporating only our families. Thus, we come to treat all acquaintances as strangers, not trusting them till payday. This is a self-protective device, but it has its costs. We may gain a reputation as a nonaltruist, and people, those we deal with daily, might come to dislike us and perhaps withhold their assistance or good wishes. The problems of a high population density are enormous. We are no longer isolated in our genetic group and we are puzzled.

Since we can no longer trust our innate feelings about how we are to behave toward those we encounter, we may find ourselves asking questions of others, looking for directives, for authority. How *should* we behave? we ask. The answer almost invariably comes back, "Treat people nice." We are told that hate is bad, that love is good. We're encouraged to behave generously toward others. And who tells us this? Others.

The world would certainly be a better place in which to live if everyone were an altruist. Read that again. Is there a catch? Better place for whom? Everyone? Including me? Is it to each person's advantage to encourage others to behave altruistically? Is that why we hear it so often?

Again, I realize how this sounds. I must therefore hurry on to say that the person telling us these things almost assuredly has different conscious motives than pure selfishness. He may sincerely want *every-*

one to be treated well. In fact, I don't know *anyone* who doesn't want everyone treated well (everyone except those deserving punishment for not behaving altruistically). But no matter what he wants, the net result is that he *will* be treated better if altruism catches on. So people who preach altruism stand to benefit and to leave their influence in the gene pool and in the culture.

Let's consider another motivation for altruism here, our ability to empathize—to put ourselves in someone else's shoes. The pain of another person can quite literally become *our* pain because we have the peculiar ability to imagine we are that person. Because of this ability to project, we are compelled to treat others well. This ability, of course, is important in helping us deal with strangers in a pleasant manner. How would *we* like to be treated? Recite the golden rule. In essence, then, we are treating ourselves well by proxy. In addition, altruistic behavior is reinforced, first, if we feel self-righteous and, second, if others see us do it.

Probably the ability to empathize arose as a mechanism to insure proper behavior toward those within our own group. But now that we live among strangers, we find ourselves applying it to them. If we can empathize with a stranger, overcoming our initial distrust, we may feel gratified. And by playing one inherent tendency (empathy) against another (dislike of strangers), we can help to build a tradition within our society from which we may one day reap a benefit. Perhaps our altruism no longer serves its original function, but since we're stuck with the tendency, there's no reason we can't use it in new ways.

The principle of applying ancient tendencies to new problems, by the way, is a critical one. We must conform to our new kind of world, but we simply don't have the time to adapt genetically through evolution. We must work with what we have, and one solution is simply to redirect or refocus our primal urges. Redirection will be infinitely easier and less dangerous than suppression. It seems that we will continue to love and hate, but perhaps we can redirect those feelings in new and creative ways to help us make this world work.

And *that's* the question. *Can* it work? Or are we dinosaurs on our last legs? Species come and species go, and we are but a species. So are we simply another group spinning, with the tuntong and the snail darter, toward oblivion? Are we just another grand experiment that failed? Have we, by our very success, painted ourselves into a corner? Can the earth exist without a bulbous-brained, introspective, gadget-minded, arrogant, aggressive, loving, and myopic species? Is this not *our* earth? Have we not clear directives to subdue it? And haven't we succeeded?

Apparently not. We have clearly changed the earth, but obviously it *can* get along without us, as it once did, and obviously we haven't subdued much of anything. We certainly haven't subdued the ancient spirit that enabled us to climb squabbling all over everything. That spirit remains with us. We are forced to admit that we are a rather primitive group with enormous pretensions. And it seems that, in fact, we *have* painted ourselves into a corner unless we can manage to shed those pretensions—those silly and irrational notions that we are not molded by our history.

Our task now is to face ourselves squarely, to try to see what we really are. This means laying aside those defenses that automatically rise to challenge anything that suggests that we are not as we wish we were. We have talked to ourselves far too long. Our rhetoric is impressive, and we have managed to convince each other that humans are, or should be, this or that. But, let's simply admire our rhetorical ability now and put it aside as we would an intricate dollhouse.

As I've said, the most popular position these days is that humans are essentially "nice." We want to perpetuate the notion that we are gentle. We want to encourage gentleness. So we say gentleness is normal. And it is. However, we cannot neglect the other side of the coin. While gentleness has its place, so do aggression and hatred. They are part of the human spirit, too. We can deny it, of course. We can pretend it doesn't exist, but we won't walk through Brownsville. By swearing that people are gentle while keeping up our defenses against them, we are at worst lying and at best remaining purposefully ignorant—choosing not to see. It's a foolish strategy, particularly at this critical time in our history. We are presently faced with an urgent need to know, to understand at the deepest level possible for us, and reciting a litany of how we *wish* things were is a hindrance. The time for wishful thinking is past. We must accept ourselves for what we are, or we are done.

Acceptance, of course, is only a first step. Accepting the fact that the boat is foundering doesn't get one to shore. We must go beyond that. We must take corrective action.

We've attempted to correct our course in the past, but we've started with the wrong premises, as witnessed by perpetually rising crime rates and the continual threat of war. We can't teach a person to love all strangers any more than we can teach him to be tall. Humans now stalk the earth in overwhelming numbers, each individual replete with his own innate desires and biases. When we see these people behaving unselfishly, we applaud. That is the way people *should* behave, we say. And we pretend to be shocked and horrified when we see them behave hatefully. But we are being dishonest. We have labeled one behavior "natural" and the other not so. But both loving and hateful, selfish and unselfish feelings permeate the human spirit. They are ubiquitous and predictable. They're *there*. We can *count* on them and *work* with them. They provide us with raw material. We can only cripple our efforts by denying that they exist. If we are to effect the great sweeping changes that our dilemma demands, we have to drop our reflexive defenses, face ourselves squarely, and admit what is.

Given that the human spirit does, in fact, encompass aggression, particularly toward outsiders, certain kinds of remedies suggest themselves. We can't remove the aggression, but we can diminish it to some extent through providing the sort of cultural atmosphere that would not nurture it. This, in fact, is about the extent of the social programs that have been attempted so far. But we have gone a bit further in another way. We have constrained the expression of hostility by social strictures: laws, rules, codes. This means, of course, that we have curtailed our freedoms. This loss should come as no surprise since freedom must dwindle as population rises. The more people there are, the more they must be governed. We really can't expect a person to behave in anyone's best interest but his own. Therefore, we must make it in his *own* best interest to behave socially in a crowded and complex world. The needs of *society* must continue to be itemized, and strong societal pressure must be exerted to see that individuals act to meet those needs, within reasonable expectations. But this means strong government.

The notion of strong government is an interesting one. Basically, governments are designed to bridle human nature. Government tends to stop its citizens from doing the things they are disposed to do. It is noteworthy that many of the strongest opponents of sociobiology call themselves leftists, but the very forms of government they espouse are among the most repressive, in that they repress the natural tendencies of the citizenry. China is apparently now largely devoid of slums, but the only way such order could be achieved was at the great cost of personal freedom. Personal freedom, of course, is a euphemism for behaving selfishly, because if we are free to behave the way we want to, we tend to maximize our own welfare at the expense of others. Such freedom to maximize is also the basis for the rightist's system of free enterprise, or competition in the marketplace. May the best man win. Or, put another way, you can identify the best man by the fact that he won.

In right-wing societies, then, we also find great repression, often because the wealth is so unevenly distributed in a system of winners and losers that the losers pay dearly. If they become disgruntled by their lot, threatening perhaps to redistribute some of the wealth, they are dealt with severely, at the mercy of a system of laws written largely by those in power—the winners.

Centrist systems, interestingly enough, seem to run on rightist business methods and ethics, but they tend to temper the sad lot of the losers by artificially taking a portion of money from the winners and redistributing it. People in such systems atone for creating losers by wearing their cloaks of guilt as their sign of success and voting themselves higher taxes. In any case, the law and order imposed by strong government remains essentially an organized attempt to change human behavior from the outside. In our modern societies, places where large populations have enormous technological prowess, human behavior must often be forced, as well as led, into the proper social channels. In fact, it seems that as populations increase, so must government, and that the noblest role of government is to ensure harmony by seeing to it that people do not continue to treat strangers as strangers. Unfortunately, strong governments have often proved themselves unworthy and unwise. The force they exert has sometimes been extravagant and excessive and the channels poorly chosen. Nonetheless, exterior pressure remains a feasible alternative in our search for ways to help us live together under the new conditions we have created for ourselves.

So I'm encouraging strong government and loss of freedom, fully aware that the very idea is anathema to many people. (Interestingly, some of the same people who demand their reproductive freedom are the very ones who are the most distressed when a rising population curtails their other freedoms.) In any case, strong governmental regulation, perhaps primarily in the form of punitive threat, can only be effective in molding our behavior within very narrow limits. We can encourage nonselfish behavior and discourage selfishness through cultural and governmental efforts. But even these efforts are not enough.

If people tend to behave caringly toward in-group members, obviously one goal should be to somehow include more people in that group. But this goal is likely to be accomplished only at great social and historical cost, and the means will be shocking or distasteful to many of us. For example, we might begin by discouraging pride in our ancestry. Forget "White supremacy" and "Black is beautiful." If blacks and whites were to give up their racial pride to freely intermingle and intermarry, we would destroy one means of discrimination. Do not be proud of your Italian ancestry. If Italian Americans deny their heritage and move out of their neighborhoods to disperse into the population at large, their descendants will go unnoticed, never worrying about being defamed. If Jews relinquish their ethnicity and move to Arkansas, their descendants will go unnoticed.

Thus, a case can be made for abandoning ethnic pride. One is tempted to say, "Forget your heritage. Mix. Mingle. Become one." Such suggestions, of course, are directly contrary to what well-intended sociologists have been encouraging for years. Their goal is undeniably admirable. It springs from a desire to tell groups that have come out on the short end in a competitive society that their loss is not due to inferiority. "Why, look at all the things your group has going for it. Were you not the first people to . . ."—fill in the blank. They are, of course, correct in their premise. A group is not inferior because it lost in a particular competitive encounter. Who would call Zulu warriors inferior? Yet in the last century many fell to the rifles of lesser men who weren't quite sure how their weapons worked. The point is, if we want to reduce aggression among ourselves, we cannot isolate. We must incorporate.

If we blend together, whom will we hate? Unfortunately, probably about as many people as we hate now. We would notice last names, birthplaces, hometowns, height, ear size—anything! We would undoubtedly find some way to discriminate. Tall people would band together and hate short people with their "nasty little feet."

Although directives to mix and mingle probably cannot contribute very greatly to the solution, we should consider the merits of blurring the distinctions between us. It may be better not to encourage people to respect their ethnic origins, as we now do in an effort to show that we respect differentness. It's a beautiful lie. We don't. Our illusions break down soon enough when our fortunes are threatened. Northerners have traditionally regarded Southerners as racial bigots, and they continue to do so even after the incidents at Forest Hills and South Chicago and the fact that there is far greater school integration in the south. So Grand Acceptance is apparently a prerogative of the temporarily unthreatened. Nevertheless, the notion of *accepting* people who are different should be abandoned in favor of *incorporating* them—to whatever extent that is possible.

So, encouragement, law, and inclusion are three ways we can mold a more acceptable high-density society. But even these are not enough. Out-group aggression, having served us so well over the eons, remains embedded in our souls. So, we must ask ourselves, what is the nature of this aggression? Can it be altered or somehow dissipated? There has been some argument over the years as to whether aggression builds within us just as the sex urge does. Is it something that builds to such a level that it must be periodically discharged if we are to remain emotionally healthy? In recent years many behavioral scientists have taken the position that aggression is learned and that it can be obliterated from society by the proper sorts of social programs. It cannot be denied that aggression, or at least its expression, can be learned. It can undoubtedly be heightened or decreased by one's experiences. On the other hand, why would evolution have left us on our own to learn something as important to our survival as aggression? If evolution has not left us with an innate aggressive arsenal, it has certainly developed in us the propensity and ability to readily acquire the behavior. In other words, if we are not born with an aggressive spirit and an eye for finding an outsider to exercise it on, we are certainly born with the ability to hastily acquire large doses of it, to meld it with our other behavioral traits, and to make it an integral part of the human phenomenon. In any case, and however we do it, we tend to end up aggressive.

We undoubtedly need to return to the hoary old question of how humans become aggressive—but this time with an open mind. Let's find out whether there are genetic directives for aggression and whether the aggressive urge can be discharged by performing aggressive behavior. If we find that it can, then let us find ways of harmlessly discharging it, such as through sports. Let's artificially select those we would confront and those we would cheer for and meet on the playing field. Let's discharge the urge in socially harmless ways. On the other hand, if we find that jingoistic activities such as sports only incite aggression and fan hateful flames, let's avoid this kind of pageant. But instead of moving blindly ahead with a fistful of wishful assumptions, let's find out. We need to *know*.

And we don't know. So far even the best behavioral scientists have shown a disconcerting tendency to support their philosophical positions with selective experimentation and convoluted conjecture. One scientist points to a small male fish that must attack something— usually another male—before he can mate. If no other male is present, he will discharge that aggression by attacking the female. Then, relieved, he will court her floating corpse. That scientist tells us that aggression is obviously innate.

Another scientist finds that soccer does not relieve international tensions but arouses them. He points to the fact that two Central American countries, Honduras and Guatemala, recently declared war after an emotional soccer game. Obviously, he says, aggression is a cultural phenomenon.

The point is, we are not in a position to make a list of our remedies because we don't yet know the nature of our illness. But it's high time that we stopped labeling ourselves and everything else in sight as if the data were in. They're not, and we're whistling in the dark while time runs out.

And we are confronted with another problem here. Do we *want* to produce a nation of nonaggressive people? I refer to a nation and not a world, because the material in this book is an intellectual exercise of the well-fed. You've eaten recently or you wouldn't be sitting here reading; you would be out looking for food. Most of the people on earth, though, are hungry and don't give two hoots about the "nature of man." And although the people in other well-fed nations may also be interested in this question, they too have hungry neighbors. And the ranks of the hungry are going to swell. Food and other commodities will continue to fall into short supply as the human population looms larger. Perhaps we are well-fed, but the time may come when we have to act against other nations to ensure our food supply. We are already in strong competition with other developed nations for many commodities. As these goods grow scarcer, can we afford to become less defensive, less aggressive in looking after ourselves? What happens if we do? Obviously, a benevolent, pacifistic, and nonaggressive nation will lose out to its more belligerent neighbors. It seems imperative that in such times as these, we keep our defenses up even while seeking ways to lower aggressiveness within our borders.

If our goal is to encourage benevolence within our borders while looking for ways to advance ourselves in dealings with those outside our boundaries, we are essentially talking about nationalism, that peculiar device that tells Minnesotans that they have more in common with Mississippians than they do with Canadians. So if the times dictate that we must be nationalistic to some degree, can we use nationalism as a device to help promote peace? Nationalism, of course, is perpetually denounced as being at the root of warfare, and so the suggestion that it can be used as a peacemaking device will undoubtedly be viewed with a great deal of suspicion. At best, nationalism is usually considered as being a way to direct our hostilities away from ourselves. It is cynical, and of little comfort, to say that benevolence within a group can be increased by a mutual hatred for others, but the principle has been effectively employed throughout history.

We cannot deny the advantages of nationalism just because it is so cumbersome and pregnant with problems. It may be that, by attempting to increase brotherly love within a national boundary while remaining a bit suspicious and distrustful of other governments, we are decreasing the likelihood of being mugged and increasing the risk of being bombed. Yet we simply cannot, in our best interest and in a competitive world, behave lovingly toward other nations. They, after all, seek our goods. Almost all of our overtures toward Russia have resulted in a net loss for us, from Salt I and wheat sales to cooperative space programs. And we cannot rationally condemn them; this is *not* bad behavior on their part. They *should* look after themselves. It is the unifying principle that works among all living things. We only call such behavior bad when it is evident that we have lost or when we have arbitrarily decided to decry selfishness, especially in others. We can expect nations, then, to behave aggressively, in their own interest.

So, although aggression has been beneficial through the eons, it is less useful today because we misapply it, using it in ways that do not advance our genetic welfare and perhaps in ways that threaten our very existence. This is not to say, however, that its present usefulness is reduced one iota when it is properly exercised. We needed it then and we need it now to ensure our own success. But now it is too often out of hand, largely because we haven't discovered how to channel it, discharge it, or in most cases, to modulate it. Only one thing is clear: whatever we've *been* doing to discourage socially harmful aggression is not working. We are increasingly subject to attack from within our own borders even as international tensions grow. It's abundantly clear that we just don't know enough about the basis of aggression.

Once again, let's see if we can use the baser aspects of our nature to promote peace. I would now like to suggest that selfishness can be used to cause nations to function harmoniously. It came home to me one day when I was reading the *Herald Tribune* at the Montesol, a little sidewalk cafe near where I was living on the Spanish island of Ibiza. A news item described the faltering British pound. I really couldn't have been less interested, but the *Herald Tribune* was a rare and expensive item, and when I got my hands on one I read it—all. It was my patriotic duty. Besides, the local newspaper was printed in Ibizincan.

In any case, the pound was down and I didn't care. I was more concerned about the fact that I was getting 55 pesetas to the dollar. Then I read a subtitle that caused me to sit up straighter. "Pound Linked to Dollar," it said. Now I was interested. The sinking pound, it said, was pulling the dollar down. Suddenly I became a pillar of altruism. "Yay, pound! Let's hear it for the pound! Damned speculators! Who do they think they are anyway?" I had suddenly become acutely interested in the welfare of the unfortunate British working class, struggling along with a weakened pound. How nice of me. Caring, I was.

Obviously (and this is a *workable* alternative), we can decrease hostilities with other groups by deliberately tying our fortunes to theirs. We can be sure, for example, that a newly powerful Japan won't attack us. Where would they sell their color TVs and spiffy little automobiles? The Russians had better not bury us until they learn how to grow more wheat. Recently, in fact, I read that the Germans were bolstering a flagging dollar. Now why would they do that? Gratitude? Because they're our friends? Or because we not only buy their Volkswagens but also act as their protector? And *why* do we protect them? It may have to do with the difficulties that would arise from competing economically with a widened Communist bloc if the Germans were overrun from the East. The Warsaw bloc must be held in check for our own good.

A partial solution to international tensions, then, suggests itself. We could very feasibly move along the economic front to inextricably weave our economic fabric into those of other countries. We would have to be vigilant, however, since each country would be seeking subtle advantages and since the United States has a rather disconcerting recent history of naïveté and gullibility in international dealings. Nonetheless it could be done. If we could increase international interdependence, we would see a proportionate increase in international good wishes, and the threat of warfare would drop considerably. We wouldn't even need to alter our frame of mind. We would be looking after ourselves as always.

The United States might also develop a better system of foreign aid. The advantages of giving money to poor countries are only short-term if it is used simply to bribe or buy their leaders. The benefits we export must reach the poorest elements of these poor countries in order to help stabilize their societies. People tend to become less radical and more conservative when they have more to conserve, and it is to our advantage to live among dependable, conservative, slow-changing countries. Our gifts, then, have three advantages: they make us feel good; they are met with approval by others; and they can be used to increase the living standards of the poorest people and thereby encourage political stability among our neighbors on this small planet.

However, we have a problem. It's related to the nature of human political systems and politicians. In most political arenas, the people who rise to positions of leadership are more likely to be hustlers than thinkers. They are, after all, the ones who succeeded in the harsh and rigorous competition of the political process. They are, almost to a person, ambitious and combative. If they weren't, they wouldn't occupy their positions. Unfortunately, an ambitious and combative person is not necessarily qualified to make difficult decisions. Shrewd is not the same as smart. In fact, the perspective of political leaders, their ability to see the big picture, may be twisted by the very traits that enabled them to succeed in the political process. They tend to view the world as an antagonistic place, an arena where someone wins and someone loses. They tend toward simplistic viewpoints, as we saw when so many American congressmen sought to enlist support for the Vietnam war. We heard them successfully arouse the indignation of many people by saying that we couldn't "bug out" or "cut and run," cowardly terms implying that it was somehow bold to vote taxes to bomb someone in a distant land.

It is, by the way, not to our credit that many of these same low-minded jingoists remain in office to this day. Nonetheless, there they are. Still making decisions for us. Simple-minded scramblers, unwilling or unable to make the hard decisions for the long run. Our task is to find a way of replacing these outdated pugilists with thoughtful people who are able to maneuver with skill and finesse in an increasingly complex world. The new breed of poitician might well consider leading us into complex and entangling international economic webs. Whenever possible, these leaders would not permit clear lines to be drawn, because where such lines exist, people will tend to get on one side or the other, setting the stage for a fight. The new leaders would make it hard to know where to stand on any issue that could lead to war.

The problem is that the public demands simplicity. So, perhaps the public is politically well represented now. But we need leaders, not representation, and if we are successful in choosing people who are able to blur nationalistic lines, we will find ourselves increasingly dependent on their expertise, their explanations.

Not representation?! "If there is no representation, there is no democracy," someone shouts. That's true. But a very good case can be made for the argument that we have *never* had democracy. The United States system is not participatory government, no matter what our civics books say. Essentially, we vote for party nominees, and, as one of our illustrious political leaders once said, "You let me pick the nominees and I don't care *who* does the voting." So a system that would let us choose leaders with superior abilities need not be less representative than the system we have now. In fact, my suggestion is that as long as the public itself is unwilling or unable to grasp complicated issues and continues to try to understand everything in simple terms, then we should aspire to *less* representation and *more* intelligent leadership. (The level of sophistication of the voting public admittedly does not encourage the hope that we could choose such leaders.) The days in which governments tend to behave like petulant individuals must be numbered. Governments must begin to supercede the meaner reflexes of selfish people.

As I've tried to make abundantly clear throughout this book, I am aware of the potential risk in full acceptance of what I've said here. Simple-minded people or demagogues will undoubtedly be tempted to use some of my arguments, particularly out of context, to support stupid or vicious claims. Thus, I hope the separate arguments I've made will be considered as part of a larger statement. Keep the ideas in the context of the big picture. Keep in mind the *premises* of the argument. Remember the compelling arguments of the Reproductive Imperative. I make the appeal for two reasons. First, I do not wish to support racist or sexist notions, and second, I do not wish to be accused of supporting them. What I've said here is not an argument for the continuance of the status quo. It is, instead, an attempt to more clearly define the nature of our predicament, a situation that we *must* address quickly and effectively. We are now in the process of destroying ourselves slowly, and we stand increasingly prepared to do it quickly. Something is wrong. Evolution has outdone itself. We have become enormously successful at manipulating conditions within the thin shell of oxygen and water swirling over our small globe, and it is here that evolution has dictated that we must live. If we are to continue to alter our fragile home, we must change it to our advantage or be lost.

We must also understand our relative position here. We cannot continue to see ourselves as conquerors in a threatening world full of usable or hostile species. It is not *us* versus *them*. Us and them need each other. We are all part of an interdependent web. If they fail, we stand to fail. Ecologists have long known that complex systems composed of many species are more stable than simpler ones with few species. Thus, as we watch species after species slide into a final oblivion, we are witnessing a simplification of our system. The resulting instability threatens *us*.

I heard a reporter on television this very morning ask a marine biologist, "Why do people need whales?" The question itself reflects our basic arrogance—an arrogance that assumes that the other species are somehow here *for* us. They are *not* here for us. But we need them. They are a part of a complex system of which we are also a part. We're in this together. Thus, even if you don't find it sad that the Russians and Japanese continue to hunt the last of the earth's great whales to render their great bodies for spermaceti to make cosmetics, you might be concerned over the fact that they are simplifying the oceans. For the same reasons, you may have been dismayed to hear a former actor, California governor, and presidential contender encourage the destruction of a great American heritage when he said of our redwoods, "A tree's a tree. How many do you need to look at? See one, you've seen 'em all." Or to hear the governor of Washington state say caustically that nothing tugs on the heartstrings like a few mallards with a little oil on their wings, even as she encouraged tankers to enter Puget Sound. Perhaps, though, you don't need a biological explanation to see the shabbiness of such thinking. Probably you regret seeing whales and mallards die for another reason, maybe reasons you don't really understand. Why not look within yourself? Look for the reason—the *real* reason why these things sadden you. You may even find a good reason for rejecting the biological explanation of human behavior.

Some sickened and disheartened people have argued that this is quite a nice planet and that it would be better for all concerned if humans would just disappear, leaving it unmolested. No intelligence greater than a mouse's need occupy this splendid place. In fact, it could do quite well if nothing more noble than the insects should succeed us. Perhaps our efforts at "development" should be viewed as a spreading cancer on a pleasant planet—a place that is now patiently awaiting our suicide to complete itself, so that doves no longer need fall from the sky under the guns of clerks who eat too much anyway. If we are gone, maybe Bigfoot could survive. A cougar and a bigfoot would avoid each other, but humans go out after church to try to hunt down a beast that, if it exists, is apparently harmless. They do it, they say, "to make the world safe for their families," or something equally meritorious. All things considered, we are indeed a superstitious, myopic, and dangerous breed. Never mind what people need with whales, what do whales need with people?

This is not to say that if humans were gone, the earth would be a gentler place. It wouldn't. Our beloved earth is essentially a hostile and brutal place. We love to look at pictures of the Grand Tetons, and we think we'd like to live there. But if we do live there, we'd better be equipped with ways to kill plants and animals for food, and we'd better have ways of shielding ourselves from that beautiful but dangerous place. Life can survive only where it has found a way to keep its components organized in the face of the environment's tendency to disrupt and disorganize. Thus animals hunt and kill other animals. They devour each other's bodies to get the energy to keep their own bodies organized. Even "harmless" plants may harm each other as they compete for scarce nutrients. Without humans, killer whales would attack leopard seals and the seals would slaughter the helpless penguins who eat fish. If life goes on, so must pain and exploitation. Thus, humans are not unique in these respects. We are not the only animal that wreaks havoc. We are not even the only animal that wages war or kills its own kind. We are only one species among many. And that is the point of this book. We are subject to the same natural laws as the other animals. Our unique bane is our ability to know what we are doing, even as we seal our fate. Our unique blessing is our ability to alter course to avoid that fate, to choose our own future.

We are here and we are destined to look after ourselves. But if we do look after ourselves, if we have not volunteered to leave the planet to less ambitious species, then we must change course. Strangely enough, although virtually everyone recognizes the problem, it remains. At this point how do we change course? Obviously, if one wishes to change the course of a ship, it would be good to know what is powering the vessel. A sailboat turns more easily if the engine is on and the screw is forcing water against the rudder. Are we under sail or power? What forces are moving us? We must know, and our best guesses thus far have not been very good ones. Perhaps the engines are on, but we can't navigate if we don't account for the wind in the sails. Are there sails? In these pages I have simply suggested that we account for *everything* before we attempt to make our critical decisions at social remodeling; that we learn more about what drives us; that we alter course. And that we do all this as soon as possible.

I do not believe that man is simply a clever egotist, genetically driven to look after his own reproduction. He *is* that. But he is *at least* that. He is obviously much more. The evidence for this is simple and abundant. One need only hear the Canon in D Major by Johann Pachelbel to know that there are immeasurable depths of the human spirit. But why am I telling you this? If you have ever stood alone in a dark forest and felt something akin to love, something utterly joyful, surge through you by simply putting your hand on the damp bark of a tree, then you know that the evolutionary explanation is not enough. What could have possessed Thoreau to walk two hours through the snow to spend the afternoon with a tree that he knew? A *tree*. I am sorry for the person who has never broken into a silly dance of sheer exuberance under a starry sky; perhaps such a person will be more likely to interpret the message of this book narrowly. The ones who will find it difficult to accept the narrow view are those who know more about the joy of being us. My biological training is at odds with something that I know and something that science will not be able to probe, perhaps because time is now too short, perhaps because it is not measurable. I think our demise, if it occurs, *will* be a loss, a great shame in some unknown equation.

INDEX